SIGHT LINES

SIGHT LINES

Looking at

architecture

and design

in Canada

ADELE FREEDMAN

Toronto
OXFORD UNIVERSITY PRESS
1990

Oxford University Press,
70 Wynford Drive,
Don Mills, Ontario
M3C 1J9

Toronto   Oxford   New York
Delhi   Bombay   Calcutta   Madras
Karachi   Petaling   Jaya   Singapore
Hong Kong   Tokyo   Nairobi   Dar es Salaam
Cape Town   Melbourne   Auckland

and associated companies in
Berlin   Ibadan

CANADIAN CATALOGUING IN PUBLICATION DATA
Freedman, Adele
Sight lines : Looking at architecture and design in Canada

ISBN 0-19-540710-5

1. Architects — Canada — Biography.   2. Architects — Biography.
3. Architecture, Modern — 20th century — Canada.
4. Architecture, Modern — 20th century — Ontario — Toronto.
5. Architectural design.   I. Title.

NA745.F74 1990   720'.971   C90-095419-1

1 2 3 4 — 93 92 91 90

CONTENTS

ACKNOWLEDGEMENTS

For their fellowship and support, always, Susan Ford, David Livingstone, Larry Richards, Colin Vaughan, Susan Walker; for that and more, Kim Cameron. For assistance on the Dickinson piece, in addition, Vera Dickinson, Robert G. Hill, Edward Jones, Horst Theis, Frederic Urban, and Virginia Wright. At *The Globe and Mail,* Katherine Ashenburg, William Thorsell, and Karen York, for their appreciation; Rick Cash, for helping to reassemble the past. At *Toronto Life,* Sheila Hirtle and Marq de Villiers, generous editors; at the Canadian Broadcasting Corporation, Anne Gibson, for being herself. Richard Teleky, my editor at Oxford University Press, gave me that needed push; Sally Livingston scrutinized a pile of prose. To everyone who contributed photographs, *merci.* And *grazie,* Franco Marenco, wherever you are.

PREFACE

This is a collection of pieces about architecture and design, most of them published in *The Globe and Mail* as 'By Design', a weekly column that began in October 1981. The remainder appeared in *Canadian Art, Progressive Architecture, Toronto Life,* and *Quill and Quire*. Together they form a record of some of the people, issues, and projects whose effect has been, for better or worse, to shape our surroundings.

My column grew from the basic conviction, shared by certain of my editors at the *Globe*, that, quite simply, people are interested in the world around them, city or chair, teapots as well as towers. Sounds simple. The reality was more complex. There was no point pretending that architecture and design were anything but an international phenomenon, unfolding according to some mysterious dialectic having to do with the national, the regional, and the personal. Objects are the visible ends of sometimes unintelligible means. The history of architecture is not written solely in buildings. Architecture is theory, polemics, major schisms, petty wranglings, whistlings in the dark; drawings, sketches, maquettes, competitions (and more competitions); exhibitions, publications, and lectures; politics and real estate; packaging and place-making; scene and scenery; glamour and grind.

I learned on-site, following my instincts and taking advice. The first time I walked into Barton Myers's office, some serious young man looked at me and said: 'But do you know what the issues are?' As I found out, there was one issue, the so-called crisis of Modern architecture. There was also the movement, or counter-movement, known as postmodernism, which few could define but which so many wore. As cities filled up with the retro and the overbearing, predictably resurged an interest in modernism, resurrected as an approach, not a dogma. In Canada, this translated into an interest in the 1950s.

Peter Dickinson, a pioneer modernist, first came to my attention through conversations with Colin Vaughan, architect turned political commentator, who once worked with Dickinson. Vaughan helped draw up a list of buildings, clients, and colleagues. In the process of investigating them. I found myself re-discovering Toronto from the point of view of those who had helped to create it. It was like finding one map of the city superimposed upon another I had stopped looking at. The first results of my research were published in *The Globe and Mail* in 1985. I decided to expand the material for this book because, fascinated, I had continued to gather information. Dickinson's story permits sight lines to a profession, an era, a city, the one, no apology, where I live. Writing it was an opportunity to join three ways of thinking about things: biography, architecture, and, my painful pleasure, journalism.

There were other highs, such as to encounter the work, and be challenged by the company, of Frank Gehry, Jane Jacobs, Shiro Kuramata, Phyllis Lambert, Ettore Sottsass, Ron Thom. Just as much, I enjoyed writing about architects, designers, and activists of more modest fame, though no less accomplishment. Looking back over more than a thousand articles, an unnerving experience, I chose as I write, unsystematically and for resonance. Interviews with significant figures such as Allan Fleming and Ron Thom, both of whom have died, and with the leaders of Memphis, the recently disbanded design collective, remain as published. I chose what I liked.

For Mary and Ben

Peter Dickinson, 1961

PETER DICKINSON:
ANGLO-CANADIAN MODERN

HE WAS 6-FOOT-4. HE WAS 6-FOOT 6. HE WAS 6-FOOT 8. HE WAS A LARGE MAN.
HE SLOUCHED. HE MOVED ACROSS ROOMS INDIFFERENT TO THE FURNI-
TURE. HE TALKED IN A BRITISH ACCENT IN A TIRED SORT OF WAY. HE SPOKE
VERY SOFTLY—VERY, VERY SOFTLY. 'SMART' WAS A WORD HE USED A LOT. HE
HAD A LONG, RUBBERY FACE. HE HAD THE ENGLISH MANNER—THE CASUAL-
NESS, THE CLASS. HE LIKED SMART CARS. HE LIKED FORDS AND MERCS WITH
DIFFERENT-COLOURED TOPS AND GADGETS. HE LOVED THE JAGUARS. HE
HAD GREAT LONG FINGERS. HE CHAIN-SMOKED—PLAYERS WITH NO FILTERS.
HE WAS A WORKHORSE. HE WAS A STIMULANT. HE WAS AN INITIATOR. HE
NEVER SLEPT. AT PARTIES HE'D FINISH A 26 OF SCOTCH AND THEN HE'D
LEAVE. HE WAS A VERY, VERY SIMPLE PERSON. HE WAS A VERY COMPETITIVE,
AGGRESSIVE PERSON. HE HAD NO OTHER INTERESTS EXCEPT ARCHITEC-
TURAL DESIGN AND GETTING CLIENTS.

A boat-train from Halifax pulled into Toronto's Union Station on a May
night in 1950. Countless such trains met the ships bringing European immi-

1

grants after the war. On board were Peter Dickinson, a young English architect, and his bride of two months, Vera. They came through the Great Hall, a neoclassical masterpiece, and emerged onto Front Street. 'Look, Peter, how marvellous! They still have wooden streets!' said Vera, remarking on what in fact was a subway under construction. They walked up Yonge Street, the main north-south axis, finally stopping a policeman to inquire when they would get to the centre of town. 'You're on Bloor Street. You've just walked through it,' was the reply. 'Mile after mile of small, sordid—even squalid—buildings; that was the centre of the city we'd come to live in!' That was how Dickinson related his impressions to Stanley Fillmore, who reported them in *Mayfair* magazine in 1957.

The Dickinsons turned left on Bloor and kept walking. They noticed a hotel just ahead—the Park Plaza, corner of Bloor and Avenue Road. It looked to be a modestly priced, European-style establishment. They checked in; the clerk told them the charge was seven dollars per night; they checked out. They had come with forty dollars. They found a rooming house near Wellesley and Jarvis streets, the red-light district—sixteen dollars a week, bugs. That night, Dickinson told Fillmore, he decided to do something about his adopted city, the ugliest he had ever seen.

Whether he had really thought this or determined that; whether he and Vera had walked all the way to Bloor or grabbed a cab: none of it matters. By 1957, Dickinson could recollect his arrival in the context of what came later. His narrative was being recorded for publication. He could shape it, using irony, and invest it with myth. He had already designed an addition to the Park Plaza. The streets he'd walked that first night had become his turf. But there were greater ironies to come. He would snare one of the prestigious building commissions in the country. He would be dead within five years. His wife would spend nearly two decades settling accounts, suing for fees. His buildings would be written off as trashy or, at best, admired without scrutiny. In turn they would be recognized as humane, urbane, and full of charm. Peter Dickinson would become history.

Although the late Alan Jarvis, arts bureaucrat and design enthusiast, wrote of Dickinson by way of obituary that 'no architect has made such an impact on the Canadian scene in so short a time', Dickinson's work was hardly ever discussed in print. Newspaper journalists strung together his controversial opinions, listed his most important buildings, and left it at that. Few books of Canadian architectural history or criticism exist, in any case, and none devoted to the 1950s, the decade that Dickinson's compressed career encapsulates. He was a man driven—to build as much as he could, whatever it took, no matter the fee; one who could be arrogant but never pompous, rude but seldom wrong; a modernist who held the middle ground between the severely reductive and the informally picturesque, in a country where modern architecture sounded as an echo of echoes of news from elsewhere.

Dickinson was 'recruited' in London by an elder statesman of Toronto architecture, Forsey Page, founder of Page and Steele, a small, fashionable, residential firm that had been in practice since 1925. Page knew what it would take to keep it going: a hotshot designer. An army man himself, proud of having risen to the rank of major in the First World War, he hired many English architects—graduates of polytechnical schools, mainly, educated on veterans' grants. They came cheap and worked hard. A background in the forces was essential: it said a man could get a job done. 'Mr Page got every inch out of everybody,' said Joan Grierson, who worked for him in 1952 and 1953: 'He was like a little rooster.' His partner, Harland Steele, was younger and somewhat more easy-going—a graduate of the Ecole des Beaux Arts in Paris in 1925, and a hotshot designer in his own right, in his own time. Like most other establishment firms in town, Page and Steele specialized in mock-Georgian: stone buildings with punched windows smaller with each storey.

Peter Allgood Rastall Dickinson was born in London on 21 October 1925. His father was Eric Carr Dickinson, a member of the London Stock Exchange like two generations of Dickinsons before him. His mother was a Crisp—and, according to Vera, 'a cold fish'. He had an older sister, a younger brother, a half-brother. His parents divorced when he was a boy. His father got custody, his mother moved out. He was raised by nannies and educated, as a boarder, at Westminster School in London, one of England's most venerable public schools. He was 17, and living in his father's house in Maida Vale, when he enrolled at the Architectural Association, an independent institution in London, in October 1942.

These were times of intense involvement with the form, content and purpose of architecture. The AA, which had 'gone Modern' in the late 1930s, was gearing up for the challenge of rebuilding—schools, housing, cities. Where Dickinson stood on ideological issues is not known. In Canada, certainly, he was never heard to utter a word about politics or theory. 'He lived modern architecture, he didn't have to talk about it,' is the spirited assessment of Horst Theis, a draftsman at Page and Steele who looked up to Dickinson. John C. Parkin, his main rival in Toronto, judged him to be, above all, 'a pragmatic man'. Either way, the AA would have suited him. Directly after the war, when the student population doubled to over five hundred, team work was introduced. Architectural models came into regular use. The emphasis was on devising real-world projects, with an eye to efficiency and economy, as often as possible in consultation with actual clients and working to actual briefs.

Dickinson interrupted his studies to do military service. He was not keen on going to war. 'Basically he was a conscientious objector—he had a social conscience,' said Vera. 'He was given a choice—the coal mines or the army. He replied: "If I'm going to be killed, I want to be killed in style." ' He was commissioned into the Grenadier Guards on 17 November 1944 from an Officers Corps Training Unit, and promoted to Lieutenant on 17 May 1945.

'They put him on a motorcycle,' continued Vera. 'He was not a military type. On some kind of exercise in England he wrecked his knee terribly. He was all alone in an army hospital. No one visited. He had a nervous breakdown.'

Dickinson made no mention of his wartime experiences to his colleagues at Page and Steele, with the exception of Joan Grierson, who remembers: 'The war appalled him. He saw action. He talked about being in hospital, in a wheelchair. His other comment was that the reason England could survive was because there were always the Guards to be thrown into the front lines. That allowed the lower classes to rise because the upper classes got thinned out.' Dickinson did not see action. He relinquished his commission on account of disability on 26 November 1945, having spent his year's service at the Training Battalion, Windsor.

He returned to the AA in October 1946. The Year Master's report, although glowing, alluded to frequent absence and 'ill health'. The image of Dickinson that remained with Ronald Sims, a student in the year below, was of a towering figure in a Guards greatcoat: 'He never took it off in the studio. He never wore it buttoned, so it always advanced before him. He exuded a kind of discontent. He was clearly protesting something.' Others were impressed by ability as well as demeanour. 'My impression was of a very aloof and opinionated person,' said Patrick Coles, then a third-year student like Sims. 'He merited the attitudes he was carrying. In that particular year he was probably head and shoulders above the remainder of the class. He was certainly a leader in activities where designs had to be co-ordinated by a team.'

Dickinson won the fourth-year prize in 1947, the AA's Jubilee year. Frank Lloyd Wright awarded the prizes, Le Corbusier spoke two days later. The next year he collected the fifth-year prize, a travelling scholarship worth £50. He graduated with honours distinction in February 1948, and sat the exam for admission to the Royal Institute of British Architects in June. He noted travel to France and Switzerland on his application. He was elected to the RIBA in February 1949. On 29 September 1949, he met Vera, who would become Canada's most conspicuous architect's wife.

'Vera was a real sexpot,' remembers Jeanne Parkin, John C.'s wife. 'At those Royal Architectural Institute of Canada dinners everyone would look at Vera. She was large and loud-voiced, she had black hair, she commanded all the attention and dominated the situation. All the rest of us were primed on how to behave. We were there to aid and abet the husbands, and make things comfortable. That was the period—the forties and fifties.' Vera, who aided and abetted in her own style, revelled in the attention. She made a point of arrogance—'one thing that was mine, and no one could take from me. When I was young, I thought people extremely ridiculous. I was a great mimic. We'd come home from parties—Peter would be amazed.'

Peter and Vera were a team. To hear people talk, they romped through Toronto like a pair of hellers, he a reckless artist, she his wild accomplice.

Vera could shock in a variety of ways: 'Drinking? I flaunted it. In those days you could only be appreciated if you were dumb and weak. In those days, if you breathed—if you laughed—in public, you had to be an alcoholic.' Still the Dickinsons, both of them big and tall and capable of the outrageous, must have made a daunting couple. 'They looked like the Himalayas,' remembers Colin Vaughan, an Australian architect who joined Page and Steele, in 1956, expressly to work under Dickinson.

Rachela Vera Dickinson is Austrian, born in Vienna. Her maiden name is nobody's business, she says. Nor will she comment on diverse speculations touching her past: 'I agree with Oscar Wilde—it doesn't matter what they say, as long as they talk.' Her mother, newly remarried, had shipped her and her sister to boarding school in England for some 'traditional polish'. The war put a stop to their education. Vera modelled, 'stockings and other things'. Her sister ran a private club in Knightsbridge. Vera and Peter met at a party. He had just been written up as an architect of promise. She liked him better the next time around, when he dropped his guard: 'From this it evolved, that was how it began—him pouring out his soul in his army coat.' He was indeed protesting something—the trauma of war, his father's remarriage to a secretary, a feeling of being adrift. 'When I found him, he wasn't so keen on living,' said Vera. 'I gave him the spirit of living, the strength of life. He wanted bacon and eggs, and mother and father sitting at the table—the loss, the loss, the lost childhood!'

They were married in London on 3 March 1950. Not two months before, Dickinson's competition entry for a vertical feature to mark the Festival of Britain had been published in *Architect and Building News*. The Festival of Britain, which opened in May 1951, was a sprawling, state-sponsored exposition of technology and the arts centred on London's South Bank—an attempt to cheer up a war-torn, ration-weary nation. The Festival signified the first prominent installation of modern architecture in post-war England, its buildings and townscapes prefiguring the New Towns of the emerging Welfare State. There were architects in England who were appalled by the spectacle, calling it populist, saccharine and 'English'; Dickinson, although he was gone before the Festival of Britain opened, knew many of the players from the AA and always remained enthusiastic. The vertical feature, or Skylon, was one of two commissions awarded by competition. Dickinson won third prize. He designed a 300-foot-high structure of concrete and aluminum from the centre of which three revolving jets would spray brightly illuminated plumes of chemical smoke.

It was the Skylon project that impressed Forsey Page when Dickinson replied to his advertisement for a chief designer in the *Royal Institute of British Architects Journal*. There wasn't much else to go on. For a time after graduating Dickinson worked in London for Wells Coates, a Canadian who came to architecture and planning from engineering. Coates's famous building, completed in 1934, is Lawn Road Flats in Hampstead, a pioneering work of British modernism—and temporary home-in-exile to such celebrated émigrés as Marcel Breuer and Walter Gropius. But Coates's career was in decline after the war: except for a Festival of Britain commission, the Television pavilion and Telecinema, he wasn't building. Dickinson formed a partnership with Richard Blow and Stephen Gardiner. He designed a restaurant and a few house renovations. He published a scheme for the comprehensive redevelopment of St John's Wood. Page would also have noted Dickinson's military background. That was about it.

The Dickinsons sailed for Canada on the *Franconia*, first-class, on 5 May 1950, docking in Halifax on 13 May. The next night they were in Toronto. On Monday, 15 May, Forsey Page wrote in his diary: 'Peter Dickinson phoned—in town—will be at the office tomorrow.' Vera came, too. Page's entry for 16 May reads: 'Peter Dickinson & wife in office at 9 a.m.—took them out to St Jo's . . .' (St Joseph's High School, a Page and Steele design, was then under construction.) On 17 May, Dickinson reported for work, at a starting salary of $70 a week. He had been hired sight unseen. He had lied about his age to get the job. He was 24—a foreigner among colonials, the nearest thing to a revolutionary the place and times would permit.

'He was talking a new language,' said structural engineer Morden Yolles, who was fresh out of university when he met Dickinson. 'There was no contemporary architecture in Toronto at the time. It just didn't exist. So when he started talking—I don't remember what he said, only the feeling— he, to me, was talking the new language, and I was very interested. He was kind of interested in me because I was representing a different kind of engineering. Both of us felt beleaguered. We'd sit around and drink and talk about architecture—how awful it looked, and how difficult it was to do anything here.' By then the Dickinsons had taken a basement apartment off Avenue Road, a residential thoroughfare within walking distance of Page and Steele. Dickinson, as chief designer, made a practice of inviting every new employee home for lunch and appraisal by Vera.

Vera had encouraged Dickinson to immigrate. Friends in Halifax had written that a boom was on. For whatever reasons he left London, the move released him. 'When we hit this country, he found himself, he found his level, he found his soul, he found his self-worth,' says Vera. He also found his patrons. The people most receptive to his new language were developers, who were seizing the day and buying up real estate. Not that Dickinson had any truck with the schlockmeisters in the suburbs who were putting up shopping malls and subdivision bungalows. He was drawn to builders no less speculative, but classier, who wanted downtown. Many of them were East European Jewish immigrants, or the sons of immigrants, who had been raised in smaller communities outside Toronto. 'You really had to be from outside the city to see the potential,' said one of their number, Walter Zwig. 'We couldn't see anything but excitement in this town. All the locals kept telling us we'd go broke. This city was developed by strangers because they were not inhibited by knowing about the past.'

A stranger himself, private about his own past, Dickinson was up for a gamble—and he had what they wanted. 'He had an intuitive flair which had a developer's perspective,' said Kenneth Rotenberg, speaking from experience. 'Established architects weren't responsive to a developer's needs. They thought more along institutional lines. That's where the big commissions were.' Both Zwig and Rotenberg, already clients of Page and Steele, were to play a part in Dickinson's success. But it was Leon S. Yolles, Rotenberg's elder partner, who spotted him first. Yolles was 'a small, beautiful man, and one of the most colourful clients we ever had,' in Horst Theis's words. Vera called him 'old man Yolles', even if he was only in his fifties, to distinguish him from his son, Morden; she pronounced him 'a free-booter, but charming'.

Yolles had been a developer since the 1920s, before the term came into fashion as a more respectable-sounding synonym for builder. He had been sitting on some choice land on a crest of Avenue Road, formerly the grounds of a stone mansion called Benvenuto. He was thinking luxury apartments. In 1950 he came to discuss design with Page and Steele. Their office was an old three-storey house on St Clair Avenue across from the Granite Club, a bastion of waspdom where Page took clients. Upstairs, in the drafting room, he found Peter Dickinson. 'My father had an immediate affinity with Peter,' said Morden Yolles. 'Father always struck a hard bargain. They just got along famously. Father was a fairly forward-looking man, Peter was showing new things—there was a lot of energy there. Peter could both insinuate a certain style of architecture and meet the needs father stipulated. That's how it all came about.'

L.S. Yolles gave Dickinson enviable opportunities. Benvenuto Place Apartments was one. Yolles liked big spaces. Although steel structures were then the rule, he wanted concrete. He wanted flat ceilings. The Benvenuto, as it is known, was constructed of concrete slabs without drops—a first for Toronto. The design of the slabs was left to Morden. The rest was Dickinson. Untried, only 26, he rose to an assured performance. Faced in cream-coloured brick, airy-looking yet substantial, the Benvenuto thrusts sharply towards Avenue Road to offer splendid vantage of the city to the south. Dickinson's signatures were already evident. He expressed the edges of the slabs to gain texture, explain construction, accentuate the horizontal. He liked thin-framed metal sash windows, balconies, flamboyant canopies—means to form, amenity, rhythm, elan. He talked Leon Yolles, who said no to everything, into a hoop sculpture for the courtyard.

He considered such detailing not only smart but democratic, not intimidating but an invitation to diverse enjoyment, not exclusive but engaging. In an article submitted to the *Royal Architectural Institute of Canada Journal*, he wrote:

'The wall is designed to keep the man in the street out, and he knows it. He can look with pleasure on windows, balconies, canopies and sculpture, but a wall stripped of these has lost its interest.' The Benvenuto interiors are simple, spacious and thoughtfully planned: no marble, mirror, or pomp. Dickinson's buildings, though stylish, are always modest. Light, landscape, and breathing space were the luxuries.

An antecedent of the Benvenuto is Chelwood House, a block of luxury flats in London designed in the 1930s by Maxwell Fry, an English modernist—but Toronto had never seen its like. The Benvenuto set standards for modern living. Even before the last phase was completed, in 1955, the Dickinsons had moved in. Soon a son, Gregory, was born. Dickinson purchased a drawing board for the living-room so he could work at home nights while helping to care for the baby. He was a patient father, an impatient architect. He had come to Canada with ideas, he was anxious to try them out. He drew, drew, drew—even when Vera's cocktail parties were in swing. Dickinson found company stimulating. He would sit at his board, drinking, smoking, chatting, sketching. It was nothing for him to complete a full set of drawings over a weekend.

At the office, more of the same. He would do a schematic study in a day and talk it out with the job captain who would see it through. 'Fast, furious he worked—I've never known anyone who could work so fast,' said architect Michael Clifford, then at Page and Steele. Dickinson's rapid free-hand perspectives, loose, witty and descriptive, were a weapon. Even Harland Steele, who resisted Dickinson's designs initially, had to admit 'they would "sell" anyone'. When he wasn't sketching, Dickinson pored through catalogues and stocklists, searching for the latest in materials and window systems. 'He thought in terms of the total thing—the system—and then worked it down thoroughly,' said Joan Grierson. 'He was very happy doing it. He used what was available, what was being produced cheaply and efficiently. There was a frontier. The world was all out there, waiting for you to solve.' Dickinson designed so many buildings, so quickly, it is hard to say where one project ended and the next began.

Dickinson's first major downtown office building, 111 Richmond Street, was ready before the Benvenuto. Built for Yolles and Rotenberg it is faced in broad horizontal bands of alternating glass and limestone. All the windows swivel open. An inclined canopy over the street shapes the entrance into a squared funnel, the better to draw you in. The ceiling of the lobby was scalloped, the floor was terrazzo, one wall was covered in rectangular tiles of multi-coloured marble. The building's most arresting feature was a solid 12-storey wall, marking the lot line on the west, entirely of green-glazed brick—'a startling sight for Toronto,' wrote Stanley Fillmore, who noted 111 Richmond as the talk of the town. That brick, which had just become available from the United States, in a variety of colours, became one of Dickinson's pet materials. He thought it classy.

Benvenuto Place Apartments

He next used it at Toronto Teachers' College, which went into the ground in 1954. Here he showed a lyrical side. The main attraction is a secretive interior quadrangle, part grass, part flagstone, otherwise landscaped with a reflecting pool planted with bamboo. Overlooking the water, a hoop sculpture. The two-storey school wraps gracefully around the courtyard, each floor a continuous loop. Dickinson experimented with walls made of playfully syncopated windows and coloured panels—blue, aqua, green; walls of windows and glass spandrels tinted pale green; wood-panelled walls; a wall of green-glazed brick. He designed a ramp, his one and only, for the lobby; and a broad wave of concrete over the front door. This controlled dispensation of random delights, sensitively inserted into an older residential neighbourhood, won a Massey Foundation Silver Medal in 1955.

That year saw the opening of Beth Tzedec Synagogue, another gift from Leon Yolles, another bang in the Dickinson explosion. The commission represented an extraordinary commission for one so young. Dickinson looked for cues to Sir Basil Spence's winning scheme for Coventry Cathedral, published in 1951. (He had entered that competition, too.) He borrowed the idea of shaping the building as staggered planes, his of buff brick, with full-length slot windows between. The fan-shaped lobby, likewise indebted to Spence, is very Festival of Britain—two flying staircases, a large painted mural, a row of tall columns wrapped in wood, decoration galore.

Dickinson would later say of the Beth Tzedec that it was the one building with which he was involved to the last detail. He wanted consistency. He specified all the materials. He chose the textiles for the two rooms for prayer and the warm finishing colours, rose and plum predominating. In the main sanctuary, cavernous, fan-shaped, and austere, luxe runs to floors of two-toned cork, blond pews with individual armrests and sprung seats, long suspended pole lights sprouting brass conical shades. The chapel is commanding, too, although intimate. Morden Yolles, again Dickinson's collaborating structural engineer, suggested the use of an exposed concrete frame, ribs arching upwards to form the ceiling. Dickinson, responsive, went on to fashion one of his most vibrant and sculpturally satisfying spaces, complete with delicately wrought altar and perforated wooden screens.

Meanwhile, Page and Steele was feeding Dickinson jobs: Juvenile and Family Courts on Jarvis Street; small office buildings on the outskirts; the Queen Elizabeth Building at the Canadian National Exhibition; schools, in Etobicoke and all around Ontario. A singular example is Humber Valley Village School, a one-storey, white-painted, concrete-block building set gracefully on a knoll, with timber framing and pitched roofs. This was Dickinson's variation on what was known, back in England, as 'people's detailing' via Sweden; he tried it, gave it his personal stamp, went on to the next project. He was evolving a clean, crisp look for apartment buildings predicated on transparent modular bases, strip windows, glazed brick, and pre-cast spandrel panels.

Toronto Teachers' College

The lobby of Beth Tzedec Synagogue

A particularly fine example is 561 Avenue Road, a building of commanding punch. Constructed in 1955 by Kenneth Rotenberg, 561 Avenue Road presents an articulate face to the street composed as recessed and projecting planes of glass and off-white brick, each sub-divided into smaller and smaller surfaces to vary the scale and punctuation. The corners are made of glassed balconies that bounce light; smartly patterned black-and-white spandrels attract the eye in. The driveway, another Dickinson speciality, makes a graceful transition from city thoroughfare to private property. At 500 Avenue Road, an all-white apartment building he would soon be designing for Rotenberg across the street, Dickinson would refine his stylish residential idiom to an extreme of simplicity.

'Always he saw things as an artist,' remembers Macklin Hancock, a planner and landscape architect who collaborated with Dickinson on both apartment buildings. 'His perspectives were wizard because his was an artistic output— an output that expressed the performance of design in landscape. In England, architects became imbued with landscape thoughts. Peter wasn't very knowledgeable about vegetation, but he could appreciate immediately the nuances of spatial relationships between structuring the landscape and structuring a building. That was related to the painters of the time. He had a Mondrianesque relation to building—I'm talking about cubism brought down to its distilled essence. When he saw things in plan form, they were composed with the same delicacy as a Mondrian canvas. To my mind, that governed a lot of his thinking. Peter worked with a basic idea in mind: if you can make a canvas look right, you should be able to elevate the landscape. Warm colours come to the eye, cool colours recede, black lines, white spaces—that was exactly what 561 was when it was originally designed. He didn't tell me about this, I didn't tell him: we were working with the same ideas and understanding.'

No two of Dickinson's canvases were alike. That was a matter of temperament—and in the interests of his strong-willed clients who were looking each for an edge. Rotenberg, for one, would not consider any facing material other than brick: it was the best and the cheapest, in his view—and the trades were there. 'That was the era of the Italian bricklayer,' said Hancock, noting that Scottish and English bricklayers were still to be found at the time. Other of Dickinson's clients were ready for a different look. Dickinson, too, kept a keen eye on the competition. 'They can copy me once, but they'll never do it better,' he would accurately boast to Theis.

The 12-storey north wing of the Park Plaza Hotel, a Yolles and Rotenberg commission started in 1955, showed yet another side of Dickinson's sensibility. He was adding to a building that had been constructed in the 1920s. He didn't overpower it, nor would he stoop to mimicry. He sited a low foyer, clad in granite and announced by an extravagant canopy, along the back end of the original hotel, connecting it to the 12-storey addition opposite by a long corridor containing retail space. This plan allowed for a landscaped drive-in courtyard off Avenue Road, with round concrete fountain and underground receiving dock to hide the humdrum. Every new hotel room had a balcony, the railings set with staggered panels of white opaque glass to cast shadows. Every inch of space and every glazed brick, here of a pinkish hue, counted. The tower occupied the block with civility, an attractive object in consonance with its surroundings—commercial streets in one direction, residential in another.

It came to this. The two hottest places to be for an architect looking to practise modernism were Page and Steele, where Dickinson presided, and John B. Parkin Associates, where John C. Parkin was in charge of design. Parkin and Dickinson were different kinds of men, different kinds of architects. Parkin, a Canadian, was International Style via the United States; Dickinson was second-generation Festival of Britain. They were perceived, however, as co-leaders of a movement aimed at dragging Toronto into the twentieth century. People were always comparing them. Parkin was considered a purist in the Miesian mold; Dickinson, a populist and individualist. 'John had a sense of elegance,' said Hancock, 'but not the same touch of catholicity that Peter had: Peter could draw so well that anything that came to his mind could show up in the result.' Fillmore quoted a musical analogy: 'Parkin would be composing symphonies—rhythmic, proportioned modern symphonies with the emphasis on form. Dickinson would be a jazzman; he would ad lib around a theme in dazzling fashion.'

Parkin was identified with institutional work; he regretted that he never got to design an apartment building. Dickinson was identified with developers. Said Horst Theis: 'If John Parkin built for twenty dollars a square foot, Peter Dickinson would build something for twelve dollars a foot that was much more satisfactory to the user.' Jeanne Parkin talked of her husband's obsession with self-image. Vera spoke of her husband's disregard for appearances. Parkin once told me: 'I hate myself, I hate my nose, I hate my buildings.' Dickinson loved his buildings. 'I like to design for the centre of the city,' he told Fillmore. 'The closer to the centre, the better I like it. Why? Because I like to look at buildings and my buildings in particular; they're easy to get to downtown.'

'Peter and I weren't rivals,' Parkin told me. 'We enjoyed each other's company. Peter was a vitriolic, sarcastic fellow, and I'm not, but I used to laugh at his ribald jokes.' They met socially, at dinners and meetings of the Vitruvian Society, a fellowship named for Vitruvius, the Roman architect and theorist. It was started by Eric Arthur, Anthony Adamson, and James Murray, three prominent Toronto architects, to build *esprit de corps*. The Vitruvians numbered around thirty, they met in private clubs, they lasted five or six years. 'It was part of both Tony and Eric's establishment attitude,' Parkin said. 'They were very much concerned with architect-as-gentleman. We all went out in our bib and tucker. Members were each supposed to give a paper. When it came to the dumb ones, we ran out of material.'

Dickinson certainly thought of Parkin as his rival. He was bitter that Parkin's entry, and not his own, placed first in a province-wide competition for the Ontario Association of Architects headquarters building in 1950. He was speaking of Parkin when he said, to Fillmore: 'It's too bad the most outrageous cubes of glass and steel are confused sometimes with modern architecture. In the right hands, a wall of steel and glass can be honest and interesting. But they're not the only materials. An all-brick wall is just as honest used in the right place. A building is the architect's statement of faith. First of all, it must serve the purpose it's built for; on top of that it must be lively, imaginative and colourful. To my mind, a building's worst sin is being frigid or dull.'

He was never dull. Robert Fulford, then a journalist in his twenties, called Dickinson for an interview around 1955, thinking to write a series on emerging young architects. First, he had to get Forsey Page's blessing. Over he went to the office. 'There was this white-haired gentleman and an enormous young Englishman. I told Forsey I was planning a piece on his chief designer. Forsey said: "That's what you're going to do if I say you can." He was so arrogant. Peter was arrogant, but he had to deal with the arrogance of people like that, who owned Toronto, who owned that neo-Georgian style.'

Page seemed to think he owned Dickinson, too. Fulford's observations, while he decided not to write them, were prophetic. Relations gradually became tense. Page regarded Dickinson as a commodity; Dickinson knew his own worth. He had single-handedly changed the firm's agenda and set it on the leading edge. He had been given to understand he would be made a partner. He began to feel cheated. Vera felt cheated. Matters would come to a head. 'The tent wasn't big enough for Peter,' said Gerry Granek, a mechanical engineer who spent time at Page and Steele. 'They couldn't fetter him down.'

He stayed put a while longer. He worked on O'Keefe Centre for the Performing Arts, a vexed project that was never properly resolved. The client was O'Keefe Breweries, which was then owned by E.P. Taylor, the financier. Earle C. Morgan is the architect of record, but not in fact. Morgan got the commission because he was married to Taylor's sister. His office was small, so he associated with Page and Steele. Conscious of his limitations, he was looking for a designer. Dickinson was eager. He thought of the O'Keefe as his baby. He spent weeks figuring out how to get its most welcoming feature, a boldly cantilevered canopy on the street, to work on the parallelogram-shaped site.

Otherwise, his work came to little. O'Keefe Centre was supposed to have been Toronto's Rockefeller Center. It was to have stretched all the way across Front Street, incorporating two theatres, office buildings, a skating rink. But the program kept shrinking; finally it came down to a single, extra-large theatre seating 3250; Dickinson's ideas were badly compromised. One Sunday he went into Page and Steele to destroy his drawings. He phoned Vera to ask her advice. 'Come home and have a brandy,' she said.

A more satisfying project than O'Keefe, as things turned out, was Regent Park South, a high-rise public housing project that featured skip-level, or double-floor, apartments. (Le Corbusier originated skip-levels in his Unité d'Habitation in Marseilles.) High-rise solutions to low-income housing have been discredited, but Regent Park South was applauded in its time: 'That was one of Peter's highlights—a breakthrough,' Granek said of the 14-storey brick towers, their plan boldly expressed on the exterior as banked windows and bright yellow spandrels. 'He proved a project could be done in a developer way without the involvement of a developer. He came up with a maisonette scheme, a three-dimensional scheme, which had been a luxury scheme.' Regent Park South received a Massey silver medal in 1958.

In January 1958, urged on by Vera, Dickinson pulled out of Page and Steele to form Peter Dickinson Associates. The turning point had come some six months earlier, when Page made it clear he had no intention of renaming the firm Page Steele and Dickinson. 'Forsey nor I ever dangled a partnership in front of him,' Steele wrote to me. 'For over thirty-five years prior to this event, Forsey and I didn't have a written partnership agreement. We trusted each other implicitly. We did not see this most enjoyable, and very unusual relationship continuing in a future partnership with Peter since we knew that we were motivated by different ambitions and values.'

Dickinson did not go alone. He raided the tent, taking architects Richard Williams, Colin Vaughan, Fred Ashworth, and John Armitstead, who were followed shortly by Jack Korbee and Peter Tirion. In the client category, he took Yolles and Rotenberg; Walter Zwig; Jack Cummings, a Montreal developer to whom he had been introduced by Vaughan; and Father J.M. Madigan, property developer for the Jesuit Fathers of Upper Canada. He rented offices in the Petrofina Building at Yonge and Davisville. There was a flag-waving ceremony. The office was still without furniture, everyone sat on the floor. Gerry Granek, who was there, remembers Dickinson saying: 'We're going forward. We are not going to malign Page and Steele.' He meant it, but subsequently things got messy. Dickinson began to claim sole credit for the design of buildings produced by the firm; Page took disciplinary action. It wasn't long before Dickinson was telling everyone he was out to bury Page and Steele. In a sense, he already had.

Unfettered, Dickinson's ambitions surged. He wanted an in-house engineering arm like Parkin had, modelled on Skidmore Owings and Merrill of New York. One day Morden Yolles was presented with letterhead that read Peter Dickinson Architects and Engineers. Yolles would have been a natural choice. He and Dickinson went back to the Benvenuto days, to the beginning. But Yolles sensed something he couldn't deal with. 'He wanted me and Granek to work for him,' he told me. 'That put me into anxiety about my own identity. I was a slow maturer, just a kid. I felt, suddenly, the power of

Peter. I felt, somewhere within me, I had to resist that power. I felt I was being swallowed up by Peter.'

Neither Yolles nor Granek came aboard; they continued consulting to Dickinson; social relations with Yolles became tense: 'I was dropped,' he said. Others would be dropped, but not for the moment. Five hundred Avenue Road was finished sometime in 1959; the Dickinsons, who were about to have a second son, Trevor, moved from the Benvenuto into a customized ground-floor apartment in the new building. Dickinson designed built-in walnut cabinets. Otherwise the decor was left to Vera, who furnished the living-room with 'abominable big couches, which Peter hated, and modern chairs thrown in-between'. The dining-room furniture, specially ordered from Chicago, was designed by Hans Wegner of Denmark. Vera's mother, a tapestry maker, sent hangings. Dickinson enjoyed listening to Debussy on the stereo: he was not a jazz fan. Vera's taste in music ran to Austrian marches.

Colin Vaughan and Richard Williams both moved into 500 Avenue Road with their wives. Peter or Vera would regularly invite them over to party. 'The thing about Peter,' said Vaughan, 'is it's hard to remember all the parties.' Hancock remembers them. 'The parties were a sort of Vera and Peter creation,' he told me. 'They had a certain way of making people comfortable. There was music, there was dancing. Any party they had was something to remember. It was a wonderful time. They lived in the city, and loved the city. It was a young city, and they could see it growing—they were helping it to grow.' Father Madigan would show up, remove his collar at the door, have a few, replace his collar, and go. Now and then, Dickinson would disappear into a bedroom where he kept his drafting board and draw his buildings. By eight-thirty the next morning, it was back to the office.

There was work. Off the top there were three office buildings, all completed in 1959: Continental Can on Bay Street, 801 Bay across the road, and the Trans-Canada Pipelines Building on Eglinton Avenue. With these projects, Dickinson arrived at a distinctive vocabulary for commercial buildings: pre-cast concrete facing panels, thin vertical fins, carefully composed roofscapes, transparent bases that make light of boundaries, suavely detailed lobbies. At Continental Can, a Yolles and Rotenberg project, he set a rectangular office block on a two-storey podium that followed the street line around a corner. The podium was a means to gain retail space and demonstrate good civic manners. It also houses the parking garage, enclosed with panels of opaque glass, on the second floor. (Parking couldn't go underground because of problems with soil drainage.)

Dickinson used the podium format again at the Prudential Building, a 21-storey corner building at King and Yonge Streets for Walter Zwig, completed in 1960. The windows were custom-made in Toronto, neoprene glazing gaskets were used in Canada for the first time, the pre-cast panels were faced with marble chips. At night, lit up, the building shimmered. For the Prudential, Dickinson designed his finest lobby, a composition of planes:

honed slate floor, reception desk of slate and glass, glass-bottomed fountain lit from below, two-storey backdrop of honed Gibraltar rock (because Prudential's symbol was the Rock of Gibraltar), one wall of light Italian marble. He detailed the whole thing overnight.

Dickinson kept pushing back the frontier. At 801 Bay, he pioneered the scissor stair—two interlaced but separate staircases inside a single shaft—so he could do away with the requirement for two exit stairways and two shafts. The scissor stair reduced the core of a building, saving space and money. When Dickinson submitted drawings of the stair to the plan inspectors in Toronto's Buildings and Development Department, they told him it wouldn't work. Dickinson had a small plastic model made and took it to City Hall, where he demonstrated the separation of the two stairs by blowing cigarette smoke through the mock-up. From then on, Peter Dickinson Associates used the scissor stair as a sales feature. 'It was one of our secret weapons,' said Roderick Robbie, an English architect who joined the firm in 1959.

But while he was exploring these and other novelties, opening to North America, Dickinson never renounced his Englishness, part of which was expressed as delight in employing a large palette of materials: brick, granite, marble, Indiana limestone, and, soon to come, fieldstone; various kinds of wood as well as concrete; slate, terrazzo, and stainless steel; metal sash windows and glass curtain wall. His architectural language was additive, not reductive; layered, never thin. 'Peter knew how to put an Oriental carpet on a slate floor, or how to create a balustrade that was more than a post and beam arrangement,' said Hancock. 'When it came to little things like doorknobs, there was always an English touch.'

It is telling that one of Dickinson's favourite buildings in the International Style was Gordon Bunshaft's Lever House, with its green-tinted curtain wall, central courtyard, and wrap-around second floor; he much preferred it to Mies van der Rohe's stark and monumental Seagram Building across Park Avenue. Dickinson may have had Lever House's perimeter massing in mind when he designed 790 Bay, but he could just as well have been thinking of Peter Jones, the 1930s department store in London that follows the King's Road, giving one last kick before turning the corner into Sloane Square. The form of O'Keefe Centre may allude to Eero and Eliel Saarinen's Kleinhans Music Hall in Buffalo, which Dickinson, an admirer of the Saarinens, drove down to see; but it is also suggestive of Royal Festival Hall, a Festival of Britain highlight. Dickinson like a broad horizon. His was not an exclusive vision.

Indeed, the one time he did pare down his palette and scrimp on colour resulted in his weakest effort, flat and drab. Regis College, a seminary in North York for the Jesuit Fathers of Upper Canada, nonetheless suited Father Madigan, who managed the project for the Jesuits. Dickinson began the design in 1958, having agreed to a 4.5 per cent fee on the $2.5-million project on the understanding that Madigan would provide more work. John Madigan, who has since left the Jesuit order, adored him. 'Peter Dickinson wanted to design the most wonderful building,' he told me. 'He was very anxious to win a Massey Medal. The building didn't look like a seminary. That always pleased me. It looked like a posh apartment building. I used to refer to it as a Jesuit country club.'

Madigan secretly arranged for a swimming pool, knowing he would never receive the necessary approval from Rome. When excavation began, he asked the contractor for a hole, 85 feet by 50 feet, in exchange for an income-tax receipt. 'I got a $50,000 swimming pool for $10,000,' he told me. 'Peter Dickinson thought it was a great idea.' The seven-hole golf course was easier to organize. It was concealed as landscaping. The building, meanwhile, is an inter-connected complex—a long residential block in the shape of a trapezoid, with gymnasium, dining, and kitchen wings off to the back; library and chapel to the front. The plan seems stilted, and for once Dickinson's walls lacked tautness and texture. The exceptional piece is a semi-circular chapel with Corbusian overtones, raised on a recessed fieldstone base, its shell punctured by projecting box windows. The interior, of exposed concrete, can no longer be savoured. In 1975, when the seminary was sold to the Ontario Bible College, the chapel was stripped of all ornament.

After leaving Page and Steele, Dickinson became increasingly outspoken. In 1959 he published an angry article in the *Daily Commercial News*, a trade paper, in which he attacked city planners, the architectural establishment, and the Ontario Association of Architects, ending in a burst of prophetic rhetoric: 'Professional restrictions and apathy on the one hand, and greed or ignorance by the developers and builders on the other hand, have created a situation where if we are not forceful, the next generation will inherit from us a wasteland of chaotic brick and block juke boxes and twisted telegraph poles, interspersed with forlorn and strumpeting grey stone elephants with punched windows.' So blunt were his criticisms that the *Globe and Mail* reported them as news.

Even when issuing a call to battle, Dickinson couldn't resist insulting the troops. In 1960, he wrote in *The Canadian Architect*: 'Let us all work to encourage sincere unpretentious architecture, well located in harmonious urban surroundings—and ring the death knell of the portly halls of ARCHAIC-TURE and the skeletal grimness of STARKITECTURE.' For archaicture, read Forsey Page and the rest of the neo-Georgian set. Starkitecture is John C. Parkin. No other architect spoke out this way. Gentlemen did not go to the press, or on television, as Dickinson did once, to praise themselves and damn their colleagues. Nor did they go about getting work so obviously.

Dickinson opened two more offices, in Ottawa and Montreal. Rod Robbie was put in charge of the Ottawa branch, where the big job at hand was a new town in Frobisher Bay, part of Prime Minister John Diefenbaker's vision of developing the north. Peter Dickinson Associates was paired with another

Ontario firm, Rounthwaite and Fairfield. Robbie remembers: 'Dickinson's brief to me was to design the project and get rid of the others.' Dickinson thought three tower slabs would do for northern housing; Robbie talked him into low-rise; the scheme was canned along with Diefenbaker, in 1963. Fred Ashworth ran the Montreal office. The firm quickly grew to around seventy architects, over three times the size of Page and Steele. Four new employees would play a significant role in Dickinson's story. Boris Zerafa and Peter Webb were hired by Williams, who managed the Toronto operation. Rene Menkes and Rick Housden entered the Montreal office.

A change gradually came over Dickinson's work habits. 'When he started Peter Dickinson Associates, it was design, design, design,' said Vaughan. 'He was working day and night at it, and it was exciting. But as time went by it became: "How can I beat out the other guy?" ' Dickinson got caught up in selling. He drew and sketched, but more and more on cocktail napkins and the backs of cigarette packages. He had his own firm to feed—and an insatiable appetite for building. 'I want to put a building on every corner of the three major cities in Canada before I go,' he boasted to his associates. 'There was a motto in that firm,' said Robbie: ' "We will fill in the spaces between the masterpieces." I was given instructions on running the Ottawa office: "Get some school work. I don't care how. Steal it off them." '

Granek noticed changes, too: 'When Peter left Page and Steele, he started to become more and more business-oriented. "Get me a job, you'll get the mechanical engineering," he told me. There was more and more hustling.' Yolles, another observer from the sidelines, summed it up this way: 'He wasn't afraid to knock on doors and go to the big boys. He was presumptuous. He wasn't considered respectable. He was outside the community of architects. He ran around getting work in a different way. Architects weren't behaving the way he was, running around and getting business. They certainly are now.'

Dickinson's work could still sparkle. In 1959, a new client presented himself, inspired by what he had seen of the Benvenuto. Isadore Sharp had a site on Jarvis Street and a dream of opening a classy motor hotel that would offer the convenience of a suburban motel in a downtown location. It had taken him five years to raise the money from friends; bankers wanted nothing to do with Jarvis Street. A builder himself, Sharp wasn't after complete plans and working drawings. What he wanted from Dickinson was a distinctive design. He offered $11,000 in fees and an opportunity to have some fun; the budget was $11 a square foot.

Dickinson, working closely with Hancock, came up with a gem: the Four Seasons Motor Hotel, cornerstone of an international empire. The Four Seasons had two floors of rooms overlooking an interior garden court— swimming pool, dining terrace, flagstone walks—so guests wouldn't know they were in a crummy part of town. The building looked clean and sharp on Jarvis Street, where a low fieldstone wall enclosed the driveway and

Four Seasons Motor Hotel

buffered the traffic. The base was fieldstone with white-painted brick above; window frames, louvres, and balcony dividers were of oiled California redwood; a comfortable bar and restaurant on the ground floor were detailed in fieldstone, terrazzo, and wood. Once again Dickinson displayed an uncanny ability to read a developer's mind. As Zwig put it: 'All one had to do was say: "Gee, I'd like to create this," give an idea of the image and dollars, and he gave it to you.'

Dickinson also designed a house for Sharp, in York Mills, one of five private residences in Toronto that bear his signature, this one a relative of Breuer's Clark House of 1949, a Connecticut residence. Low and lovely, Sharp's house hides from the street behind a small, gently curved, fieldstone wall. There's a corresponding wall of fieldstone inside, just beyond the front door, defining an entrance lobby. Off to one side, down a corridor, the bedroom block; to the other side, around and behind the wall, the living-room and dining-room, separated only by a two-sided stone fireplace. Partition walls throughout are of wood, 7 feet high. The kitchen is at the front, the side window overlooking an entrance court. The house is sited to take full advantage of a golf course next door, the social rooms affording continuous views, the bedrooms, privacy.

'When he said he'd do the house,' Sharp recalls, 'my wife and I went out for a drive to show him what we would like. We looked at a beautiful house— what could be wrong? Peter Dickinson said: "Well, if you'd like to build something mock-Georgian, you don't really need me. If you'd like me to do a house, allow me to do something that would suit you." He wasn't being insulting, he was being honest. I don't think he charged me for the design.'

Penny-pinching clients like Sharp were not going to make Dickinson rich and famous. Indeed, Hancock insists, contrary to some, that 'he wasn't searching for immediate fame; he believed painstaking, solid design had to emerge over time.' Jobs and money were rolling in. Dickinson bought his suits from Eaton's but he liked his luxuries—a Mark 8 Jaguar drophead, or convertible; Johnnie Walker Red Label; travelling in style. Intending to build a house, he acquired a ravine lot in Rosedale, an old-money neighbourhood of which he once said to a reporter: 'It's beautiful because you can't see the buildings for the trees.' He paid his associates well. His flourishing practice was envied and recognized. Four projects by Peter Dickinson Associates won Massey Awards in 1961: Trans-Canada Pipelines, The Four Seasons Motor Hotel, the Ontario Hospital Association building in Don Mills, and the KLM Dutch Airlines Ticket Office, an interior with ceramic floor tile, rubbed walnut panelling and cabinets, and suspended tile ceiling with one panel of 'leaf-lite', a baffle randomly notched with little metal medallions to simulate leaves.

These projects were overshadowed by the biggest plum of all, the Canadian Imperial Bank of Commerce and Windsor Plaza in Montreal. Design began in 1958, when Dickinson was just 33. Even more unusual was the fact that

Sharp residence

a colonial got to break a rule of colonialism. In post-war Canada, bank headquarters went to big-name architects based in the United States—I.M. Pei, Mies van der Rohe, Edward Durrell Stone. Dickinson was the exception. The man who unlocked the doors to Montreal was Jack Cummings, the developer. Like so many others, even those who resented Dickinson's arrogance and brashness, his intimidating size and smooth sell, Cummings relished his panache—his persona.

'Peter was a very interesting, exciting man,' Cummings told me. 'He had a sense of quality, of space, of space in relation to the human scale. Peter had a very powerful ego. I'm not sure, and I say this with affection, that he considered any architect up to his standard. He had a powerful intellect and a good humour. He initiated thoughts and ideas. He had an unbelievable reservoir of energy. He wasn't a plagiarist. He started from degree zero with his own creativity. The CIBC, 30 years old, is as gracious and contemporary as it was when it was built.'

The CIBC was both climax and distillation. Again, Dickinson was working for a developer who believed in him and drove a hard bargain. Again, he cut a deal that left him short: a flat fee of $750,000, engineering costs included, for a building budgeted at $25 million. Morden Yolles got $60,000—and 'innumerable letters from Peter before the deal was made, saying it was too much'. (Had Yolles not received another $120,000 from the bank later on, he would have gone under.) Complicating matters was the fact that none had done a 43-storey building in Canada before. At first, Dickinson made light of it. Gerry Granek tells of receiving a phone call from Dickinson on a Sunday afternoon: 'I'm at the airport. Can you give me a price on two buildings in Montreal? Oh, and another thing, they're one on top of another.'

But inexperience became a problem. The tower was being fast-tracked, that is, constructed as it was being designed. To speed things up, Granek, the mechanical engineer, consulted New York firms with computer technology unavailable in Canada. Still, the job dragged. Another drag was Neil J. McKinnon, president of the CIBC. Dickinson didn't get on with McKinnon from the start. When the bank and some investors purchased the site from Cummings and took over project management, relations did not improve. One consideration was uppermost in McKinnon's mind. His tower had to be taller than that of Place Ville Marie, headquarters of the Royal Bank, which was going up at the same time. 'A millimetre higher than Place Ville Marie was the motivating force,' said Cummings. 'I resisted it, Peter Dickinson resisted it. McKinnon was an animal—you can quote me on that.' Dickinson's term was 'a fucking peasant'.

Dickinson went out of his way to antagonize McKinnon. 'Peter at his worst was the bank,' said Granek. 'McKinnon was a very strong person. Peter kept on showing him what he had to sell. He showed three renderings, 8 feet tall, of three styles. There was very very heavy sarcasm in the sketches: "This is what you want." "This is what it would look like." "This is what you should

Canadian Imperial Bank of Commerce, Windsor Plaza

have." McKinnon walked out and never talked to him again.' McKinnon, nevertheless, was responsible for one of the building's most unusual features, Westmoreland slate cladding. Dickinson did not think stone appropriate. He wanted the tower clad in lightweight curtain wall and steel. McKinnon wanted Canadian granite. Slate spandrels were a compromise: stone, but not the stone favoured by McKinnon, which proved too expensive, in any case. Stone, but of a shade of green that Dickinson found pleasing.

He refused to let the matter lie. 'I always remember when Peter bumped into McKinnon and his wife at a party,' Rod Robbie recalls. 'They were fixing up their house and garden. Peter turned to Mrs McKinnon and said: "It just occurred to me, we have these slate rejects, why not use them on the patio?" McKinnon was outraged. The man was already paying for it—and Peter had insulted his wife! When Peter told us what happened, we told him he was dead. We were after more bank work. For developers, we cut fees.'

That Dickinson got off such a fine building says something about fortitude and skill. The CIBC is a petite, elegantly proportioned tower with tiny floor-plate, standing in subtle relationship to a tiny plaza. The skin is glass, pre-cast concrete mullions faced with stainless steel, and slate spandrels attached to insulated concrete panels, which provided all the advantages of prefabrication and speedy construction in addition to the desired character of stone. Fascinating, too, is a helicoidal staircase of laminated stainless steel bars and teak treads in the main banking hall—a design so original that a test model was first analysed for strength and stiffness at the Department of Civil Engineering at the University of Toronto. The fifteenth floor of the tower was reserved for the management office, a restaurant, and a barber shop; a small elevator serves the observation gallery on the 43rd floor. The 16th floor and 42nd floor were entirely given over to mechanical services. All the different functions are expressed on the façade.

Dickinson could design even a skyscraper that was sincere and unpretentious. Construction began in October 1959. Meanwhile, trouble was brewing at the office. Ashworth, in Montreal, who had a number of apartment buildings, Elm Ridge Golf and Country Club, and a Loyola College residence to worry about, on top of the CIBC, was concerned about finances. So anxious was Dickinson to get a project that he would grab a figure out of the air, leaving his associates to get the thing done. Williams, in Toronto, had similar complaints: 'His desire to expand transcended his financial capability. Money was always a problem. I questioned why he always had to make a deal—people were coming to him.'

There was resentment of Vera, who was having more and more say in the business. She swept into the Toronto office with her German-speaking accountant and took home the books. She came and sat. She expressed strong opinions about clients. When Dickinson and Zwig fell out, during construction of the Prudential Building, Vera declared a vendetta. 'It was us against them,' she always held. Some architects on staff were for Vera. John

Armitstead thought her 'an elegant lady who provided strength and direction.' Peter Tirion maintains that 'Vera did a lot of good for the firm; she was very supportive; she got a lot of publicity.' Vaughan remains unconvinced: 'It was like a little family business, Peter and Vera. We were going to be the biggest broke firm in Canada.'

The associates decided the only way to get the business on track was to have a say in running it. They wanted partnership. They requested a meeting. 'We realized it was committing suicide, in effect,' said Vaughan, who aired the group's grievances. The four wanted Dickinson to play down developer work and go after universities and hospitals. No more fly-by-night, no more sketches on the backs of airline sickbags. Dickinson didn't say much. This once, he would not cut a deal. 'It was like King Peter,' said Williams. 'He didn't want to give anything up.' Vaughan delivered a parting shot: 'If you sat down and did more design, you'd be a lot better off.' Dickinson sniggered. Vaughan and Williams carried their cardboard boxes out of Peter Dickinson Associates in Toronto on a January afternoon in 1960. Vera rushed in, wearing a black cape, and stormed down the hall. 'Open the windows in here!' she shouted. 'This place smells.'

Vaughan, Williams, Robbie, and Ashworth formed a partnership that lasted a dozen years. Kenneth Rotenberg gave them their first job, a small addition to the north of Dickinson's addition to the Park Plaza Hotel—just enough to keep them going. Vaughan would eventually leave architecture for city politics and television. Robbie and an Ottawa engineer would win the competition for SkyDome, Toronto's sports and entertainment playground. Williams has his own office. Ashworth is based in Vancouver. None ever saw Dickinson again. Said Robert Osler, who was in the office: 'One day they were there, the next day they weren't. The work went on.'

Dickinson appointed new associates in Toronto and Montreal: Peter Webb, Boris Zerafa, Rick Housden, Rene Menkes, Peter Tirion, Jack Korbee. Dickinson had never felt at ease with Zerafa. Williams tells it this way: 'Peter said to me: "Every time I go to the bathroom, Boris' eyes follow me." I said: "If you want to fire Boris, fire him yourself." ' Vera had a different take on Zerafa. 'This man will not stop until he has taken Peter's chair,' she said to Korbee. She was not mistaken. Vera took to calling her husband's new group 'the boyscouts'—to their faces, even in front of clients. Dickinson, hearing her step in the hall, would look up and say: 'Ah, it's the countess.' Together, Peter and Vera visited the office on Saturday afternoons to look at what was being drawn and done. During the week, Dickinson was on the road, in Montreal and elsewhere. 'He'd see lots of people, and come up with sites— two, three, four,' remembers Justin Klim, a junior at the firm. 'He would come back and say: "We need a 40-storey hotel here, a 30-storey office there." We worked like mad to produce floor plans, proposals. It was pie-in-the-sky. They never went through.'

Sometime in 1960, Dickinson was off to Rome to knock on a very big door. The Societa Immobiliare, the construction and investment company partly owned by the Vatican, was building in Montreal and Dickinson wanted a piece of the action. Place Victoria, the proposed headquarters of the Montreal Stock Exchange, interested him particularly. The obvious strategy was to see Pope John XXIII. Could Dickinson have sold the pontiff with charm and sketches? The audience he thought forthcoming, with the help of Father Madigan, who had contacts in Rome, didn't happen. 'Things got a bit muddled,' said Vera, who went with him. 'Madigan told us not to worry, another time.' There was not to be another time. In July 1961, Dickinson was in Mount Sinai Hospital. Cancer of the bowel, nothing to be done. Vera, beside herself: 'Peter, why us?' Dickinson: 'You can't have everything, Vera.'

There had been signs. Dickinson ignored them. Even at Page and Steele, Vaughan recalls seeing him, occasionally, doubled up in pain. 'I don't know, I really should stop drinking; I'm having an awful problem with my stomach,' he told Janis Goodman, an interior designer with Peter Dickinson Associates. Ashworth witnessed frequent collapses. When David Yolles, Morden's brother, finally arranged for Dickinson to see a specialist in Toronto, it was too late. Still, he had hopes of recovering. Kenneth Rotenberg visited Dickinson at Mount Sinai and remembers him 'looking out the window and telling me about the great things he was going to do out there'. Isadore Sharp arrived to discuss his next project, a hotel in the middle of nowhere to be called Inn on the Park: 'I told him: "We've got to do something even more dramatic than before—so dramatic people will want to drive there to see it." Dickinson said: "Leave it with me." I came back. He sketched on a pad the way the hotel looked when it opened. This building, when it opened, was identical to the sketch.'

To everyone who came, Dickinson said the same thing: 'Take care of Vera, take care of Vera.' Vera, who practised numerology, kept having his room changed in hopes of changing their luck. Her mother sent a tapestry, an English garden scene, to hang across the hospital bed. Dickinson talked of reducing the size of his office if he pulled through. They would have retired to Cornwall, Vera says: 'He would paint me, we would watch those big waves, have a nice cottage. That's what we were dreaming about. He loved the sea.'

In September, Vera moved her husband to Montreal, where they had bought a flat-roofed house in Westmount when Dickinson was designing the CIBC. 'I thought I could leave it behind, it was a grotesque bargain you can make with the devil,' Vera said of her decision. Dickinson was taken to Royal Victoria Hospital. Of his associates, Korbee was the first to know he was ill. Vera swore him to secrecy, but when she started to talk about selling the firm to John B. Parkin Associates, Korbee insisted she tell the others. On 12 October, the six of them met with Vera at the house. On 13 October, Dickinson made a will leaving his estate to Vera.

On 14 October, a Saturday, Korbee opened the Champlain Secondary

School in Pembroke, Ontario, for Dickinson. That night Webb and Tirion went to the hospital at Dickinson's request. 'Whether he pulled two names out of a hat or not, I don't know; I felt honoured,' said Tirion. 'He was quite lucid, very, very thin. He usually weighed over 240 pounds. He was down to 95—a pretty sad sight. Peter asked us to carry on. Within a week, the thing came apart.' The seminary of the Jesuit Fathers of Upper Canada was opened on 15 October. That morning, six days short of his thirty-sixth birthday, Dickinson died.

The next day, in Toronto, Boris Zerafa, just 28, made the announcement. 'We were totally flabbergasted,' said Justin Klim. 'There was the whole opera comique after that. Everyone was ready to leave and look for work. Boris said: "Listen. Don't move. We have projects, and we will try to continue." Boris told Peter Webb: "This is the chance of a lifetime." ' The projects referred to by Zerafa were the Telegram building for Yolles and Rotenberg, Inn on the Park for Sharp, and Lothian Mews, a retail and office complex surrounding a courtyard, for an English client, Angus Critchley-Waring. (Lothian Mews was conceived as a temporary installation pending approval of a phased in-fill project anchored by a 40-storey tower.) All were begun under Dickinson and completed, after his death, by his former henchmen.

Negotiations between Vera and the Parkin firm broke down. John C. and a business advisor travelled to the Montreal office within a few days of Dickinson's death to examine legal agreements and project records—'too many fees at too low prices,' they concluded. Parkin remembered something else about the visit: 'They were already scraping Peter's name off the wall and all the drawings, with those electric pens.' Webb, in Toronto, and Menkes, in Montreal, the only associates registered at the time, sought advice from two lawyers. One was John Turner, future Prime Minister of Canada. The architects were told to obey orders and not ask questions. There was a decampment from both offices organized, said Korbee, like a military operation. Isadore Sharp, anxious to see Inn on the Park built, gave the fledgling firm a weekly payroll. Kenneth Rotenberg offered the Waterloo Trust building in Kitchener. 'On those two jobs they went on to become one of North America's largest architectural firms,' said Sharp, who has been using Webb Zerafa Menkes Housden, or WZMH, ever since. Sharp has one regret: 'The sign on the hotel site should have had Peter Dickinson's name on it, too. Peter Webb wouldn't have minded—he was so grateful to get the job.'

Dickinson's body was cremated on 17 October 1961. A small private ceremony was held at the Joseph C. Ray Funeral Home. Vera, although she told reporters she would scatter the ashes over the ocean near Halifax, dispersed them from a plane over Portland, Maine. 'To me, sinking, New England was closest to England. Since he was an Englishman, I thought the ocean was the thing.' Vera remained in Toronto with her sons, who were 5 and 2 when their father died. She sent them to Upper Canada College, and after that, to Trinity College and Osgoode Law School.

All three now reside in California. The house in Montreal was sold to Franz-Paul Decker, a former conductor of the Montreal Symphony Orchestra. Vera still owns property in Toronto. Whenever she visits, she takes a furnished apartment at the Benvenuto. It was during one of her stays, in 1989, that I met her in person. 'You'll see a fat, old broad and you'll recognize me,' she said on the phone. She turned out to be a beauty—fine skin, striking hair, high cheekbones. She refused to be photographed, offering instead to send 'pictures of my legs on which I earned my living'. Decidedly visible were lots of jewellery and an ornate lorgnette, a handy instrument when it came to perusing a luncheon menu and wondering: 'What the hell is a paillard of chicken?' She still commands attention.

After her husband died, Vera waged a long and bitter battle with Webb, Zerafa, Menkes, and Housden over authorship and rights to drawings. (The Ontario Association of Architects will not show the Dickinson file, even to researchers, for fear of inciting controversy.) Vera sued the Jesuit Fathers, in 1965, and the Canadian Imperial Bank of Commerce's realty arm, Dorchester Realty, in 1977, alleging unpaid fees. 'I wasn't suing, I was defending,' she says. 'I had no choice. How many other women have you heard of that fought? I had proved myself as a woman, a mother and loyal wife—what else is there? I fought.'

On 29 January 1990, the Benvenuto became the first building of 1950s vintage to be designated by the Toronto Historical Board. Others of Dickinson's works haven't fared so well. The Canadian Red Cross Society headquarters,the first building he worked on for Page and Steele, was also the first of his designs to be demolished, in 1989. In 1986, the lobby of the Prudential Building was stripped and redesigned, to its detriment. The base of Trans-Canada Pipelines, an award-winner, was encumbered with a protruding greenhouse addition. The Four Seasons Motor Hotel has been torn down. The north addition to the Park Plaza is to be refurbished and re-skinned beyond recognition; the connecting link between the old and new wings will be replaced by a modish palm court entrance. The base of the Canadian Imperial Bank of Commerce tower is being dolled up and renovated into an atrium that will swallow the plaza under glass. There are plans to sling an overhead walkway across the courtyard of Toronto Teachers' College.

There's probably no single building by Dickinson, with the exception of the Benvenuto, whose alteration or demolition would bring defenders to the ramparts. He did not design masterpieces. His big inning lasted all of eleven and a half years. Yet his career is in many ways exemplary. Dickinson's strength lay in his continuing search for an appropriate modern architecture, in a country resistant to modernism, for clients who prized economy at least as much as style. That alone is sufficient cause to treat his easy-going and street-smart buildings with respect. For Dickinson did not design isolated objects, as modernists are always accused of doing. His theme was building-in-landscape-in-city. His style was Anglo-Canadian Modern, pictorial and personable, faithful to the moment, sensitive to locale and circumstance.

Dickinson's professional stance is likewise admirable. Because he was not an ideologue, he did not become a victim of modernism: he did not pretend to heroism, he wasn't out to save the world. As long as he engaged with people of intelligence and imagination, he enjoyed collaboration and shared responsibility. He could abide imperfection. He wasn't haunted by eternity. Nor, for that matter, is Vera. She is not distressed about the physical abuse of her husband's architecture: money talks, owners have rights. She only regrets that her sons have no memory of their father. Others do.

PETER DICKINSON WAS ONE OF THE PEOPLE WHO SPAWNED A NEW ERA. HE WAS A FORERUNNER. HE SET A PACE. HE WAS ALWAYS EXPLORING. HE WAS FREE AND MODERN FOR THE TIME. HE HAD A FREEDOM IN HIS MIND TO USE MATERIALS IN AN EXCITING WAY. HE HAD AN AMAZING ABILITY TO ENVISION A DETAIL. HE BROUGHT STYLE TO THE DAY-TO-DAY ARCHITECTURE OF CAN-ADA. HE HELPED ELEVATE THE QUALITY OF APARTMENT AND OFFICE BUILD-INGS. HE COULD CREATE, WITHIN A BUDGET, A LOOK THAT COULD ATTRACT PEOPLE. HE COULD EXCITE PEOPLE. HE CERTAINLY SAW BIG CLIENTS AND BIG PROJECTS AND BIG DEVELOPMENTS. HE COULD VERY WELL HAVE DESIGNED MUSEUMS. HE WOULD HAVE DESIGNED A GREAT CIVIC BUILDING. HE WOULD HAVE EVOLVED MUCH MORE IN HIS THINKING. HE DIDN'T REALIZE THE FULL POWER OF HIS CREATIVITY. HE WORKED HIS HEART OUT. HE NEVER TAILORED THE WORK TO THE FEE. HE WAS FOREVER DESIGNING THE NEXT BUILDING. HE NEVER STOPPED. HE NEVER QUITE BELIEVED HE WAS GOING TO DIE.

HE MUST HAVE BEEN OUTRAGED HIS LIFE ENDED SO SOON.

PEOPLE

Allan Fleming

Something about the living-room jars your sense of boundaries. Eight assorted chairs comprise the furniture. Straddling every available window ledge, a fine collection of antique moulded bottles glints like an eccentric stained-glass window. The bookshelves boast a complete set of the Nonesuch Dickens and a near-complete run of King Penguins. A number of old wooden letterforms, salvaged by an employee at Dayton Signs, decorate the wall in a neat cluster. And there in the midst of this tastefully assembled literary flotsam sits Canada's most distinguished graphic designer, Allan Fleming, with a Roy Rogers pin stuck to the lapel of a worn jean jacket, Shakhti sandals on his feet and a cravat wrapped haphazardly round his neck.

It's soon apparent that there's a poetic logic at work here. The droll sitting-room bearing signs of Fleming's restless intelligence, penchant for collecting, mistrust of regimentation, and love of letters—even the coloured bottles are saved for their letterforms—houses a free spirit.

Fleming himself uses a metaphor from palaeontology: 'In a sense,' he wrote in a recent issue of *graphicaids* magazine, 'I am a sort of classical dinosaur in my approach to typography. I feel like a Brontosaurus struggling around in the tar pits, trying vainly to do my own thing but sensing, with my mini-brain, that the end is near.'

The first thing that pops into mind when someone mentions Fleming isn't his brontosaural qualities so much as his virtuosity. His output over twenty years has been profuse, as anyone who caught the recent retrospective exhibition of his work, at the Vancouver Art Gallery, where it originated, or at the Art Gallery of Ontario, must surely have noticed. The logos reverberate impressively: CN, Gray Coach, Ontario Hydro, Trent University, the Toronto Symphony. His gallery invitations, most of them executed in the 1950s for the now defunct Gallery of Contemporary Art, still sparkle. Posters, catalogues, book jackets, the sumptuous pages of *Canada, A Year of the Land*—everything is stamped with the quality, wit, and class that impart something of the feel of Georgian silver to Fleming's designs. Moreover, the exhibition clearly illustrates Fleming's belief that designing 'is really a great deal of fun. For there is nothing quite like the kick of putting a page together.'

The wayward sense of fun and freedom that nourishes Fleming's work stands in direct contradiction to current typographical modes laid down by the so-called Swiss School. The Swiss designers, basing their principles on those of the Bauhaus, advocate the careful use of Helvetica typefaces, a good system on the page, the controlled use of space—all guaranteed to give a cold, scientific look. Compared with the rational Swiss, Fleming's passion for letterforms is positively tropical. 'I consider myself a Romantic designer,' he said. 'I hate the grid applied to the printed page.'

Fleming first encountered letterforms early in the 1950s while working in a commercial art studio. To this day he speaks of alphabetical shapes and styles with unreserved enthusiasm: 'I think letterforms are funny; they're marvellous and romantic.' His sensuous attachment to them naturally carried over into his work as a book designer. 'He wants everything to be lovely and beautiful,' commented Laurie Lewis, Fleming's former assistant at the University of Toronto Press. 'He's just like Sir Lancelot.'

The bulk of Fleming's work as a book designer was accomplished at the University of Toronto Press, which he joined in 1968, a year after the runaway success of *Canada, A Year of the Land*. He'd spent the previous five years successfully pursuing a career in advertising and no one quite understood why he took a big cut in salary to join the Press. Nonetheless, there he was, supervising the design of between 80 and 100 books a year, many of them honoured and awarded. His most daunting assignment was *The Collected Works of Erasmus* (UTP), published in 1974. It took six months for Fleming and his assistants to turn the enormous manuscript with its nightmare of footnotes and line notes into a set of beautiful physical objects.

How does he do it? With self-assurance he replies: 'Most designers enforce design decisions on the printed page, I don't. I'm too respectful of the material.' His former colleagues readily elaborate on the Fleming method. Ken Rodmell, art director for *Toronto Life*, worked with him at Cooper and Beatty in the 1950s. He singles out Fleming's 'respect for traditional typographic design'—rare among contemporary designers—as the outstanding feature of his approach. 'He taught me,' Rodmell continues, 'that a designer should design for the problem; he's not an illustrator. He has to pick the typeface that's right for the message: you don't set Dickens in Helvetica.'

Over at Dreadnaught Press, designer Robert MacDonald mentions the same theme. MacDonald was so impressed with what he saw of Fleming's work and personality at Maclaren Advertising that he followed him into publishing as an $80-a-week apprentice. Fleming changed MacDonald's orientation to graphic design. 'The most important thing he taught me was to subordinate your personality to the text. You have to identify with what you're designing. It's the standard number but he's the only one that does it.'

In addition to this kind of chameleonship, Fleming is an acknowledged master of the more practical aspects of design such as estimating costs, laying out pages, selecting paper and typefaces, and choosing among different printing methods. His expertise as well as his emphasis on the primacy of the material at hand lie behind the notion that there's no distinctive Fleming style. In other words, his style is so appropriate to whatever he's designing that it's completely subsumed in the product and thus invisible. 'The problem is that his style is not obvious,' muses Rodmell. 'His very approach negates the idea of style. If there *is* a style, it has evolved naturally instead of being consciously imposed.'

If there's no Fleming style, there most certainly is a Fleming *purpose*. His romanticism is related to the need for organization. In his own words, he tries 'to design something which should be noticed, and then read. In a visual life which is so active, you've got to have some peace in reading. What I'm creating is an island in the storm where people can read with respect for the material.'

There's no doubt that he succeeds. His books are so attractive that your eye is guided in a kind of Platonic progression from form to ideas. The horizontal movement of eye across type is accomplished with ease and luxury. You're hardly aware of it. There is always enough space provided for the contemplation of a drawing, illustration, or argument. Fleming hovers behind the books he's designed as though they were so many masks disguising his protean pursuit of beauty.

Given Fleming's typographical sorcery, it's not surprising that his years at the University of Toronto Press coincided with the upgrading of university press productions. As Laurie Lewis remarks, 'a jury at the Look of Books Show will now say of a university press production that it's a "typical university press book, excellent in every way". Eight years ago, this would never have happened.'

Even more dramatic has been the rise in status of the graphic designer in general. When Fleming hung up his shingle in 1957, no one knew what he meant. The quality of book design and corporate design was indifferent. But, thanks largely to Fleming's designs and to his tireless campaigning on behalf of visual quality, interest in graphic design has burgeoned. 'He has set the standards for an entire country,' wrote Robert Fulford in a recent essay about Fleming.

Right now Fleming is on leave of absence from the Press, or as he describes it, 'I'm out in the cruel, cruel world where I have to perform.' He's still active in book design, having just completed *This Land, This People* for Gage, and Freeman Patterson's *The Joy of Photography* for Van Nostrand Reinhold. Fleming first encountered Patterson's work in *Canada, A Year of the Land* and found the photographer's point of view congenial: 'He didn't enforce his imagination on a certain dewdrop.' In addition, he's directing the design of a book to be published by John Sime, *Joy and Ivy*. It's a collection of letters from Beatrix Potter to her Canadian milliner. Also with Sime, he'll be overseeing the design of a *Portrait of Eric Gill*, using the text of a radio program on Gill.

Fleming has undertaken other kinds of work. He designs *TV Guide*. He lectures on typography at the Ontario College of Art. But, like the audience for the books he's designed, he too feels the need for an island in the storm. He clearly regrets his decision to leave U of T Press, and hopes to be back there soon. Freelancing is not the easiest way to make a living, particularly for someone who has suffered several heart attacks and strokes over the last half-dozen years. Moreover, Fleming finds the philosophy of commercial publishing houses alien, if not hostile, to his own. 'For them,' he says in his forthright way, 'publishing is ephemeral; for me it's holy.' The upgrading of the commercial Canadian book has not, to Fleming's disappointment, proceeded at the same rate as other fields of graphic design. 'The designers who were promising in the sixties,' he claims, 'have been squashed by their clients, frozen at the stick, locked in power drive. Designers are in a sense ahead of their time; Canadian publishers are very much behind the times.'

The gap he's talking about isn't just a feature of design. Fleming may very

well be sounding the lament of the 1970s. If it weren't for the crazy eclecticism and educated flair of people like him—people who keep their rear-
view mirrors polished—there'd be little to nourish the senses except disco,
Big Macs, and offset.   — *October 1977*

Alison Smithson

One look at Alison Smithson and you know she's her own person. 'It's
difficult to escape from fashion—none of us can,' she insists, and yet there
are no visible signs that she's been infected by it. Wearing a beige cable-knit
dress and sensible white nurse's oxfords, her grey hair pulled back, her bird-
like face cosmetic-free, she was the daisy in a sea of silk flowers at the
Courtyard Café.

As in her costume, so in her architecture. Smithson is a radical from
way back; she's one of the few women whose names appear in surveys of
architectural history. Born in Sheffield, she qualified at the University of
Newcastle in Tyneside in 1944, at the age of 21, and the same year married
Peter Smithson, an ex-serviceman who trained as a town planner at the same
institution. Straightaway the Smithsons rushed into revolution, taking up
arms against postwar English architecture as practised by the local housing
authorities. Under the dignified title of The New Humanism, the English
working classes were being provided with homogenized public housing
distinguished by cute, picturesque details such as pitched roofs, bricky materials, and wood-framed picture windows. 'People's detailing', it was dubbed
by its critics, and it simply wasn't good—or real—enough for the Smithsons.
(Or, for that matter, the English.) Their response to The New Humanism
was something they called Brutalism, the first and most famous example
being their steel-and-glass Hunstanton School, completed in 1954.

Truth to materials, honesty of intent, no curlicues, no shtick—this is what
the Smithsons, eyes trained on social and cultural realities, preached. Over
the years they continued to refine their ideas and grapple with the challenge
of rebuilding Europe, always ready to contest received wisdom once it had
fallen into the hands of bureaucrats and to substitute new ways of thinking
about urban problems. 'We've always received a lot of flak, but our ideas
have entered into the ideas of others,' says Smithson.

The osmotic metaphor is important. As Smithson sees it, if an architect is
good, the history of architecture flows through his bloodstream, not through
his index cards. 'It's like cultural food. The way the English have eaten
Palladio, for example, is not the way Sweden has eaten Palladio. That's the
real divide between our European attitude and the collage attitude of North
America. We're incredibly puritanical. We think it's immoral to cut up and

rip off.' Although she doesn't mention names, they come to mind: Michael Graves and his plaster garlands, Philip Johnson and the classical hat on his AT&T building. Borrow from here, tack on there. 'A form of escapism', comments Smithson of so-called postmodern classicism. 'It has nothing to do with real needs. Everybody misses out—the doer and the consumer. If you do something everybody understands, society is pulled together and it puts energy into everybody.'

Palladio, as it happens, was one of the influences on Brutalism, but his name wasn't drawn out of a hat. 'Even sixty years ago,' claims Smithson, 'a great many people in Europe had a classical education. They went to look at ruins, or the site of ruins, with the Greek or Roman writers as ghostly company, as it were. The information they had made them as people, made their minds, connected them with others in general and gave them a key to the place.' In other words, they earned the right to use Palladio as a source, and, likewise, people didn't have to run to their architectural dictionaries to understand what they built.

The same applies to Brutalism and its subsequent development, New Brutalism. The Smithsons came across the term in a newspaper cutting that referred to *concret brut*—concrete straight out of the mixer. 'The English being a literary culture, it just took,' says Smithson. 'The definition of Brutalism is being able to work with the as-found. If it's steel and glass, let the qualities speak—the old Miesian thing. And it's also the way people are living—patterns of change.' These principles, she implies, must still apply if architecture is to be real.

Although 'things are getting smaller and smaller in England', meaning that opportunities to build are few, Smithson continues to teach, write, and reflect, guided by her interests and instincts. You never know when or where the as-found will strike your consciousness. The 'big discovery' she stumbled across in Canada—she came to give lectures in Ottawa and Toronto—was the Rideau Canal. She's now collecting information about the Canal, believing that if you start from one discovery you can begin 'renewing and re-energizing everything'.

In the present-day world, there's no alternative, Smithson believes. What do you do with the buildings you have? If you do design an urban garden, what do you hope to maintain? It's hard work finding the answers to these questions, and glossy magazines aren't the place to look for them. Solar energy, shadow, wind—these are the subjects, perhaps the only ones, that Smithson would assign architecture students.

Which brings her back to the subject of fashion. Most architects, she maintains, go places with preconceived ideas instead of being receptive. Experience or, better, wisdom is a far trustier guide. 'You know,' she says, 'architecture is such a long-term art. That's why it's called an old man's art: you have to know certain kinds of things are passing. You have to be fairly calm and relaxed and think what it is that will serve people over the next forty to sixty years. What's quality enough to receive change is worth receiving change.' Having delivered her message, she subsides into silence, a Sphinx.

—*January 1982*

Eric Arthur

Eric Arthur, who died on Monday at the age of 84, was a legendary and idiosyncratic figure, both pioneer preservationist and champion of modern architecture, who made an art of living. In no particular hierarchy, he was professor, architect, author, editor, *raconteur*, correspondent, perambulator, fisherman—a gentleman. He wore wonderful tweed hats and carried exotic canes and umbrellas. He could dash off a letter to the editor in praise of women who crochet on the subway at the same time as he was digging into the history of Canadian ironwork. In the course of his long life, he touched many people's lives. Says architect George Baird: 'From as far back as the thirties, insofar as Toronto architecture had a patron, he was it. In our terms, in our times, he's just like a mountain.'

Baird's tribute combines appreciation of Arthur's role as an architectural activist with warm regard for his person: 'He didn't discover Niagara-on-the-Lake but he did document the major monuments there, many in derelict condition, very early. He was strategic in getting all that stuff taken seriously. His book *Toronto: No Mean City* [University of Toronto Press, 1964] had an enormous impact. A lot of his writing is quite sloppy, but don't forget, he began all this. He was the professional adviser on competitions for a generation. He went out on a limb personally to rescue St Lawrence Hall from demolition. These days, we can have a debate; before him, we wouldn't have had anything. He was extremely charming and an extraordinarily natty dresser.'

Born in New Zealand, Arthur arrived in Toronto from England in 1923 to take up the position of associate professor of architecture at the University of Toronto, where he remained until 1966. In addition, he shared a practice with William Fleury from 1937 to 1965. 'The thing that always impressed me,' says Stephen Otto, former head of the provincial Heritage Conservation Programs, 'was how early he began. In the Ontario Archives are photographs he took beginning in 1929. He went round Ontario for three or four summers taking photographs of buildings he thought of value—before there was an inventory to guide him—using his own sense of what our architectural heritage was.

'With those photographs, he interested students in doing measured drawings—drawings done by actual measurement on site. For many buildings which have since been destroyed, they're the only accurate records we have.

That endeavour resulted in monographs that came out of the school in the late thirties, published as "Early Architecture of Ontario". It's the first inventory of significant buildings in Ontario, and still a damn good guide.'

From 1939 to 1944, James Murray, the editor of *Canadian Architect*, studied under Arthur at the University of Toronto. 'In a real sense, Arthur was Mr Architectural Education in Canada,' Murray says. 'He taught us architectural design through the five years of the course, and also the history of architecture, particularly modern architecture. When he taught us design, he wasn't looking at the past. He was a marvellous interpreter and analyst of the origins of the Modern Movement—Gropius, Le Corbusier, Frank Lloyd Wright. As an indication of his interest in modern architecture, he spearheaded the idea of an international competition for Toronto City Hall.

'He was a marvellous guy and had a marvellous wit. In first year, students actually used to design buildings. He gave us a little house to do. When I showed him my drawings, he made some suggestions about the doorway. A few days later, he saw my new drawings and said: "Murray, where did you get that pathetic door?" "You gave it to me two days ago," I answered. From that day on, we became lifelong friends. For years he edited the *Royal Architectural Institute of Canada Journal* [now defunct] but when I founded *Canadian Architect* against the wishes of the RAIC, the person who supported me was Eric. When he wrote, he would fish a pen out of his pocket and write elegant prose and never cross anything out.'

Another person who met Arthur in the 1940s is Edith Firth, former librarian in the rare Canadiana section of the Toronto Public Library. Arthur thanked her profusely in the acknowledgement section of *No Mean City*, and again in his last book, *Iron*, which he co-authored with Thomas Ritchie (University of Toronto Press, 1982). 'The thing about Eric was he made you see things you were familiar with,' Firth says. 'In *No Mean City*, he says St Paul's Roman Catholic Church is the most beautiful in Toronto. "Don't be silly," I told him. "It's dirty, dingy, run-down." It's been cleaned up since. "Come down and have a look," he insisted, and dammit, he was right. He could see it, I couldn't.'

According to Firth, Arthur 'wasn't a wild preserver. He wouldn't join the stampede to save everything, believing a city has to continue living. He didn't want a museum. But he was tremendously enthusiastic about everything connected with buildings. He got terribly excited about things. He kept phoning with his latest discovery, his latest idea. Two weeks ago, he was still working, still discovering. I drove him around to a helluva lot of cemeteries.'

Arthur was working on a history of cemeteries and funeral customs before he died. He never learned to drive because of his contempt for automobiles. Taking a stroll with him, however, was a treat. Says Blanche van Ginkel, former dean of architecture at the University of Toronto: 'When I came here in 1977, Eric was the first person who asked me to lunch—it was quite touching. He came down to the school and walked with me down St George

Street to the York Club, all the way regaling me with stories about the houses on St George and complaining about the offensiveness of ivy. He was very testy about ivy. He was the first, or one of the few, who wanted to introduce into Toronto a sense of the twentieth century in architecture.'

Journalist June Callwood met Arthur about eight years ago at a luncheon. 'We just loved one another, or at least I loved him. We began to have regular lunches. I drove him around to look at ironwork. We exchanged gifts. He took me to what he called his beanery, the York Club. When he received an honorary doctorate at Guelph University last June, I was there. A week before he died, copies of the *Iron* book were delivered to his friends, each with a personal inscription. He carried on an enormous correspondence in tiny, tiny handwriting. Rarely did a week go by without a note from Eric. His idea of a note was to attach a clipping and add an anecdote about the Duchess of Bedford.'

Arthur also valued the spoken word. 'He felt that conversation should be witty and have content,' Callwood says. 'He never talked about the weather or gossip—he was unaware people did in conversation. He gave you jewels— perfectly told stories. My lasting-forever impression is of his deep courtesy. He was incapable of unkindness or gaucherie because of the pureness of his interest. He enjoyed excellence. He and I would stroll along and he'd see a manhole cover with a design on it. "There's another one at the corner of Adelaide and Queen," he'd say. I never see a manhole cover without thinking of him.'
— *November 1982*

Ron Thom

The house that Ron Thom designed for himself in 1974 sits on a steep wooded hillside overlooking the Scarborough Bluffs. The site is the next best thing to a secluded parcel of land in beautiful British Columbia, the province that nurtured Thom's imagination and architecture. To reach it, you pass a Dead End sign and drive as far as you can without falling over the ledge. The house sits up to the left, practically disappearing into the backdrop of tree, rock, and sky. At night the only proof of its existence is a vertical band of light slashing through the darkness—windows revealing a seductive glimpse of staircase.

The four-storey house is made of unpainted cedar, another reminder of the west coast and a material Thom likes because it's 'the most durable' (also the most soft-spoken). The immediately notable qualities of the interior are warmth and unpretentiousness. No flash, no gimmickry. Lots of dark stained oak and glowing colour—tiny red and blue paper birds suspended from the ceiling, a chair draped in a crocheted afghan, hanging lights made of twisted balsa wood, endless bouquets of dried flowers, a baby grand standing in a triangular skylit niche, leaf-patterned wallpaper in the bathroom, pottery jugs, giant Inuit sculptures, paintings and prints by west coast artists propped on shelves or tacked to the wall with pins.

Thom, 59, came to national prominence in the 1960s with the design of Massey College (on the University of Toronto campus) and Trent University, for which he also did the master plan. Among his other projects: the design and master plan of the Metropolitan Toronto Zoo, the Shaw Festival Theatre, the renovation of the St Lawrence Centre, and a variety of colleges, hotels, apartment buildings, offices, and private homes, including that of Murray and Barbara Frum. 'Ron is unique in this country,' says fellow architect Jerome Markson. 'He's very special. He does his own thing and he follows it true. He doesn't drift with fashions every few years. He loves our Canadian landscape. His buildings fit in the landscape very intimately. He's creative but modest.'

A 'man of tall timbers', as Walter Kehm, a landscape architect, described him, Thom is not one for gossip or long perorations. He tends to converse by reaching for a handy piece of paper and doing a quick sketch. 'Look, dear,' he'll say softly, flourishing his pen, 'here's what I mean.' From time to time, he loosens one of the bundles of his emotions and explodes with something on the lines of: 'All our lives are frustrated in one way or another. We've all got our set of things we're frustrated about. The idea is to relax people, ease them. And it doesn't just come to me—it comes to city planners. Who makes the choices? And it comes back to the schools, too, although never having gone to one . . .'

Thom is an artist by temperament, an architect by vocation. His Scottish father did sheet metal work—'he kept us warm during the Depression'—and sang in the Vancouver Bach Choir. His Irish mother, the second woman lawyer in Canada, desperately wanted him to become a concert pianist, insisting he practise five hours every day. Says Thom: 'I'll never forget the day I looked out the kitchen window and saw my girlfriend playing baseball with a whole bunch of boys—practising piano didn't mean a damn thing to me.'

Drawing and painting did, thanks to the 'incredible lady' who ran the art class when he was in the seventh grade. When he reached grade 12, he went to high school in the morning and the Vancouver School of Art in the afternoon. In his spare time, he sold shoes. The fall after graduation, he was conscripted: 'I couldn't stand the thought of the army. Mom and dad were totally against war.' Instead, he joined the air force. Navigation was not his strong point. Once, missing his cues, he discovered he was flying over Winnipeg, not Vancouver.

In 1945, he went back to art school, graduating in 1947. 'It was an electric time,' he says. He met artists Molly and Bruno Bobak and Gordon Smith, and came under the influence of two teachers at the school, Jack Shadbolt and B.C. Binning. Binning was in the habit of inviting internationally known artists and architects to Vancouver, putting them up at his house and holding regular soirées. One night, he invited Thom and Arthur Erickson to meet Richard Neutra, the great Viennese architect who had emigrated to the United States in 1923 to make contact with Louis Sullivan and Frank Lloyd Wright.

'Did Neutra ever turn me on,' says Thom, who learned as much from Wright—'I sometimes call myself Frank Lloyd Thom'—as he did from Neutra. 'He was a sociologist. He would tell us things about the effects of highrises on human behaviour. By the end of that year, I couldn't see myself sitting down and doing drawings all my life.' Thom approached Charles Edward (Ned) Pratt, a principal in the Vancouver firm Thomson Berwick and Pratt. 'He said he wanted to come down and work for me,' says Pratt. 'He did anything—he swept floors. He learned so quickly . . .' Thom would return from work, nap, and then 'get the books up' every night until 2 a.m. 'I learned everything in the office—those damn books are so stupid,' he flares.

'Let's talk post-war,' says Thom, relaxing on a well-worn sofa upholstered in forest green velvet. 'We on the west coast were more conscious of Japanese, California, and northern architecture than anything out east. [He reaches for a notebook and sketches a Chinese pagoda balanced by a huge weight at the end of a chain.] The Chinese figured out cable grounding back ten centuries. But, also, there was the beautiful detailing of the wood joining—good strong stuff. So we played all kinds of games with wood. We were all very oriented to natural materials. If I built you a wood house, there's no damn way you're going to get away with painting that thing.'

A sip of wine, a cigarette and: 'Say we were building a house, the first thing we always did was really look at that site. We took topography into account—a building has to make love to a site. [Here he plays a minuet in the air with his fingers.] See this house—from the bedroom windows, you see the sunrise. The breakfast room faces east, and I put that 60-inch slot right of the fireplace so the last rays of the sun flicker into the study above.'

It took eight years for Thom to become a registered architect—he was 34. The next year, 1958, he became a partner in TBP. In 1959 came the first round of the competition—'the fairest I've ever been in'—for Massey College. Vincent Massey flew four architects he felt were appropriate for the job—Thom, John C. Parkin, Arthur Erickson, and Carmen Corneil—to the family home in Port Hope for a three-day seminar on the English residential college system on which Massey College is modelled.

Thom got the job. Still with TBP, he drew the college in Vancouver and travelled to Toronto periodically to supervise construction. By the time this unassuming masterpiece was completed in 1964, Thom had broken with the Vancouver firm and set up his own office in Toronto—he'd been offered another prestigious commission, Trent University. 'There was a fair amount

Massey College, exterior

The courtyard of Massey College

of strain,' Thom says. 'Suddenly, here I was running an office by myself, something I never did in my life before. I did have a drinking problem years ago—it was one of those emotional things.' 'He was a genuine poet,' says Jack Shadbolt, 'and phenomenally intelligent. But he didn't have a chance. He had a chip on his shoulder about the establishment in general, which was due to lack of education. He wasn't an intellectual at all, and that griped him. He couldn't take to forced discipline.'

Architecture, at least as it's practised by people like Thom, is a romantic profession that demands everything you've got. Drinking and divorce— Thom has been divorced twice—are occupational hazards. 'Ron's a tremendously sensitive guy,' says Murray Beynon, a partner in Thom's firm. 'It's hard enough when he's presenting the logical aspects of a building to a client, but presenting the humanistic aspects is very difficult—it's taken its toll.'

Seeking out gurus to act as mentors, as Thom did Pratt, comes with the territory, too. Vancouver architect Paul Merrick is one of many who sought out Thom. He'd 'become aware of him' in 1942, as a high-school student, and when he decided to drop out of architecture school—Thom eventually persuaded him to go back for his ticket—he called Thom.

'He was doing Massey College at the time,' Merrick recalls. 'I wanted to learn what I could from him. I enjoyed his company and admired his work. I felt he perceived, as few others do, that there was a realm of art in architecture, that the two things are inseparable. That's difficult to perceive, and Ron always has perceived it. The other reason is that Arthur Erickson, one of my tutors at the University of British Columbia and then at an early stage in his career, advised me one day to get close to whomever I wanted to work with.'

After finishing his degree, Merrick spent three years in Toronto working on Trent University. One of his jobs was designing the Reginald Faryon Bridge—with M.S. Yolles, the structural engineers—two concrete arches standing on hyperbolic paraboloids. ('Hell, I couldn't even draw that thing,' says Thom admiringly.) 'Exciting? To be sure,' says Merrick. 'It probably wrecked my first marriage—she went, I stayed. It's not easy to talk about Ron's style but certainly his work has a quality—there's an atmosphere about it. It's warm, humane. It requires purposeful application—that thoroughness ends up showing.'

Says Pratt: 'Thom and Merrick are the only two architects Canada has ever spawned who design from the neck down. They have an Elizabethan mix of heart and mind. I'm sick to death of architecture from the neck up.' Neck-down architecture isn't an easy thing to pull off in the commercial market, which has succeeded universities and private homes as the big market of the 1980s. 'The seventies and eighties—pah! What's left?' says Thom, flailing his glasses, which hang from his neck on a chain. 'When he has a super client,' says architect Jack Diamond of Thom, 'he does what you expect of him. When he has a lousy client who doesn't push to the possible limits, he's no better than the average architect.' Says Beynon: 'He's still a real human being. In the business world of today, he hasn't reacted well. If a client rubs him the wrong way, he washes his hands of him.'

Beynon, 36, joined Thom's office seven years ago, after working in Paris and Japan. 'He's the most natural designer I've ever seen,' he says. 'It comes so easily, so fast. He always asks the common-sense questions. He gets those straight and look for the order and logic in them. He doesn't look at things in a tremendously complex way. Because he's so comfortable in the artistic sense, he doesn't feel he has to focus on that. What he does at the beginning of a project is pull in the structural and mechanical engineers to have their say. He lets his artistry flow from the requirements.' Says Morden Yolles: 'Ron is one of my favourites—I like architects who draw me out and make me work. Certain architects really draw on you; they have their own vision.'

Beynon was the project architect on two recent commercial projects, low-rise atrium buildings in Calgary and north Toronto. Thom and Beynon walked the Calgary site many times talking about colour and form. 'A flat field with yellow straw coming out—that decided the materials right there and then,' says Thom. 'It's a very light anodized aluminum colour. Poof—right into the landscape.' Beynon refers to the Toronto building, which won both an energy award and a Governor-General's medal, as 'a real Ron Thom building in the eighties'.

'Just in terms of the humanity of the place, this is a great place to work,' says architect Stephen Quigley. Thom's office feels a lot like his house, or as Beynon says: 'He will not try to dominate and control. The philosophy of the office is freedom. He lets me do my thing and I respect his incredible talent.' Thom reviews all the design work in the office, follows up leads, writes letters and articles. He still designs private houses but will involve himself in big projects close to his heart, such as the submission to the National Gallery competition. (The job went to Moshe Safdie.) Most important, he is passing down his attitudes and values—human scale, texture, colour, harmony with the landscape or cityscape—to a new generation.

Thom, who has just sold his house on account of his divorce, leans forward on the sofa and points a finger in the air. 'You know what makes me happy? You work through something with somebody—say, their house—and really, it's just like you were born together, or something. They still live in what you did for them, and they're still happy. They never forget you.'

— March 1983

Douglas Cardinal

Even wearing a pinstriped suit and loafers, Douglas Cardinal doesn't quite project the suave and carefully managed image of a successful architect. It's as though he is observing custom without having to believe in it. For all he seems to care, he might be dressed in a kimono or a toga—he would still be Douglas Cardinal, his eyes would still be fixed on some dimension beyond the physical reality of his immediate surroundings, in this case a room in the National Museum of Man [now the Canadian Museum of Civilization] in Ottawa, for which he was selected last February to design a new home.

Cardinal's appointment propelled him into the limelight, not kicking and screaming but complaining softly about the heat. The choice was bound to be controversial. Cardinal is a Métis from Red Deer, Alberta, with a dozen small buildings to his credit—credentials hardly likely to convince eastern Canada's professional élite that he's deserving of a crack at a $90-million-plus, 420,000-square-foot culture palace on the Ottawa River. Furthermore, the dozen small buildings, of which ten are in Alberta, don't conform to any of the currently fashionable definitions of the cutting edge. They're characterized by curvaceous façades inspired by natural forms, translated into brick with the aid of a computerized graphic system.

Consequently, Cardinal's style has been called 'gopher baroque', his design for the new museum likened to a stage set from *Planet of the Apes* (or dismissed as 'fifties Futurism'), and the man himself written off as a provincial. 'I lock myself up and do my thing,' says Cardinal, not the least concerned whether the sentence qualifies as a rebuttal or not. 'I haven't thought of where the rest of the profession was. I'm not playing to my profession. I appreciate what they're doing, that's great, that's nice for them. But what if you're just excited about taking a different course? I don't think I've got any royal jelly or something that makes me different. I believe every creature on this earth is an architect—they all design their own houses. Why should a few select people set themselves up as an élite? We all have it in us—all animals do.'

The pinstriped legs cross and the pinstriped arm becomes a chin-rest: 'I'll do my thing. If people like it, great. If they don't like it, that's okay, too. It would be nice if people would say, "You're acceptable," and they did this year—they accepted me into the Royal Architectural Institute of Canada—and I thought, "That's nice," but it was trying, you know, sitting there all day. I did it for them, if you understand what I mean.'

Cardinal, 49, talks a lot about acceptance and rejection and his 'native background'. Most architects would be embarrassed to talk about their buildings in relation to their ethnic origins, although that hasn't stopped them from saying Cardinal got the museum job because he's an Indian. Cardinal talks about his background because he's proud of it, because it has troubled him, because his work derives from it, and because a lot of Canadians couldn't care less.

He wanted to become an architect as early as the age of 6, while a student at the St Joseph's Convent School. At the convent he discovered the work of the great architects of the Roman Catholic Church—Michelangelo, Sangallo—in the form of etchings, drawings, books. He studied piano, painting, and sculpture but, he says, 'it was almost like painting wasn't enough, like music wasn't enough. Architecture was the ultimate challenge.'

In 1953, when he was 19, he left Red Deer for the University of British Columbia. He was excited by architectural history, 'but when it came to trying to develop my own style, there was no way that could be achieved. There seemed to be a mould I had to fit. You were supposed to be interested in early Le Corbusier and the Bauhaus School, a lot of analytical kinds of things. That left me cold. Corb's Ronchamp—now that's what I'm interested in. [The curvilinear chapel is late Corbusier and one of his most revolutionary buildings.] The professor said: "Forget it, he's gone against all the rules." '

Cardinal lasted 18 months at UBC; the final blow was being told by the director that he didn't have 'the right background' for architecture. He put himself through the University of Texas in 1956 by doing drafting jobs and graduated seven years later. His first important commission after returning to Red Deer was St Mary's Roman Catholic Church. Its form was so controversial that it scared off potential clients. Between 1967, when the church was finished, and 1977, when Cardinal's Alberta Government Services Centre in Ponoka opened, he had designed exactly two buildings.

Meanwhile, he had undergone a spiritual transformation. When St Mary's failed to bring more work and Cardinal began to suspect he might be crazy (a divorce didn't help, either), he sought out the elders on Alberta reserves for guidance. Adopting buckskins and braids, he participated in rites of purification and became involved with pressing community issues. Thus liberated, he got a haircut, bought a grey suit, and went back to work in Edmonton, where he'd relocated his office. (He now lives outside the city with his second wife.)

Perhaps the only architect who has ever championed Cardinal, and without being bothered by his 'native background', is Philip Johnson, the most powerful elder on the North American architectural reserve. Johnson was sitting on the jury for a prestigious American award for which Cardinal was being considered after designing the Ponoka building. Struck by Cardinal's way with brick and his fresh approach, Johnson tried to award him the prize. Failing to persuade the rest of the jury, he called up Cardinal in a fighting mood and said he wanted to promote him.

Thanks to Johnson, Cardinal was included in the 1979 travelling exhibition organized by the Museum of Modern Art entitled 'Transformations in Modern Architecture': 'He gave me a boost just when I needed it—"at least Philip Johnson likes me, I can't be that crazy." So I went back to being an architect.' The two men have talked on the phone, but their first meeting took place only a couple of weeks ago. 'We talked about what it meant to be an individual and the problems relating thereto; he talked to me in a fatherly way,' says Cardinal, flashing something near to a smile.

'I'm not trying to do anything but try for my own individual experience,' Cardinal murmurs. 'I'm not trying to break the rules. Corb took the rules, evolved them, and put something more into the rules than an analytic formula—a sense of soul. I thought I was in step with what Corb and Alvar Aalto [the late Finnish architect] and Felix Candela [the Spanish-born Mexican architect] were doing. I felt they were taking shapes and forms and providing a sense of drama and excitement. I don't see much in a Mondrian painting. I say, "That's nice for my head, my head is happy," but it doesn't do anything for inside me. I think the mind is one organ. It's not your whole being.'

He elaborates: 'With my church, I tried to evolve a form growing out of the functional requirements and to show respect for materials, much in the same thinking as the International Style—form follows function, less is more, all that jargon. But instead of using rectilinear forms, I used curvilinear forms. I think in curvilinear forms. My sketches are all curved forms, amorphous shapes. That's the way I think, the way I'm made. Even music I see in pictures.

'It seems I've got two parts. I feel that when I design, I design for my right hemisphere. So I will design intuitively, solve a function intuitively. Then I analyse it as criticism and figure out how I can build it. I'm very right-sided. It's part of my native background. Native culture is very right-sided—it's almost that analysis doesn't mean anything. I always found it difficult when I had to relate to left-sided society. I used to think I was odd.'

Left-siders still think he's odd, perhaps because they speak a different language. When architects talk about trees and grass, for instance, they talk about landscape—Cardinal talks about Nature. 'I have a feeling of man as part of nature and I'm part of the life chain and I have to be sensitive to what I'm doing and sometimes I'm not. Engineering has evolved to a fantastic point. We have the flexibility to create some organic forms. I'm talking about how forms evolve in nature, whether it's here, in Ontario, or in the west. I don't think it really matters. I would like to see our buildings very dynamic. They should close up at night and then open to the sun. I don't see why we can't have buildings that open and shut—that respond to the sun and close to the rain.'

Right now, however, Cardinal is devoting most of his time to the National Museum of Man, churning out computer graphics that will plot his longest and most audacious curves to date. For him, computers are left hemispheres: 'That's what a computer is, artificial intelligence that can do anything that's totally logical. I find it a very useful tool, not a threat. I look at my left side as an imperfect computer, but my right side has an imagination that can create a thousand different rooms.'

Douglas Cardinal is living out a set of contradictions. As a Métis, he's part-native, part-European (and Métis have traditionally enjoyed a lower status than treaty Indians). Although he was inducted into architecture in a convent school, he has contempt for missionaries and 'that save-our-soul trip'. In Canada he's called a provincial, Philip Johnson takes him seriously. Before he got into computerized design, his curvilinear forms were called 'aboriginal' and nobody wanted to know how much work it took to make them real; now they think he'd be nowhere without the fancy software.

Yet Cardinal manages the tensions with dignity: 'I feel that the important thing is to just know who you are and what you can and can't do; and some of the values you have, you can expand on and then try to contribute something to the people around you by giving them what you have. That's what I should do as a human being—because I believe that we should evolve to be better creatures, to a higher life form.

'I have a native background and I don't want to give up my native background to be The Professional. I can't see why I shouldn't go to a sundance and celebrate the earth and life one day, and sit down behind the computer the next day. It's supposed to be denied to me? That's bullshit. I'm proud of being part of that culture, of using it as a basis for living in the future. But people object to that. A lot of people have objected to that.'

— February 1984

Jane Jacobs

Jane Jacobs, who studies cities with a lover's passion—hope and despair—is sitting in her backyard, enjoying the view of her neighbours' backyards in her adopted city, Toronto. It's only a two-minute walk from Bloor Street, but her garden is the next best thing to a forest clearing. Instead of a lawn and flowerbeds, piles of raked leaves and the remains of Christmas trees have been allowed to rot into the ground, year after year, forming a lumpy perfumed carpet.

'The needles are what really give it body,' says Jacobs enthusiastically, as though discovering the virtues of the pine tree for the very first time. 'I love to walk the alleys and look at all the backyards and arrangements. Once, when I was going around Edmonton, I saw a hammock, and underneath it were leaves and needles. "Hey, that's the thing—just recycle what you've got," I thought. We've been doing this ever since. My daughter, who plants trees in British Columbia, said it was called making duff—that's what the forest floor is called. Sometimes we even collect other people's Christmas trees. It's a pleasant surface—the more trampling, the better it gets.'

Inhaling the heady aroma of duff and chain-sipping vermouth, Jacobs, 68, looks the picture of radiant satisfaction: she's earned it. She doesn't have a degree in planning, or architecture, or economics—she's a writer—but her observations of the way cities work and don't work, published in her first book, *The Death and Life of Great American Cities* (1961), revolutionized the urban planning profession, and her new book, *Cities and the Wealth of Nations*, might just do the same for economics. Thanks to Jacobs, ideas once considered lunatic, such as mixed-use development, short blocks, and dense concentrations of people working and living downtown, are now taken for granted.

'She's one of the most significant writers and thinkers I have ever encountered about the city,' says Kenneth Greenberg, head of Toronto's Urban Design Group. 'In the first book, which I read in the mid-sixties, she managed to look at the city in a completely different way, outside all the orthodoxies of the planning profession. I was stunned by it. My education had been full of Team 10 and the Modern Movement. That book was a revolution . . . The biggest single thing for me was her looking at the way people were using cities: you didn't have to remake the world but you worked with the realities.'

In Greenberg's view, 'Toronto is the one place on earth that, as a society, took her book to heart. The proposals that led to the Central Area Plan document—people were looking at the world through her eyes. She created a new language about the city. Previously it was loaded in favour of urban renewal and large-scale redevelopment. She's the first person to put "city blocks" back into the language as a professional term since the nineteenth century. And "stoops"—that's a New York word, and stoops didn't exist in modern architecture.'

The fact that Jacobs and her family moved to Toronto in 1967, for reasons to do with the Vietnam war, added to her influence. 'When she's stirred up, she's like a tiger,' says her husband, architect Robert Jacobs—and shortly after her arrival, she leapt to the support of the Stop Spadina movement, which halted plans for an expressway through the downtown. Next she came to the rescue of the Dundas-Sherbourne neighbourhood, which was about to be levelled by developers. Architect Jack Diamond joined her on the barricades as the bulldozers swung into action: 'Jane took one look and suggested we pull down the hoardings and call the Inspector because bulldozing crews can't work without hoardings. We took down the hoardings and called the Inspector. He stopped the bulldozers. It was extraordinary.' (The city eventually took over the property and the site was in-filled.)

Jacobs continued to challenge received opinion, speaking out against the concept of Metro government in 1974 and, more recently, against the Metro Toronto Convention Centre: to no avail. But last May she and economist David Nowlan led the fight against another proposed expressway, the Leslie Street extension. Metro Commissioner of Roads Sam Cass, when asked to comment on Jacobs, said: 'It won't be printable. I don't know her. I've never heard of her. I read her name somewhere once. I don't know anything about her ideas. Goodbye.' Jacobs, when told of Cass's reaction: 'Oh, that's nice. He had great highway plans for this city. He was going to Los Angelize this city. He just identifies me as a spoke in the wheel of opposition.'

In the little-known book *The Question of Separatism: Quebec and the Struggle for Sovereignty* (1980), Jacobs backed secession. Now, in *Cities and the Wealth of Nations*, she's challenged the articles of faith of the economist establishment. In it she argues against the nation-state as the unit of economic theory—Adam Smith was wrong—and says cities and their regions, the only sensible entities of economic analysis, can survive only by replacing imports. Reprisals have been quick in coming. 'The element of courage is always there,' says her husband. 'Walter Lippmann once wrote that there were two kinds of courage, military courage and civilian courage—she's got civilian courage. Often I think it's characteristic of women, who will face up to opposition and won't be intimidated. Most of us men will be intimidated.'

In her books as well as her actions, Jacobs champions the concrete over the abstract, local decisions over imposed solutions, people over statistics— and the sort of common sense that leads to recycling old shrubbery into duff. For all the change and controversy she's stirred up, she remains a very private person, grounded in her family, her writing, her city, and the wonders of everyday life. She has no patience for myth-making if it gets in the way of reality—and the myth of Jane Jacobs repels her most of all.

'I think I always was interested in cities,' she says simply. The city she knew first was Scranton, Pennsylvania, where she was born and raised. 'When I was a little girl, I just loved to go downtown. We lived in the suburbs— nice houses and lots of trees. That gave me an attachment to trees I'll never lose. But I even loved to go to the dentist when I was 10 because I could go around in the downtown. It was always a wonder to me. And, of course, that's where all the bookstores were, and I loved to read. But this is so egocentric—do you want all this egocentric stuff?'

Her intellectual rebelliousness was already apparent in the fourth grade, when she began studying geography: 'The teacher gave the standard line that cities were formed where there was a waterfall. I absolutely didn't believe this because there was a waterfall in Scranton—it was lovely but it didn't have anything to do with the economy of Scranton. Mines were the thing in Scranton. I was very suspicious. I didn't think the waterfall could account for it.'

Jacobs graduated from high school when she was 18. Fed up with formal education, she learned shorthand and typing and set out for New York to seek her fortune. 'It was the Depression and I was looking for secretarial jobs,' she says. 'It was very difficult because I would find a job and the company would close down. But as I looked for jobs, I became happy learning about the city.' Inspired by her wanderings, she wrote articles on New York's fur, diamond, flower, and leather districts, which were published by *Vogue*— 'so that was encouraging to me. Later, I wrote an article that *Cue* magazine took about manhole covers and what they told you about what was running underneath. Now do you understand about me and cities?'

The 'egocentric stuff', whatever there was of it, disappears into the duff like so many curling leaves. Jacobs doesn't mention it, but she eventually enrolled as an extension student at Columbia University: courses but no degree. She neglects to say she's been offered numerous honorary degrees—and turned them all down. She touches on her job with *Architectural Forum* (as a writer, not a secretary) but doesn't comment on raising three children for fear of exploiting her family.

'This seems ridiculous,' she does say, 'but actually, I like attention being paid to my books and not to me. I don't know who this celebrity called Jane Jacobs is—it's not me. My ideal is to be a hermit, to a certain extent, and do my work. And I just detest it when I'm around somewhere and strangers say, "Are you Jane Jacobs?" and engage me in conversation in this obsequious way. That has nothing to do with me. You either do your work or you're a celebrity: I'd rather do my work.'

Her work has been criticized for offering brilliant insights without the programs for implementing them. She scoffs: 'What I try to do is tell how things work. If I'm right about it, and I try as hard as I can to be right, then lots and lots of other people have to think about this. I'm not some kind of Atlas holding up the world. The last thing I want to be is someone who hands down the truth from a superior position—"do this, do that"—no, no, I don't believe in that.

'The most useful thing I can do is try to explain to people what are the wrong things to do. Then you put your mind to what can be the right things. But prescriptions—the whole point of my writing is that prescriptions have to be local, empiric, and based on real life at that time. That means prescriptions for Toronto have got to be made in Toronto—and when Toronto does that, it's just wonderful. The City Home infilling and the St Lawrence development were both made in Toronto... Toronto is better than any other city I know at mixing in residences with workplaces. That's for the City of Toronto. As for the suburbs of Toronto, it's incredible how benighted they are when they have the example of what's been working in Toronto.'

It's no wonder people wish Jacobs would play fairy godmother: she has a way of making the most abstruse issues seem simple. As reviewers have noted, sometimes back-handedly, her books are a delight to read. But not, she says, to write: 'Oh, I'm so chaotic. I just scramble as best I can. Sometimes people say, "You use such wonderful examples to illustrate what you're saying—how do you find them?" It's just the opposite... The example comes first. I think from the concrete. I can't think from the abstract. If there's any common denominator in the whole thing, which I believe there is, it's real life, the way the world works—and that directs me, and it's disturbing to me sometimes.'

The book on separatism is an example: 'This was a very hard thing to me when I started to think about it. My grandfather was in the Civil War and fought hard against secession; his favourite brother was killed in the war. I was brought up to believe this was an enormous triumph. But when reason tells you one thing and the myth you were brought up with is at odds with it, the myth has to give—and that's not easy.'

Her readers haven't found it easy, either: 'In my first book (*Death and Life*), I got castigated terribly by planners because it went against everything they'd been taught, and I can understand it. It's hard to be told by someone: "Hey, you learned a lot of junk, you should reconsider." For a long time, I thought my book wouldn't have any influence—and it wouldn't have had if it weren't for young people. I have a feeling the new book will be like the first one: if it will have any effect, it will be on young people.'

Yet Jacobs savours growing older. 'It's a fact of life, and also it's delightful to grow older and see how things have turned out,' she says, eyes dancing behind the horn rims. 'You see you're a link in the continuum of life. There's that phrase "The unexamined life is not worthwhile"—it's true, I think. The older you get, the more you can examine it—not only your own life but the life that's come under your view. My mother lived to be 101 and was still interested in what was going on. I would like to live that long, but I'd also like to live to 201, or 501. My only regret is that the human span is so limited. I'm just so curious to see what happens.

'On the other hand, I believe in youth and its ability to revolt against ideas that already exist and try new avenues, and that the old have to be cleared out so new ideas can come. The young mustn't just accept.' Which reminds her, even though she's 68: 'You know what I miss about New York? Toronto is so polite, it's like talking through a pillow. I wish people would say straight out: "I hate what you've said." I'm happy and proud and pleased to be a Canadian, but I sure wish Canadians would be more argumentative and not so afraid of offending.'

Beyond her belief in the promise of youth and the wisdom of age lies her hope in human intelligence and the human heart: 'By this I don't mean just believing in geniuses and wheeler dealers—not them at all. I just have such enormous faith in the brains of human beings, and that makes me an optimist. But if you look at history and all the dreadful forces at work, you can't help being a pessimist, too. So, my heart is the heart of an optimist, and my brain is the brain of a pessimist, maybe. But being temperamentally an optimist, I hope our intelligence and love—why not mention love? it's basic—will win out. That's our only hope.'   —*June 1984*

Andrée Putman

Andrée Putman, looking like Lillian Hellman in her Sunday best, is receiving on the top floor of the Roots department store in Toronto, which last week became the exclusive home of the fine line of 1920s furniture she has been producing since 1978 under the label of Ecart International. How is it that a woman who has designed interiors for Karl Lagerfeld, Yves Saint Laurent, and countless other somebodies, who has been wearing black and white 'since ever', whose taste has become synonymous with Taste, has taken an interest in the Roots beaver?

The answer is Michael Budman, who, in addition to having co-founded Roots, a clothing and accessories chain, is the publisher of *Passion*, a monthly English-language newspaper distributed primarily in Paris. 'Once,' says Putman, dragging on a perpetual cigarette, 'he walked into my showroom in Paris. [This was in the spring of 1981.] He said: "I'm Michael Budman, I hear you have some nice things in your showroom." So, we talked. So, he walked away and said: "I'll get back to you again." He invited me over for a drink. He lives over the most delicate pastry place in Paris. He had the most wonderful cakes. So, we became friends.' Six months later, Budman's apartment had been outfitted with nice things from Putman's showroom, including Eileen Gray's Black Magic rug and chairs designed by René Herbst. 'What a place,' sighs Putman. 'He had so much luck to find such a place in Paris. I love people with so much luck.'

Indeed. 'Putman helped us incredibly with *Passion*,' Budman says. 'She was the person most responsible for the success of the magazine. She opened so many doors. Helmut Newton did six covers for us, and Lagerfeld gave us a cover interview—and it's all Andrée's doing, which is so un-French. Andrée is someone who puts people and things together.' Last August, Budman and Don Green opened their new Roots headquarters, designed by Putman. And now Torontonians are getting an eyeful of the vintage design masterpieces rescued from obscurity by a woman with an immodest talent for 'putting pieces together like a family'.

Putman is sitting on the reproduction that started it all, Eileen Gray's Transat (for Transatlantic) chair, designed for the Maharajah of Indore in the early 1920s. She's not the only one reproducing furniture by Gray, a pioneer of modernism who died, forgotten, in 1976, but she was the first. 'I made Eileen Gray famous,' she says, firing every syllable like a gun. 'They— the other ones, the merchants—didn't touch it until I made it. The man who got all the rights, without paying one cent, never produced one thing till I started. After I was approached by Eileen Gray's niece in London to do something, I went to him. "What do you think of the rugs?" I asked. "They're not interesting. They get worn out in a showroom so I will lose a lot of money if I produce them." So, I knew about what kind of man he was.'

By the time she was through, Putman had acquired the rights to 'everything I thought the most beautiful'—the rugs, the Transat chair, the Satellite mirror with its revolving arm, two lacquered cabinets. 'The people at the Victoria and Albert Museum were so touched someone was working seriously on the Transat chair, they even let me in to sit on one,' she laughs. 'So, I sat on it—and I thought it was the best chair I ever sat in.' The V&A organized the first tribute to Gray, and in 1980, it was presented by the Museum of Modern Art in an expanded version that included Putman's copy of Gray's Blackboard rug—white blackboard markings on a black background. The only clues to recreating the rug were little bits of paper from Gray's estate.

'It's something I love to think about,' says Putman, pursing her lips in something approaching a smile. 'Because how can we calculate what happened to these images between 1925 and the 1980s? There were spots, marks, things she had erased. She was so used to being not understood—forever she was not understood—she didn't think of herself as a genius. So, there was a kind of messiness. I made some interpretations. And don't forget, Le Corbusier started his furniture after he saw this.' Here she taps a Transat arm.

Putman expanded her family of reproductions with chairs, tables, and lamps designed by Mariano Fortuny, Antoni Gaudi, Van Ravenstyn, Jacques-Henri Lartigue, J.J.P. Oud, J. Michel Frank, Robert Malley-Stevens, René Herbst, and Michel Dufet. All of them were born before 1900, but their designs remain startling and fresh. 'They never knew each other, they didn't belong to a movement, they weren't so interested in success,' she says. 'They were just doing what they thought was the most exciting thing at the time. I think of all these people, though I never met most of them, as friends of mine. In my imagination, they participate in my success.'

That success hasn't come easy, but Putman, who will not reveal her age, wears her wrinkles with the same elegance as she does her clothes. Like the designers and architects she champions, she's a rebel, and proud of it. 'In the stone ages, I started to like Deco—when I was very young, when everyone thought it was a shame for the nation to have such bad design,' she says, peering mischievously through a wave of carrot-coloured hair, the only dash of colour in her ensemble. 'More than unhappily, I belonged to a very narrow city that looked to Versailles as the future.'

A pause, a puff, and: 'When I was 12, I knew I would escape from that fairy tale where everything must be old to be respected, which is the opposite of a fairy tale for me. That auto-satisfaction which is so French made me unhappy very, very early. I fought from a child against that attitude. The second I had my first job, I went to Knoll and bought a Mies van der Rohe chair, as a first statement. I lived with my mother in a very nice apartment filled with wonderful things. She offered me some space. I said to her: "I don't want to offend you, but what I buy will be like nothing you see in these rooms." My mother was a total eccentric. "I can hardly wait," she said.'

Next she began buying paintings. 'I met wonderful people like Riopelle— I speak about Riopelle because we are in Canada. I was totally involved in that group.' She met Beckett, Ionesco, Peggy Guggenheim. She started designing interiors for friends and did a house for herself, in the south of France, 'which was published and published and published—I don't even know why.'

Notwithstanding, she says, 'I never thought of myself as someone who was going anywhere. I was just a hard worker trying to do the best possible in a modest job—I was cleaning up objects for Mr Tout Le Monde, the average person, just trying to make day-to-day life less ugly.' That was in the 1960s, when she worked for Prisunic, the French budget store chain. Under Putman's influence, Prisunic produced a catalogue of well-designed household objects at affordable prices, everything from furniture by Gae Aulenti to baby clothes. (Today, Mr Tout Le Monde is very likely to think twice before picking up many of the pieces being sold at Roots. Prices start at $195 but quickly rise to the $6,000 range.)

Other design crusades followed in the 1970s, only to end in failure. 'I didn't have the timing or the luck I needed to succeed,' says Putman. 'But everything changes in a person's life. Suddenly I had the timing—and the ideas were always there, like a volcano waiting to explode.'

Putman exploded after ending her marriage to art critic Jacques Putman in 1978. 'I was under the rug with miseries of all kinds,' she says. 'When I started Ecart, I had not one cent at all. We were never backed by anyone. I was leaving a wealthy husband who had spoiled me. That's why I found the energy. It was only a few weeks ago that we made a little money. Now we know we will succeed.'

Putman will continue adding to her collection of timeless objects and promoting her approach to design. In a nutshell: 'My approach is very non-colour. I cannot live without art, and art brings so much colour. To me art is so much the basis of life, I would never compete. I think of places as shells to be very friendly to art.' When she rises from the Transat chair, she leaves a vacuum.   — *September 1984*

Michele De Lucchi

'My feeling is that the vacuum cleaner is a mass-produced object that is capable of communicating.'   — *Designer Michele De Lucchi*

In a nutshell, Michele De Lucchi is of the school that believes vacuum cleaners can, should, and absolutely must do more than swallow dust. Like tables, chairs, fans, hair-dryers, and toasters, all of which he's designed, they aspire to becoming metaphors of reality and models of change. De Lucchi, 33, is fond of quoting his mentor, Ettore Sottsass, on this point and others. 'Ettore Sottsass,' he claims, 'was the first to say that when you design an object, you don't just design the object, but also the environment in which the object will be put. And you also design the behaviour of the people who will use the object.'

It will come as no surprise that De Lucchi is both Italian and a member of Memphis, the design collective hatched in Milan in 1981 under Sottsass's leadership. Memphis is shorthand for humanoid cupboards sheathed in patterned plastic laminates, textiles that reverberate like tom toms, penile ceramics, and all manner of totems dedicated to violating modernist taboos. Memphis, according to critic Barbara Radice, originated 'not from monuments, truths, or programs, but from a generic, biological, existential happiness; from the consciousness of life as an indifferent cosmic-historic event and from the desire to taste it, consume it, communicate it physically, almost chemically or molecularly, as a vibrant, neutral, enticing, seductive presence.'

De Lucchi was in Toronto recently to say things along these lines at the Art Gallery of Ontario, in connection with its current exhibition, 'The European Iceberg'. His contribution to the exhibition is a lacquered wood and metal table, designed for Acerbis International, which illustrates many of his preoccupations. The rounded base looks distinctly like a face whose expression can be altered by the addition, subtraction, or manipulation of its features. The table is important, De Lucchi feels, because it is mass-produced by a factory that produces square wooden panels. Asked to design something using panels, and working within the rules and regulations of industrial production, he managed to create a personable and expressive piece of furniture.

'Memphis objects want to be participants in the industrial design world,' continues De Lucchi, who tends to speak of Memphis as though it were a person, not a collection. 'The first goal of a Memphis piece is to try to do something more in institutional industrial design. All Memphis pieces are very functional. They work very well, most of them. One or two pieces in a house would be enough. They are pieces with a lot of intensity. One bookcase of Ettore Sottsass is enough to furnish a room.'

De Lucchi keeps talking: 'Memphis is communication with images. We are working with all the images available in the world. I think Memphis has so much energy because it comes after ten years of conceptualism. It's a reaction against conceptual art and architecture. I was in the conceptual movement, and I became so tired of conceptual art, body art, congresses. We felt inside ourselves the necessity to create images and work with images.'

Memphis has taken off. It is now a company with a catalogue of sixty items—not the full collection, but everything is available as long as time and money are no object. But sales are not Memphis's problem, according to De Lucchi: 'Our problem is what to do with the Memphis idea. My personal position is that today it's very important for every designer in Memphis to work in his own iconography. I would like each designer to take a different position. Another idea I have for the future is to spread the Memphis idea beyond industrial design to architecture. We're always working in interior decoration, mainly in Germany, but I would like to apply the Memphis idea to other objects—jewellery, rings and so on.'

De Lucchi has taken the step of setting up his own office (with sister Memphisite Martine Bedin) instead of continuing to work directly for Sottsass Associates. 'Normally,' he smiles, 'it's impossible to leave the family of

Sottsass without being considered against Sottsass. I'm in a fantastic position: we are still good friends. Sottsass is the owner of the basic idea of Memphis—the idea of design that gives pleasure to use, see, touch. And I realized from this theory that today it's possible to work by *adding* figuration instead of *subtracting* figuration. It is possible to create a new kind of decoration—not flowers, but new kinds of patterns. This is revolutionary. It's important for us to show that a piece of furniture can be an item of communication, that it can participate in the up-to-date image of the world.'

There's no stopping him now: 'I try to make a connection between my work and punk iconography. The phenomenon of the world today is the phenomenon of the distribution of images. The world needs images, and Memphis objects want to show images and drive the machine so it's able to produce images, images, images. I believe in free images travelling the minds of people. I believe there's a kind of stratum of images floating above the land—that everyone knows that but no one is able to understand which are the right images of today. Every day, the world is making its own iconography, adding images on top of images. There is no single object that symbolizes an epoch. I'm working to produce a thousand images which, all together, will be an image of this world.'

As De Lucchi sees it, the path to Memphis was cleared by a change of attitude to consumerism: 'In European culture, for a long time, consumerism was considered very bad. It was synonymous with dirty business, smog and equality: everyone would have the same objects. We tried to remove consumerism from the future. We considered industrialism positive and consumerism bad. Now we see that it's impossible to live without consumerism. We have to use the qualities of consumerism—mass communication—to communicate free, happy, optimistic images.'

How does he define image? Says De Lucchi: 'When you see an up-to-date car, for example, you feel something that makes you understand the relation of this car to the world. This, to me, is the image of the car—a global sensibility that puts something in your head. It is a problem to find the real meaning of image. It's an over-used word.'

Of one thing De Lucchi feels certain: Memphis has had an impact. 'It's important today to activate public creativity,' he insists. 'A lot of people who have seen Memphis think they can do a Memphis piece, that it's possible to use colour in a house—strong colours that have never been used before. This is a very simple but real example of what happened after Memphis. We don't speak about revolution. It's enough to say we're changing something.

'But Memphis will not continue to exist if we only work for furnishing houses. Memphis wants to do more than furnish houses. You're right: Memphis is full of contradictions. Sometimes I wonder about them. I wonder where it will all go.'

— *March 1985*

Frank Gehry

20 September 1986. A crowd is milling around a curvaceous 6.7-metre-high glass-scaled fish in the concourse of the Walker Art Center in Minneapolis. They've been arriving all day in waves, from Milan, California, Chicago, New York, and Toronto, to celebrate the opening of 'The Architecture of Frank Gehry', an exhibition honouring the Toronto-born, Los Angeles-based architect who has reserved the right to comment on the world in a vocabulary that runs to chain-link, plywood, cardboard and, increasingly, fish. Gehry's work is so personal and inclusive that it is often put down as irrelevant to architecture or, insult of insults, populist. The fact that he's never made any secret of being influenced by art and artists has added to the confusion: is he an artist who stumbled into architecture, or an architect halfway to becoming an artist?

By organizing a travelling exhibition in Gehry's honour, the Walker Art Center's adventurous design curator, Mildred Friedman, has sounded the countercharge. Gehry is indeed an architect—a 'contemporary master builder', in fact, whose work 'bridges the gap between the art of building and the arts of painting and sculpture'. The pronouncement is, of course, controversial. The term master builder is not taken lightly in architectural circles, either by architects vying for the coveted title or critics competing for the right to crown the next king. The mantle of Frank Lloyd Wright, the greatest architect in American history, is up for grabs—and everyone who's anyone wants a say in who's going to inherit it.

That Gehry's candidacy was being announced in Minneapolis, and not New York, where important matters such as succession are usually decided, is also controversial. Friedman offered the exhibition to the Whitney Museum of American Art, but it was refused—most likely, she says, because the Whitney has commissioned an addition from Michael Graves (who, incidentally, has been declared Wright's heir by the tireless, tiresome promoter of postmodernism, Charles Jencks) and would naturally prefer to give Graves a show. Not for nothing does the T-shirt accompanying the Gehry exhibition bear the inscription: 'Being accepted isn't everything'—a comment made by Gehry in 1984 and seized upon by Friedman as quintessentially Frank.

These were only some of the currents rustling through the conversation of the opening night crowd. Some guests had already been upstairs to see the show, others were saving it until after dinner for maximum impact. What they all experienced, sooner or later, was a double whammy to the consciousness. Not only had a twenty-year sampling of Gehry's projects been collected in one place, but the architect had designed his own exhibition as well, making architecture to show architecture.

The installation looks a lot like one of Gehry's recent houses, and cost more to build than most. Gehry fitted an entire little village of one-room buildings into the gallery space, co-opting the skylight, staircase, walls and windows to achieve his own ends. Each room is an elegant piece of sculpture, a miniature art gallery for the display of models, drawing, furniture and lighting, a separate quartier in a magical city mysteriously implanted in Minneapolis. Together, and with an intensity bordering on confrontation, the installations communicate the full range of Gehry's palette and preoccupations.

Gehry's village is made of sleek Finnish plywood, copper, galvanized metal, corrugated cardboard, steel, lead, wooden posts and raw plywood. Three of the houses are free-standing sculptural entities, the remaining two are joined at the façade to commemorate his early experiments in exploding a building into fragments and joining the pieces together in unexpected ways. The drawings and immaculate wooden models have been placed both inside and outside the five structures so that to take them all in, you're obliged to move along streets and plazas, slip through cracks and fight your way through a forest of posts niched into the stairway and arch dividing the two-tiered gallery space.

The exhibition encourages voyeurism. The temptation to peek through doorways and windows is irresistible, creating the condition whereby a tourist can become a *flâneur*—Walter Benjamin's word for a practised explorer of the labyrinth known as the modern city. The passer-by sees the most astonishing things through Gehry's windows. To show his cardboard furniture, the objects that first brought him to national attention, he designed a room in the shape of a trapezoid, made entirely of laminated, corrugated cardboard. The walls are thick and rough-edged, their colour and texture suggesting a remnant of a long-gone civilization. A large opening provides a tantalizing glimpse of the contours of something resembling a whale. It is covered in lead scales. The metallic leviathan turns out to be a showcase for Gehry's fish and snake lamps.

The dissection of a building into pieces and their reconstruction as a miniature city, the contrast between a formal exterior and a casual, incomplete interior, the use of angled openings to create unexpected views, the play of manufactured and organic, abstract and figurative, the subversion of expectation, the joy of manipulating space, texture, form and colour—all these hallmarks of Gehry's architecture are present and accounted for. "And to think this is happening in Minneapolis!" exulted Chicago architect Stanley Tigerman, one of Gehry's greatest supporters.

Like the exhibition, the opening-night crowd bridged art and architecture; like Gehry's buildings, it was composed of colliding fragments. Claes Oldenburg and his wife, Coosje van Bruggen, were in attendance, he a much dourer presence than might be expected of the designer of a monumental clothes-pin. So were Italian curator-impresario Germano Celant (the man responsible for 'The European Iceberg' at the Art Gallery of Ontario in the spring of 1985), Los Angeles artist Charles Arnoldi, important clients, and a gaggle of art historians and hangers-on. The warmth came mainly from

Gehry's family—his Panamanian wife, Berta, his 83-year-old mother, Thelma, his sister, Doreen, his Uncle Kalman Caplan and his Aunt Ruth from Toronto, his kids—and, of course, from Gehry himself, who responded to Mildred Friedman's introduction by welcoming everyone to his bar mitzvah.

In his funny way, he was being serious. When Gehry turned 13, in 1942, his family was living in Timmins, where his father sold pinball and slot machines. Growing up Jewish in northern Ontario during the Second World War—think about that one and you've got the makings of a treatise on character-building—Gehry, who was born Goldberg, encountered so much anti-Semitism as an adolescent that his parents had to talk him into having a bar mitzvah. Forty-four years later, friends and family in attendance, he was being confirmed as a master builder. Being accepted may not be everything, but it can make up for a lot.

Gehry travelled a tortuous path to architecture. He was born in Toronto in 1929. His family lived on Dundas Street near Dufferin, in a neighbourhood with a large Jewish immigrant population. The family pet, he loved hanging out at his grandfather Caplan's hardware store, fascinated with the inventory. His grandmother took home wooden shavings that she and Gehry turned into cities and roads. Just before his father moved the family to Los Angeles in 1947—his livelihood cut off because slot machines had been declared illegal and he was in ill health—Gehry looked up the University of Toronto architecture exams in the library. By reading the questions, he knew the school wasn't for him. At this point, confused and upset by his father's illness, he wasn't sure what was.

In Los Angeles, the Goldbergs had it tough. For two years, according to Doreen, she and Frank took turns sleeping on the fold-out bed in one of two rooms occupied by the family. Like all Jewish sons, Gehry was under pressure to succeed. He drove a truck, delivering and installing breakfast nooks for a cousin. He enrolled in fine arts part-time at the University of Southern California, where his ceramics teacher encouraged him to transfer into the architecture program. Slowly, he found friends and mentors. In 1952, he married. His wife, a legal secretary, helped him through college. When he graduated in 1954, she insisted they change their surname to something less Jewish-sounding—a common practice in those days. She looked through the telephone book under G until she found something suitably aristocratic. Later, the whole family changed their name to Gehry, in a gesture of solidarity.

Gehry set up his own practice in Los Angeles in 1962, after spending time at Harvard, in Paris, and in the office of Victor Gruen Associates, a company that does a lot of developer work. He was divorced in 1966, remarried ten years later. An outsider by birth, upbringing, and sensibility, Gehry has managed to wrest from a life of upheavals and eruptions a strange sort of beauty. It's the way Gehry's architecture has evolved out of his experience and his commitment to reality that makes it so compelling.

Gehry's relationship with art and artists is complex. Over the years he has designed studios for artists, collaborated with people like Richard Serra on exhibitions, built houses for collectors, mounted exhibitions, exhibited major works in his house, and designated art works for his own commissions. He thought a lot about painters like Cézanne and Giorgio Morandi and he counted artists among his best friends and major influences—Carl Andre, Donald Judd, Serra, Robert Irwin, Ed Moses, Larry Bell, Arnoldi, Oldenburg. He's learned from all of them, but what he takes, he transforms with the part of his mind that thinks like an architect. He specializes in buildings pared down to simple forms, or 'dumb shapes', as he calls them, exposed lathing and joists, tough sculptural shells concealing incomplete interiors, illusions of perspective and space, the play of light, shadow and reflections— preoccupations that resonate with contemporary art concerns.

But at the same time as he's striving for simplicity, he's striving for richness and presence. He seems to inhale the context of a project, the forms and colours of the city, so he can exhale it as architecture. Memories, images, hunches, and observations of social behaviour keep surfacing; and, of course, there is the program, the budget, the client. Out of all these, working by free association, he makes buildings where one dimension frequently contradicts another, creating surprising juxtapositions of forms and materials, textures and colours, insides and outsides. Gehry's is an architecture of simultaneity. He's dealing with everything at once—and most of all, he's dealing with himself.

For Gehry, art is a kind of paradigm for the intensity and contact he wants out of making architecture. His houses, made of one-room buildings, each expressing a different function, came to him from the idea of somebody confronting a blank canvas. 'That's an incredible moment, I would guess, before you make the first stroke. How do you get close to that experience? You simplify all the stuff, you take away everything extraneous, and a one-room building was close. It's very simple: you have to face yourself.'

These are not the words or attitudes of the architectural establishment, particularly now that architects have all but rejected the utopianism and social ideology of modernism and turned back the clock to classical standard time. Gehry knows his history as well as any architect, but the designer classicism favoured by his colleagues doesn't get his vote. (In fact, one of the things that troubles critics who appreciate Gehry's talent is that he could never become the leader of a movement or school.) In this context, Gehry's align-ment with artists is a political statement. He refers to his work as a visual commentary: 'The materials you pick, the way you deal with projects or the criticism of your colleagues—whatever you know, you criticize. You criticize yourself, you criticize your times. I'm more a streetfighter than a Roman scholar.'

One of the most lyrical of Gehry's commentaries is the Norton House on the beach in Venice, California, which from the outside looks like a collage of boxes turned inside out. It's as though a building had been cut in half by a wrecking ball so that you could peer at the remains of the interiors. The inside is filled with light and flows with a gentle rhythm. Gehry designed a one-room studio on a perch for his client, a screenwriter who has fond memories of being a lifeguard. The elevated office overlooks the busy beach but maintains its distance. (Privacy is a prime concern for Gehry. However exhibitionist his buildings may look, they remain sanctums.)

Gehry has designed buildings of only one room, buildings with two interconnected parts, and lately, buildings with so many pieces they become villages. These can be of large or small scale. At Loyola Law School in Los Angeles, one of his finest projects, he separated the moot court, two classrooms and a chapel from the main building so that students, on what was once a shabby site without character or dignity, could move around a campus village and experience a sense of community. To create a feeling of diversity he had one of the classrooms clad in brick, another in wood and the chapel done in Finnish plywood. From the upper floors of the administration building three sculptural open stairways turn down to the courtyard below— a visual metaphor of human action freeing itself from the rule of law, and a simple way to animate a space.

No two of Gehry's canvases are alike, although the vocabulary of forms and materials he has used over the years is recognizably his own. The Sirmai-Peterson house under construction in Thousand Oaks, California, another series of one-room buildings, is majestic in character. The room/buildings cascade down a slope in five or six directions from a central cross-piece. They're joined by stairways and corridors, some open to the elements, others covered or even submerged. Where the living-room and bedrooms come together Gehry created a courtyard. Instead of each piece being clad in a separate material, the house will be covered in stucco and sheet metal. The whole composition resembles a Romanesque church quietly going out of control. This isn't a case of chaos-for-chaos's sake—Gehry's seemingly casual compositions are strictly calculated—but of opening up a structure to many viewpoints, many interpretations. Compared with corporate neoclassicism, say, his work connotes anti-authoritarianism. Wherever you stand to view the Sirmai-Peterson house, the house faces you.

The Winton guest house in Minnesota is almost a commentary on Sirmai-Peterson. The main house was designed by Philip Johnson in the 1950s, and the Wintons didn't want Gehry to upstage it. His solution was to go sculptural. He gave the Wintons a pretend sculpture garden to be viewed from the terrace of the main house—no windows or doors will be visible from the terrace—as an abstract ruin, a still life. The guest house is only 167 by 186 square metres, but it's been broken up into six pieces, the claddings to consist of fire-brick, Finnish plywood, limestone, and lead-coated copper. Each piece is a pure form and connected to the others in a way that maintains the illusion of separateness. The feeling of a town is preserved by the variegated shapes that make up its miniature jagged skyline. Because the connections have been suppressed, the guest house gives the impression of

Loyola Law School

stillness despite its many skins, while the Sirmai-Peterson house conveys spatial excitement despite the reduced palette of materials.

Gehry's collaborations with Claes Oldenburg are a highly visible way to explore the junction of art and architecture. They met in the 1960s and by the time of their first project, in 1983, they were ready for each other. Oldenburg was designing monumental (or anti-monumental) outdoor projects that involved working with context, building codes, engineering and structural teams; Gehry had begun working with representational forms like fish, eagles, and snakes. In 1983 Oldenburg and Coosje van Bruggen designed a piece for Loyola, but this wasn't a true collaboration.

That had to wait until 1984, when at the invitation of Germano Celant, the trio worked on a project in Venice that combined performance and architecture. They chose the image of a Swiss army knife to link the performance and architectural parts of the project and 'to reconcile historical Venice with its present status of tourist city'. The knife was an apt image for Gehry, who makes a point of cutting away buildings to reveal their bones. Working with students, Gehry plotted a new section of the city in the form of a complex of islets. They made two models, one of the area around the Arsenale, and the other of Coltello Island, a structure to house artisans and to include a bank, a medical clinic, a fire station and a theatre. The buildings would appear to slice up out of the water. A Gehry snake turned up as the fire station form, next to an office building by Oldenburg drawn as the opened lid of a grand piano. To house the library, van Bruggen and Oldenburg suggested a brick façade shaped like binoculars, and Gehry and van Bruggen proposed a theatre whose rear wall would serve as a drive-in movie for gondolas.

The three had problems reconciling and justifying their images, but they went on to collaborate on another commission, a mountain summer camp for kids with cancer, to be called Camp Good Times. They designed it as a village filled with the imagery of boats and sails. Their ideas really jelled in the dining hall. They decided the roof should be a literalization of a wave form—sliced frozen waves, says van Bruggen—and the kitchen an Oldenburg milk can to harmonize with the bucolic surroundings. Nothing came of the project because the camp administration decided to go with traditional huts.

Recently Gehry and Oldenburg have been collaborating on an office building for Chiat/Day, a Los Angeles ad agency, called Main Street 1975-1986. Oldenburg's binoculars reappear as the centrepiece of the project, forming the entrance and containing a library. Gehry's contributions are a curved boatlike shape to one side and a forest of tree forms on the other. 'Rather than be influenced by dead artists, as many of my colleagues tend to be, I have always felt that living artists are working on the same issues I am,' Gehry has said. But he's influenced by dead artists all the same, in a mysterious, dialectical way.

'When I started doing one-room buildings,' he says, 'I started seeing Morandi in a different way, and then I started looking at Cézanne's still lifes, and other still lifes, in a different way than I had. I'd always looked at them as a total composition. And now I started looking at the pieces as individual pieces, and at their relationships to each other, and then the spaces between— which made it possible for me to see Matisse's cut-outs differently. I didn't get them before. I remember seeing them when he was doing them, and I thought: 'The guy's off the end.' But now I've started to see the singular pieces playing off each other—it's objects next to objects—and they're so beautiful, because you sense the hands-on, the cut of this masterful scissor cutting through the thing, quietly, effortlessly. I hope when I'm that age— he was in his seventies—I can do something like that.'

But he's already done something equally daring. Given the long and laborious process by which buildings are put up, the fact that he's gotten so many of his artistic visions built is itself an achievement. Next to most practitioners he's a one-man Paris in the Twenties—a commentary on the compartmentalization and conformism of his profession. By the time his next bar mitzvah rolls around, Gehry will be recognized as the true thinker of his generation. —*Winter 1986*

Gae Aulenti

'It is the first time, and I love,' says architect Gae Aulenti, oval face, tailored jacket, mannish watch, speaking of Toronto. 'It is very calm—how do you say it?—harmonious.' A first impression, but coming from Aulenti, who speaks only what (and when) she feels, the remark has the ring of a Sphinx-like truth. So does everything else she says, in an English more polished than she cares to admit.

Aulenti was in town this week to lecture at the University of Toronto architecture school about two recent high-profile projects. The first is a glory project instigated by French President François Mitterrand: the mammoth conversion of the Gare d'Orsay, the 1900 Paris railway station, into a museum of nineteenth-century French art to be known as the Musée d'Orsay. The second is a refitting of one floor of the Centre Georges Pompidou, designed by Renzo Piano and Richard Rogers, as the Musée National d'Art Moderne.

Aulenti does not make a habit of public speaking—'they ask me to talk because of my work, but if I talk, I no can work'—but she met her match in Francesca Valente, the dynamo director of the Italian Cultural Institute, which sponsored her visit. 'I didn't invite,' says Valente. 'I insisted.'

Elegant to the tip of her Chesterfield cigarette, intelligent to the point of intimidation, Aulenti, 58, is one of Italy's most accomplished designers. Like most Italian architects, but entirely from conviction, she designs just about everything—furniture, exhibitions, stage sets, showrooms, buildings. A telling difference is that she's female—the only woman of her generation to make it to the top in Macholand. (As far as architecture is concerned, the entire world is Macholand.)

How did she do it? A subsection to the question was put later by an admirer: what must it have taken to deal with François Mitterrand, who visited the Musée d'Orsay site three times to discuss materials and finishes, and the machinations of French politics in general? Aulenti smiles. Graciousness is second nature, a powerful charm. 'The important thing about the relationship to men is to be very natural,' she says—and foremost, she adds, never to try to be male: 'For me—I was beginning thirty years ago—it was difficult. I was the only woman on the editorial board of *Casabella* [the influential design magazine].' Though she counts herself a survivor, she says, 'I think it's better not to remember certain things. I never tried to have a man as a colleague. I began with myself, and this is my little world.'

Aulenti's 'little world' spans Milan, her city of choice, Paris, Barcelona, and New York: she has projects going in all of them, and offices in all but the last. 'It's completely different working in Paris than in Italy,' she says, 'because the work rapport is different. In France, they love engineering, technology. In Italy, no. You can do the same thing, but the behaviour is different. At the same time, it is difficult. I want to work with intensity—to study the general thing but work in detail, to see the two things at the same time.'

The word Aulenti uses to describe her approach is 'analytical', a term that encompasses depth of understanding, the making of relationships, the reconciling of differences; she never talks style, only process. 'I do not have an ideological attitude. Building in Toronto or Paris is very different, and this is what engenders the possibility of good architecture. Our tradition is the modernist movement, with all the differences our epoch of transformation offers us.'

The importance of context follows. For example, Aulenti designs all her furniture for specific houses. 'Afterwards,' she says, 'it goes into production, it adjusts to a new environment. When I design sets for the opera, there are two other points of consideration: the text, or script, and the relationship between the theatre, the set, and the town where the theatre is. The theatrical context is much more complex than everyday life. This gives me the energy to go back to architecture.' For Aulenti, integration is everything. 'You have one mind: the global vision is very important,' she insists. 'If it's true that we must have an analytical approach, the more complex the situation, the better.'

The single most complex project she has had to date is the Musée d'Orsay: 'It is a very big museum—40,000 square metres: *enormo*. It is the transformation of a train station to a museum—the relationship with the architecture of the past, the relationship of the year 1900 and contemporary architecture, the foundation of contemporary architecture not in a square, a street, a hill, but inside the station. I saw the station *come una terra*—as land, earth, ground for building on: no pastiche! And then, the possibility of designing to the very last detail—the doorknob, the window. This was very important for me, the possibility to really show this kind of thing could be done.'

And with a staff in Paris that never exceeded twelve: 'I don't like work division, the whole office is creative. I don't want to be a manager, I want to be an architect.' At present, Aulenti alternates weeks in Paris and Milan. 'In Italy we don't build many things, but the cultural debate is very important,' she says, sounding the call to harmony again. 'Our cities are small, and we have an exchange with writers, musicians, composers. Everyday life is enriched. Paris is too big, impossible.' (Her own circle of friends includes writer/philosopher Umberto Eco, conductor Claudio Abbado, and pianist Maurizio Pollini.)

It would be forward to suggest that Aulenti's sensitivity to differences derives from a highly developed sense of her own difference, her essence. She puts it another way: 'We are nomads. I don't mean we are uprooted. *Nomadismo*—it's a little bit like people of the desert. We have our own culture, but we want to see other things. It's positive. It creates exchanges, which makes things even more elaborate and complex. I believe it is important that we at least have the instruments to understand the differences. This is richness.'   — *March 1986*

Douglas Ball

If workers are ever driven to rebel against the open plan office, it won't be Douglas Ball's fault. Born in Peterborough and educated in industrial design at the Ontario College of Art, Ball has earned international distinction as a designer of office systems for SunarHauserman a US-based company specializing in contract furnishings; his superior work stations and furniture show how endless, bland office space can be transformed into elegant zones of human habitation.

Ball, a quiet, reflective man whose studio is just outside Montreal, appeared at Via Design, the consciousness-raising event at the Palais des Congrès, to describe what it takes to see a product through from conception to reality. He referred specifically to his office systems and a revolutionary children's wheelchair he's developed for Everest and Jennings, but his presentation ran to slides of tree bark and cloud formations. His message, simply put: if a designer hasn't got the time, or is incapable of regressing, he's in trouble.

'Time is the greatest single variable in the development work we do because we're involved in the process of discovery,' he said, noting that he enjoys photography because pictures are developed quickly. It took him nine years to develop the award-winning Race office system and nine more to reach the prototype stage of an adult wheelchair that may never be produced. 'The biggest single problem is the ability to see what's there,' he said. 'As we get older, we see less and less. A child can see because he's learning. The brain of a child is receptive to questions that have no immediate answer. Adults aren't able to achieve clarity in a project. In order to survive, an adult has developed a brain that tends to repress dissonance. Our problem is how to see through the eyes of children.'

How, indeed? Designers such as Ball are bombarded with information in the form of trade publications, conferences, seminars, exhibitions. 'The total effect can be devastating,' Ball said. 'The more we see, the more we create a maze. With the brain giving us six weeks of messages in any one day, we refuse to advance. We suffer from sensory overload. This becomes a source of tension, and tension is part of design. We have to live with the rush of adrenalin.'

One way to alleviate tension is to reduce the variables of a project, to take things one stage at a time. 'You have to force yourself to think in black and white, to turn a problem upside down like a picture to prevent associations. One moves from an area of many chaotic thoughts to an area of higher pattern recognition and a sense that everything is falling into place. Beyond that is more confusion.'

Remaining focused is paramount: 'I have to shut myself up completely. I don't answer the telephone or open my mail. The brain knows it has the information you want, but you're not getting it. Focusing through all the complexity is a skill that can be learned, but it's hard.' The trap is 'hasty closure'—a tendency to think a problem is solved before it actually is. Preconceptions are the enemy: 'There's a constant need to update what is right and wrong so you look at what you want to look at and not see anything else.'

Ball updated his thoughts about office systems in 1970 after observing a huge installation of his PAS office system, which features high panels to prevent distraction and provide acoustic control. 'I condemned those people to a working hell.' He thought about the problem for five years without putting pen to paper or constructing a model. 'I wanted to arrive at a new starting point. I wanted to produce something as different from everything before as possible. We were so close to this problem that we couldn't see it clearly.'

When he finally realized what he wanted, he started sketching madly to get an idea of what his new system could—and should not—look like. When he opened his bursting sketch pads, certain forms leapt from the page. Soon, he had it. A prototype of the system was shown at Neocon in Chicago in 1978. Ball studied it. He started from scratch again: 'We knew we could solve problems we thought were unsolvable, that if we hadn't reduced the variables, we wouldn't have gotten this far. Now we started to put it all back together. Nine years after we started, the product was out'—Race.

Is Ball, 48, condemned to spend the rest of his life designing office systems? Is the open plan office here forever? 'Once there's a certain mindset, it's hard to undo it,' he said. 'That's why it was refreshing to design a wheelchair. There will be a renewed interest in walls and closures. One reason I won't get tired of doing it is because, when I look out there, I'm not happy with what I see. It is architects who are putting people into systems—standard ceiling and lighting systems. We can only do so much with furniture. It has to start with architecture.' And the development industry, surely. The question Ball didn't put publicly: can his customers learn to see?

— *November 1983*

Herbert Irvine

Herbert Irvine, the *premier cru* of Canadian decorators, arranges himself in the corner of a sofa that Arthur Rubinstein used to occupy when he came by the house. 'Rubinstein must have been here twenty times,' says Irvine, 78, but with a complexion of pink satin. 'He was very funny, very entertaining, and not a bit conceited. I met him through my sister who is married to an actor. She met Rubinstein on the train called Twentieth Century, the most deluxe there ever was, going from New York to Los Angeles. He taught her to play poker. This was the only place he'd visit in Toronto—do you know why?' A dramatic pause. 'Because we didn't have a piano.'

An hour or two in the company of Irvine, and the clock turns back to the 1940s and 1950s—'the good days,' he calls them, when Toronto 'was a very bright town and there was far more unself-conscious gaiety than there is now.' It was then that Irvine was at the height of his three-decade reign at the Eaton's College Street decorating department. His superior taste and feeling for period design were sought after by the cream of the country's architects and matrons. ('If you didn't get Herbert Irvine,' says a woman who did, 'you didn't exist.') He worked out of an oak-panelled office on the fifth floor called The Clifford Inn Room, a replica of an eighteenth-century room in the Victoria and Albert Museum carved by Grinling Gibbons. What more appropriate setting for a self-styled 'late-seventeenth-and-eighteenth-century person' who adores Mozart and Madame de Pompadour?

'Eaton's had a gold mine,' says fabric merchandiser Robin Vaile, Irvine's assistant for four years. 'Herbert taught everyone. He started the whole chain of taste in Toronto.' Adds decorator Harold Babcock, another Irvine protégé: 'He was involved in the simplification of decoration after all that late nineteenth-century Victorian-Moorish stuff. I learned more from Herbert than in four years at the Ontario College of Art. You can go to an art college and study the history of furniture, but to be exposed to someone who had entrée into homes where people had all this furniture . . . To appreciate antique furniture you have to touch, you have to feel.'

The man himself is more modest: 'I helped decorating out of the side door into the front door. There were others who did the same thing. It wasn't really a recognized trade, it was a sideline. It was only a cultivated person with taste that took you seriously.'

Irvine came to Eaton's in 1935, when he was 27. ('It was like joining a nice club,' he says.) He reported to no one except the man who hired him, first vice-president O.D. Vaughan. He worked for architects like John Lyle, Marani and Morris, and Mathers and Haldenby. 'The best modern I ever did was with John Lyle for R.S. McLaughlin's residence in Oshawa,' says Irvine. 'It was very like Leleu [the French *ébéniste* of the 1920s]. Lyle was one of the top people in Toronto. McLaughlin kept smooth stones in his hands when he was being driven around, to keep the muscle tone in his arms. He didn't want a chauffeur, but he had to have one because he was so important. He wanted very much to live to 100. He lived to 101.'

Irvine outfitted residences, banks, clubs, insurance companies, hotels, apartment lobbies, theatres. (Probably his only public interior in Toronto still intact is the Royal Alexandra Theatre, which he redid for Ed Mirvish, a favourite client.) Then there were the embassies, lots of them, a favourite being the embassy residence in Paris he decorated in the early 1950s using Bagues chandeliers ('they're the best fixture firm in the world'), a salon rug from Savonnerie, suppliers of carpets to the Crown ('they made it to my specifications—their colours were strong. I wanted it done in faded colours') and an English Sheraton dining table ('the ideal dining-room table of any country'). 'There was nothing spartan about the Vaniers,' says Herbert of the first occupants of the 1805 embassy. 'Madame Vanier had taste in clothes. She was dressed by Worth.'

Prime Minister Louis St Laurent's official residence was another Irvine job: 'His wife was the most devoted bridge player. She asked for a hand-painted bridge table with a drawer that could take a cheque book because she liked people to pay their debts before they left.' He did Government House for the Vaniers and Légers, too, although Madame Léger was so knowledgeable in French furniture he just helped pull things together.

Irvine always preferred residential work. He travelled extensively in Europe in search of fabrics and furniture—antiques and good reproductions—for the Canadian rich and private. 'I was the first person in Eaton's who bought important furniture in France and Italy,' he says. 'It was the first time a decorator had done the buying for the decorating department.' He also exerted enormous influence on the furniture, textile, and accessories buyers. 'His clients were the best in Eaton's and they bought the best things—

the buyers would listen to Herbert,' says interior designer Murray Oliver, who worked in the design department in the 1950s.

By the time Irvine retired from Eaton's in 1972, Toronto had exchanged its neo-Georgian architecture for steel and glass, and a new generation of designers had come on the scene for whom the fifth floor at Eaton's represented the enemy and Irvine's exquisite colour sense counted for naught. 'At the end of the sixties,' says Vaile, 'the hard core was still going along with Eaton's but the young decorators were very avant-garde. When you were with Herbert, there was no such thing as today's look.' Says Oliver: 'He was a marvellous character in the fifties and sixties world. He just soared through the sixties as though nothing had happened.'

Irvine, still a marvellous character, now works (with his partner, Julie Lombard) out of his home, originally the residence of Sir John A. Macdonald's nephew, where he and his Chilean-born wife, *née* Mélisande Guerrero, have lived since 1947 surrounded by beautiful objects from Irvine's favourite period. Among them are the first thing he bought with his own money, a drawing by Marie Laurencin acquired when he was 14, and the first pieces of furniture he ever bought, a pair of palace chairs made for Fontainebleau purchased in Paris in 1937 for $35 each.

Irvine has a story about everything he's bought and everyone he's worked for or even collided with, including the Duchess of Windsor, whom he once knocked over in New Orleans. 'We were looking at a furniture window from opposite sides and bumped in the middle,' he says. 'She had great taste but she never paid her bills.' As for Peggy Guggenheim, 'She never washed her neck. I saw her once when she was married to Julian Levy, who had lots of taste. She was wearing dirty running shoes, a pleated serge schoolgirl's skirt and a middy with a big collar—and she wasn't very clean.'

Where did Irvine get his taste? 'I come from Brampton,' he says. 'It was a sweet little town. I was the eldest of four. I wanted to be an architect but I was so bad in math that I chose the next thing to it, interiors. At 14, I knew I was going to be a decorator. I read everything I could lay my hands on. I traced the furniture with tracing paper and a coarse black lead pencil—that way you remember it forever. There was no decorating school in my day. I just kept reading and keeping my eyes open. My three Irvine aunts had a lot of taste. My sister Marion has great taste.'

The Irvine family was in the lumber business. Their advertising folder read: 'Irvine's Brampton is the spot / For clean coal and lumber.' 'My father didn't work in his life that I remember,' says Irvine. 'The business was inherited from a bright grandfather.' His mother played the piano. His Irish grandmother was a 'marvellous cook and hostess', but she didn't have much taste in furniture. Irvine remembers her exchanging a set of Irish Chippendale chairs with her washerwoman for black leatherette chairs: 'I was younger than 6. It was just shocking.'

His three aunts, who lived together, had a 'marvellous library' and often presented their nephew with books on classical architecture. 'They were great friends of Charles Comfort Tiffany. They used to holiday with him. There were about fifty signed Tiffany shades in the house—far too many. I hated them and I still do. I only use them under duress. I hate everything about them.' (When Irvine's aunts died, his mother called the Salvation Army to remove the offensive lighting.)

Irvine came to Toronto when he was 21 to work for Minerva Elliot, a decorator who had worked at Wanamaker's in Philadelphia and then at Eaton's before setting up shop on Bloor Street with an assistant, Malcolm Slerman, who 'did very good English decorating' and had also passed through Eaton's. Irvine started with Elliot on 10 January 1929, at a salary of $15 a week. He stayed for three years. 'Minerva was a slave-driver,' says Irvine. 'I was fired four times a week and quit three.'

Next he went to Simpsons, where he began doing rooms at the Canadian National Exhibition—something he continued doing at Eaton's. 'That was a very important thing in those days. The rooms cost a fortune. Fashion was shown along with the furniture. There was no modern in the sense of *moderne*—it was all traditional—but it was expensive furniture. Simpson's and Eaton's had six rooms on different ends of the Manufacturers Building. They were all sheeted off so no one saw them until 9 o'clock the night before the CNE opened. They were far too good for the CNE.'

The prestige job that Irvine did for Simpson's was the Toronto Ladies Club. Eaton's was upset at not getting the job—'Lady Eaton was a member of the club and Simpsons didn't even know where it was'—but they made sure they got the decorator on side. O.D. Vaughan took Irvine out to lunch twice. The first time he never mentioned Eaton's or Simpsons. The second time, with two bottles of wine on the table at a time when wine was scarce, he made him an offer of double his salary at Simpsons plus 5 per cent of sales. Irvine jumped, particularly as 'Simpsons never made any effort to improve decoration or the profession. Eaton's bought the first contemporary furniture in this country, they were the first people who bought directly from mills, the first people to have things printed in their own colours.' The rest, as they say, is history—but history of the near-forgotten, undocumented Canadian kind. — *November 1986*

Phyllis Lambert

Phyllis Lambert, Canada's doer extraordinaire, wants to 'make a case for architecture'. The usual ways of doing this are to organize a walking tour, write a book, start a journal, get a panel together, or, perhaps, even encourage an architect to design a good building. Lambert supports such activities, but she has never learned to obey stop signs. In this instance, she has opted for the arduous route of building, designing, filling, staffing, programming, and endowing a big-time institution. Heiress to a sizeable chunk of the Bronfman family's Seagram fortune, she has the resources to do it. The will, however, is her own.

Lambert, officially an architect, started the Canadian Centre for Architecture, a non-profit corporation, in 1979. What it consisted of then was the founder's already substantial private collection of material related to architectural theory, practice, and history—prints, drawings, photographs and books purchased over a twenty-year period—and her single-minded determination to use them as the cornerstone of a museum. A great museum. In less than a decade, thanks to her open-purse policy and shrewd, aggressive way of doing business, the CCA collection has burgeoned to more than 150,000 objects, valued at $50-million, the rate of acquisitions making calculations instantly obsolete.

No published catalogue of the CCA's complete holdings exists yet, leading one curator to remark that 'one of the fascinations of the CCA is that nobody knows what's there.' Still, enough material has been logged, publicized, and consulted to cause scholars and auction bidders around the world to gape. Toronto architect George Baird, one of Lambert's advisers, says of the collection: 'It is the best one in the world devoted exclusively to architecture—and not only that, the combination of things is unique.'

But the CCA is not just a lot of pricey paper. It is also a building, designed by Montreal architect Peter Rose, with Lambert as consulting architect and principal client. In addition, it is a lesson in respect for the past. Rose's U-shaped building wraps deferentially around an 1875 mansion, the Shaughnessy House, which Lambert, once a modernist, then a born-again conservationist, purchased for $600,000 in 1974 to prevent its demolition. The house is being restored down to the last newel post to hold administrative offices, a restaurant, and a lounge. Like the old, the new building is clad in solid limestone, the greystone Montreal is famous for, making it a kind of bridge to the city and its architectural history. Remember, too, that Lambert made her commitment to Montreal—the CCA could have gone anywhere—when the city was turning into a departure lounge for jumpy anglophones. Lambert has more agendas than an arms-negotiator.

With the building scheduled to open in September 1988, the CCA is in a critical period. The collections themselves, multiplying by the minute, are being entered into data bases. The photography collection, stored in New York, is making its way to Montreal, a rare example of cultural treasures' being repatriated rather than exported. Exhibitions tied to the new space are in the works. (One inaugural show will be about the collection, with emphasis on representation, co-curated by Eve Blau, the CCA's curator of exhibitions and publications, and Columbia University professor Edward Kaufman;

another, curated by Larry Richards, will be about the building.) Policies are being hammered out, public programming is under discussion.

'It's an opening out,' associate director Timothy Porteous, former head of the Canada Council, says of the CCA's full-throttle transition from a one-person collection to a permanent seat of study and investigation. 'I don't know what the full range of activities is going to be,' he continues, 'but they will be of a high level. This is a new type of institution. It hasn't been set up by a government or a university—research-oriented institutions in this country are either one or the other—so it's one-of-a-kind.'

The same goes for its founder and director. Comparisons have already been made between Lambert and great American collectors and patrons like the Fricks, the Rockefellers, the Mellons, the Gettys. 'We haven't seen her like before, and we won't again,' says CCA board member Christina Cameron, chief of the architectural history division of Parks Canada.

The skeleton biography of this human *non sequitur* bears repeating. She was born sixty years ago, daughter of the late Samuel Bronfman and Saidye Bronfman. She studied sculpture as a child, and in 1948 graduated from Vassar; in 1963, the interval marked by a brief marriage, she received an MA in architecture from the Illinois Institute of Technology. She had already emerged as an architectural force, having recommended Mies van der Rohe, in whose office she later worked, to her father as the designer of the Seagram building in New York. When Samuel Bronfman died in 1971, Lambert resumed residence in Montreal, becoming a spokesperson, even activist, on behalf of neighbourhood preservation, the renovation of heritage buildings, public consultation. In 1975 she founded Heritage Montreal as a permanent reference centre and foundation devoted to historic buildings. In 1979 she founded the CCA.

Lambert has such an obsessive personality that it is hard to know where it ends and CCA begins. Safe to say, without the one the other would not have come into existence. Second-guessing her motives has become a pastime for Sunday shrinks—but no one wins a popularity contest by building and floating an odd, rarefied, and complex venture such as this. 'I don't see this building as a monument to myself,' says Lambert, piqued by one theory about her anomalous behaviour. 'It is consistent with everything I have done.'

Single-minded in her devotion to a nameable if undervalued cause, she is wearing her familiar habit—workmen's overalls, long-sleeved shirt, scarf wound tightly around the neck. Woollen socks complete the ensemble. That she is in a position to afford Chanel is irrelevant. The hair is clipped short, the face untouched by make-up, the gold-rimmed glasses are severe. It's as though she's determined to demonstrate that, as one architect remarked, 'she has a very tough, reductive notion about the way things should look.'

She also has a fair notion of who she is. Lambert has designed buildings, the best known being the Saidye Bronfman Cultural Centre, in the Miesian mode, but it is doubtful she will go down in history as a designer—and she knows it. 'I guess I have to think of myself as an architect,' she says, gruff and fidgety. 'As an architect, you have to enjoy what you're doing. But an architect wants to make a statement about something. An architect has ideas about what she thinks a building will accomplish. It's a set of ideas about the history of architecture, where it is, how people relate to it. By making the CCA, one is extending one's capacity to make statements enormously. The exhibits, all the activities, the publications—well, okay, this was something I found that I really loved to do. If I had had a stronger sense of form—if that were the overriding consideration for me—I would have been drawing all the time. I would want to make my statement that way. I have chosen to make it this way, by making a place in which ideas are discussed, argued, put forward.'

The key is the collections, which will draw students and scholars to Montreal, advertise Canada abroad, and feed into exhibitions, publications, and seminars. 'We're interested in it as study material. The major thing about the collections is one wants to make material that provides for study—complete, not just a piece here, a piece there.'

The focus is on the way architects think and work—how they've thought and worked from the fifteenth century to the present. Should someone wish to investigate the influence of travel on the architectural mind, there are city guides, field notes, printed guides dating from 1544, early photographs of faraway monuments, diaries, travel sketches, measured drawings. But there are many different kinds of groupings. In some cases, an individual architect's *oeuvre* has been reassembled in the form of original proposals, contemporary periodicals and later photographs. In others, an architect's entire library has been purchased: books by architects used by other architects. The archives department contains the complete written and graphic records of certain individuals and firms, the star attraction being the vast Ernest Cormier archive. Coming at it another way, the CCA has assembled successive editions of key texts—fifty-eight editions of Vitruvius' *Ten Books on Architecture*, for example—that illustrate how ideas spread from country to country and across time.

The CCA's programming will interrelate in similar fashion. 'A study centre without interaction is academic,' says Lambert. 'Exhibitions without commitment are entertainment. We want to engage people's attention. We have to do that in different ways. My conviction is that by keeping on slowly, year after year, presenting different aspects, one will build a society that is literate about architecture. Seminars, films, television productions: it makes a subject.'

Reactions to Lambert's grand scheme have been mixed, ranging from nit-picking questions about her credentials to larger issues: is there a true clientele out there for that richness of collection? What sort of access will people have to the works? What happens if separatism becomes a force in Montreal again?

What has been accomplished so far, however, is beyond question. Says Michael McCarthy, University of Toronto professor of art history: 'She's put Canada on the map in a way greater than any building or work of scholarship in Canada has, by her sheer acquisitiveness. Canada has become a foremost contender at auction houses. To know Canada is taking the best of the collections at auction, and it would be available to me and my students—you'd never have a Canadian buyer in a sale of drawings in Rome or New York before. Everyone is terrified that Canada is going to sweep the board. Sheer, crass commercialism has given Canada clout, not its architecture.'

Lambert's capacity to make statements has already ben demonstrated, and so has her largesse. The CCA can't help being her monument, but in these niggardly times, in this anti-heroic country, we need more monuments like this, not fewer. — *March 1987*

Ettore Sottsass

The North American mind is ill-equipped to fathom the polemics and passions of Italian design. What for us may amount to no more than visually titillating luxury objects are, for Italian designers and critics, an expression of theoretical positions embedded in a convoluted socio-political matrix that is the subject of endless debate. Talk to a North American designer and the conversation usually turns to form, function, and the way things are made. Talk to a master from Milan and the discussion is likely to touch on Fascism, Rationalism, Utopia, semiotics, and the meaning of life.

Ettore Sottsass, eyelids at half-mast, a man of a certain charisma, speaks of all of these, with particular emphasis on the last. Nearing 70, a spliff in one pocket, fated for radicalism from youth, Sottsass made headlines in several languages for his role in siring Memphis, both the collective and the collection. When the first Memphis furniture, glass, ceramics, and textiles were exhibited in 1981, they caused a sensation. The strange-looking stuff was cheered for being exuberant, funky, and upbeat; Sottsass was credited as the guru of a band of designers half his age who followed him over the top. It wasn't long before funny tables with squiggly legs in the Memphis mode were popping up all over the Western world.

'When we did the first exhibition, we knew it had great energy inside, like the scientists who discovered the atomic bomb,' says Sottsass, in Rochester to address a conference on style sponsored by the Rochester Institute of Technology. 'But we didn't know it would explode. We didn't know that, particularly in America, it would be taken the way it has been taken—as a style, an artistic attitude. It's been schematized very much. I don't share this kind of figure the media has given to Memphis.'

Or to himself. Sottsass doesn't consider himself an artist. 'Normally,' he says, 'people who design speak of art a lot, or beauty. They consider art something above politics. They divide the world into practicalities and art. I almost never speak of art. I don't consider myself an artist of that kind. We're people dealing with languages, other people, the process of culture: that's it.' Moreover, says Sottsass, Memphis is not that optimistic: 'It was just the contrary. We were very pessimistic. We were looking for a new kind of innocence. That means not playing, but risking a lot. If an old man like me goes to a young girl for innocence, it's a risky proposition.'

Memphis has changed since 1981; so has Sottsass. In the beginning, there were strong links with American postmodernism; Michael Graves even contributed a piece to Memphis's debut exhibition. Admiration for Graves didn't last. 'There's a general movement in the world looking for greater communication in design and architecture—more elements, more information, more memories—but the world isn't as clean as we thought ten years ago. It is a mixture of corruption and technology. That's why I can say Graves in those times could be with the Memphis people. We wanted to share our trip with somebody, but we are not the same.'

One difference between postmodernism and Memphis, he says, is that 'all the iconographic references in Memphis come from suburbia, but all the memories of postmodernism are coming from academia.' Sottsass dismisses Graves as a conservative and postmodernism as 'homemade culture revisited'—a form of nationalism of which Tom Wolfe is the principal theoretician. 'The right stuff is very perverse stuff,' he says. 'It will go on.'

So will Memphis, but with a few changes. 'The energy and desperation of the first days are getting softer,' says Sottsass, adding that two years ago, fed up with being described as the grandfather of Memphis, he left the collective, no longer attending meetings and making decisions but still designing pieces for the collection. 'I didn't want to have the figure of an old man playing with colour. It's not my goal to become a master, just to do things. If one is old and one gets into an environment with students, immediately you're the old man. You can no longer have contact with people. There's a screen. I thought if I went away, the young people would have more responsibility. The whole situation is more relaxed. I am formally part of the Memphis Group, but I refuse to be their leader.'

Sottsass is a sworn enemy of systems and rigid ideologies. In un-European fashion, he got turned on by American 1960s culture, by the beats and hippies and Hell's Angels he met in California whose interior decoration—slashed refrigerators, cardboard boxes filled with the last remains of middle-class respectability—he greatly admired.

Another country that has influenced him is India, which he has visited frequently. 'It's the way of seeing life as a floating possibility,' he says. 'Everything they do, if they put a cup on the table, they always stay very high. They don't descend to vulgarities.' That has something to do with information:

'The way information was given to a peasant culture was through the sun rising and setting, and very few elements to live with. Indians don't have tables and chairs, so they don't have to mean anything. The rest is seasons and geological drama. That gives the idea that space and time are very slow. If you don't have anything, nothing changes.'

As for us, says Sottsass, 'it's a totally other thing. We belong to the air-conditioning, to the fluorescent lamp. Every day we have a lot of information. Time passes fast because we're consuming things. No one thinks today you can do something for eternity. You can't be a classicist any more. You don't put stones anywhere any more.'

All of this, somehow, bears on the objects and environments that Sottsass designs, everything from ceramics to Esprit showrooms to Memphis. They partake of the nature of totems, of mysterious presences that appeal not to the head but to the senses. 'Probably, already as a child I had this feeling. I had to create a sacred space for myself where all this river of information could pass over me without touching me too much. It could be that my totems have this kind of function.' But why do totems have to be designed in Milan? Sottsass smiles: 'I am not at the animistic stage. I'm at the intellectual stage.'

And we Westerners are in the capitalist-consumption stage. Sottsass tells of visiting an apartment in St Moritz recently that was done up exclusively in Memphis: 'It's really horrible, like taking twenty aspirins at once.' Karl Lagerfeld's Montecarlo apartment, designed by Andrée Putman using Memphis, is 'on the edge of the knife', he says. Sottsass's rule of thumb: no more than two Memphis pieces in any one place.

Take his ideas far enough, and you're in a dimension where the boundaries between subject and object, work and play dissolve, and the production of snob-value design becomes obsolete: the success of Memphis would spell the end of Memphis. 'We want to build a real democracy, if possible,' says Sottsass, 'and a real democracy is anarchism, which is very difficult to reach, although I must say, Italy is very near.'

He smiles, then he looks sad. 'I have always been a sad person,' he says, 'full of nostalgia for something that isn't happening. The feeling is always that everything is so fragile you really don't know what's happening with yourself. I am too much in love with everything. And when you are in love, you are sad all the time.' *— April 1987*

Witold Rybczynski

With the publication in 1986 of *Home*, McGill University architecture professor Witold Rybczynski became an overnight authority on the subject of comfort. A 230-page meditation on the evolution of domestic interiors over the centuries, *Home* has gone through five hardbound printings totalling some 25,000 copies, and is now in its second paperback printing. These statistics are a measure of Rybczynski's persuasive way with words, coupled with the fast-fed hunger of the 1980s to blame modernism for every human affliction, including backache.

It was in the cards, but nonetheless wearisome, that a champion of intimacy, privacy, cosiness, convenience, and pragmatism would blame 'modernity' for banishing comfort in the name of aesthetics. *Home* often reads like a whispered sequel to Tom Wolfe's noisy bestseller *From Bauhaus to Our House* (1981). Wolfe sends up modern architecture; Rybczynski takes a hammer to modern interiors, with special emphasis on seating. Marcel Breuer's chrome-and-leather Wassily chair and Mies van der Rohe's Barcelona chair are joined to everything Le Corbusier ever said and did about houses to demonstrate that the modern interior, in Rybczynski's phrase, 'attacks the very idea of comfort itself. That is why people look to the past.'

Well, a man is entitled to his opinions, even if he has conveniently overlooked Le Corbusier's LC4 chair and sofa, otherwise known as Le Grand Comfort, as well as entire housefuls of twentieth-century furniture that would shame the horsehair off a Victorian settee. But right, wrong, or consciously naïve, Rybczynski is not at all apologetic. 'I wasn't an anti-modernist before I wrote the book,' he said during a visit to Toronto, where he lectured on nineteenth-century domesticity at the Royal Ontario Museum. 'But I began to understand pre-modern architecture, which I hadn't as a student, and now I can actually look at buildings like I listen to Mozart—not as an antique, but to what it sounds like. The book enabled me to appreciate old furniture, which I hadn't done before.'

So writing *Home* was an adventure, not a pre-conceived plot. In fact, Rybczynski says, letting a cat out of a bag, he changed his mind about Le Corbusier between starting and ending the book. He wrote his chapter on the modernist's modernist before he touched anything else, thinking he'd then go back to the beginning and work forward. By the time he caught up with Le Corbusier again, he realized his original chapter needed a rewrite. He found himself, begrudgingly, 'pulling down a hero'. And his hero's chairs: 'These objects I'd admired for so long were so awfully uncomfortable.' He even turned against the Wassily, which he happens to own, because 'it didn't really work as a chair'.

Rybczynski still isn't sure whether 'modernists set out to destroy comfort or whether what was a by-product of their attack on bourgeois values, but it turned out the same.' To which one might add that it makes no difference whether Rybczynski set out to destroy modernism or whether it was an inevitable by-product of his case for comfort. It turned out the same. One-dimensional is one-dimensional.

The success of *Home* has given Rybczynski 'more confidence in writing and pursuing personal interests' because he's realized 'they may be other people's interests.' It's difficult to make architecture a 'readable subject', he feels, meaning he's never been keen on writing architecture books for other architects. Now that he's found his public, he's at work on a book that is 'much more about architecture'—something 'a bit like a travel book in that it takes you into various ends of architecture that have interested me.'

On the narrative level, Rybczynski's new book is about designing and building his own house, which took him five years. But that's really an excuse for describing how architects work and think: 'Faced with a sheet of paper, they come up with a building. That's why people are intrigued. You can produce this totally complex thing, and it's there.' Tracy Kidder's book *House* (1985), which describes the construction of a US dwelling down to the last toothsaw and nail, comes immediately to mind—and Rybczynski almost flinches: 'I was nervous when that book came out. It was really a book an architect should have written.' Himself, for example.

Rybczynski has high hopes for his new book, not because he's an architect but because he's a different sort of architect. 'I don't think my house is important as architecture,' he says pleasantly. 'I'm not making the case I'm a great architect who wants more work, which is what most books like this would be about.' His book will include self-criticism, or as he puts it: 'The process of design involves a lot of dead ends, mistakes, and coincidences. Of course, architects don't like to talk about that because it makes them out to be not so masterly. I'm more of a writer than an architect.'

But he is an architect. His specialty is low-cost housing in countries such as India and China. 'Because I work at that end, I feel good talking at this end—I've paid my dues at the other end,' he says. 'A lot of people don't have housing, let alone a home. You get architects building multi-million-dollar houses who get quite defensive or arrogant, which I personally don't feel. The modernists at least didn't negate housing. A lot of architects say housing is not architecture, but if you go to other countries, like China, it's only housing. It's their number one problem.' Rybczynski is now preparing to scour his home and native land for 'civic-minded developers' prepared to build affordable housing in Canada. That promises to be an even greater challenge than taking on Le Corbusier. *— November 1987*

Moshe Safdie

Moshe Safdie is no longer simply an architect: he's an architectural phenomenon. With the announcement that he's been selected to design the proposed ballet-opera house in Toronto, Safdie extended to four his list of glamour jobs on the go, or just completed, in Canada: the other three are the Musée

National de la Civilisation in Quebec City, the National Gallery in Ottawa, and the addition to the Museum of Fine Arts in Montreal. What's so special? Plenty, when you consider the projects are all prestigious public buildings; that they were all commissioned within the last six years; that not a single one went to Arthur Erickson, Safdie's match for political savvy; and that Safdie, in every case, was applying from abroad. Born in Israel, educated in Montreal, employed by Harvard, he has lived in Boston for a decade. Although Safdie has built a lot in Jerusalem (where for four years he directed the Harvard Jerusalem Studio), he seemed to disappear in Canada following Expo '67, only to reappear some fifteen years later to compete for every big job in sight.

Expo was the scene of Safdie's first triumph, Habitat, that odd-looking knobby structure billed as revolutionary prototype of twenty-first-century social housing. (Actually, it became an apartment block for the wealthy.) Habitat got as much attention as any building deserves, but it didn't seem to go anywhere, nor did Safdie, except to Boston and the Middle East. Now he's back, radiating confidence, with a brace of museums and an opera house slung over his shoulder.

'It is amazing,' Safdie said of the fifteen-year intermission between acts one and two of his Canadian career. An hour earlier, he had been introduced as winner of the ballet-opera house and posed for ritual photographs of architect hovering over model; reporters were waiting their turn at the door; all in all, a nice day. Safdie has had a lot worse, he acknowledges, particularly after Expo '67.

'Habitat was very controversial, it frightened a lot of public clients,' he explains, speaking in the relaxed, direct manner that has gained him the nickname of Mr Charm. Other obstacles stood in the way of a brilliant Canadian career in the 1960s. 'Then, in Quebec, it was a very nationalistic period; the provincial government was a closed shop. Jean Drapeau [former Montreal mayor] hated my guts—he wanted a tower at Expo instead of Habitat. So he finished me in Montreal.'

It wasn't as if he didn't give it his best shot, he continues, letting plots and subplots fall where they may. He was still resident in Montreal when he entered the 1976 National Gallery competition, but he didn't even make the short list of ten firms in that contest (which, in any case, came to nothing). 'I wrote [Pierre] Trudeau and we discussed it: I'd been blacklisted,' he said. He tried for the Quebec City opera house, but didn't get that, either. 'So I got work in Jerusalem and the US, which I did from Montreal. When Harvard asked me to come, I went.' He became director of the urban design program at Harvard's Graduate School of Design in 1978; he currently teaches architecture and design.

But Safdie didn't burn all his bridges in Quebec; Pierre Trudeau wasn't his only correspondent. The 'breakthrough', in his words, came in 1982, with the commission for the Musée National de la Civilisation. 'The whole thing happened because a Quebec City firm [Belzile, Brassard, Gallienne, Lavoie] asked me to join with them in the invitational competition. I warned them: "You're crazy." When we made it to the short list of five, there was a petition from certain architects saying I should be disqualified because I wasn't a Canadian.' Winning that competition changed everything. 'I wouldn't have had the National Gallery in 1983 without that. Jean [Sutherland Boggs, who ran the competition] liked it. Trudeau liked it.'

The other architects in the running for the gallery didn't like it one bit: Safdie, they complained at the time, had been invited to submit for the Museum of Man (now the Museum of Civilization, designer: Douglas Cardinal) and not the gallery—and besides, he wasn't even living in Canada. To which Safdie responds, in part: 'The years I did live here, I didn't get any commissions.' Now that he's getting them with astonishing regularity, he is going to open a permanent office in Toronto, which will become his 'main Canadian office'. That means his Montreal office, considered by his rivals to consist only of a telephone-answering machine, will play a less important role in his plans for a full-scale invasion of Canada.

One of Safdie's most instrumental patrons, however, lives in Montreal—Bernard Lamarre, head of the giant engineering firm Lavalin, and president of the Montreal Museum of Fine Arts. (Lavalin were the engineers on the Musée National de la Civilisation project.) In some quarters, Safdie is considered a creation of Lamarre, to the point where Odile Hénault, in an editorial published in *Section a*, in 1985, identified two controlling forces in Montreal architecture, each with his/her court architect. One is Phyllis Lambert, promoter of Peter Rose; the other, Lamarre, promoter of Moshe Safdie. Montreal, Hénault concluded, could become the 'biggest company town in the country'. 'Imagine me being called Lamarre's court architect,' says Safdie, who had raised the issue himself. Does he disagree with Hénault, then? 'She's absolutely right. Sure, Bernard Lamarre appreciates my work.'

Well-connected and proud of it, master strategist, expert in the politics of charm—is it any wonder Safdie won the ballet-opera house? If the response at Thursday's press conference is any indication, Toronto actually had its doubts. When Safdie's name was pronounced, and not that of James Stirling, the British architect that both Safdie and Barton Myers considered the man to beat, entire rows of jaws were seen to fall open. But Stirling is not well connected in Canada, so he wouldn't be much use in helping to raise money to get the hall built; and neither, for that matter, is Myers.

Stirling had one thing going for him: namely, the support of juror Phyllis Lambert. But Safdie had something even better going for him: the selection process. Remember, the Ballet Opera House Corp. was looking for an architect, not a design. Recall that there were only four architects on the selection committee, and eight lay people representing the two performing companies and the board. Finally, think back to the requirement that the finalists were asked to consult with the companies every two days during the three weeks they were given to come up with sketches and a model. (Safdie produced four models, each more elaborate than the one before: 'Making models with lights? That's my thing.') Stirling resented having clients peer over his shoulder; Safdie did not: 'What I had going for me was the relationship that evolved with the members of the company.' And, by comparison with Stirling, whose building in miniature is quiet, processional, self-contained, showing a nose for Toronto taste in the 1980s, Safdie's design is glassy, showy—a people-pleaser.

Safdie, with reason, is expecting more work in Toronto and the country in general. 'I see a shift in emphasis of my professional activities into Canada,' he says. 'Jerusalem is ongoing, but I will shift from the United States into Canada.' Partly, the shift has been arranged for him by the recent cancellation of Columbus Centre in New York, which he considers a painful setback. But Safdie has a way of overcoming failure, both in deed and in word. 'I think I produced all my best work in Canada,' he says, 'from Habitat to the National Gallery.'

— March 1988

Shiro Kuramata

Shiro Kuramata introduces himself this way: 'My strongest desire is to be free of gravity, free of bondage. I want to float. I don't like heavy things.' This quiet confession, relayed by an interpreter, may help to explain how Kuramata came to design a transparent glass chair, furniture, and even a boutique of expanded metal mesh, a floor lamp with a clear acrylic shaft filled with a colourful tangle of wire, an illuminated floor surfaced with sandblasted glass, terrazzo floor tiles inlaid with stainless steel chips, and a table with a round acrylic top embedded with diodes that glow red in the dark. We're talking poetry here, not prose—a glistening anthology of inklings, ambiguities, and flickering boundaries in danger of disappearing altogether.

Kuramata has been exploring the skeletal, shiny, and luminous for over twenty years, although he did not become internationally known until the 1980s. A man of compact frame and cherubic curls who happily admits, 'I haven't grown up yet,' he has been on the leading edge of design in Japan since there was an edge to lead—that is, since the 1960s, when Japanese design shook free of architecture to become an independent discipline. Drawing on ancient traditions of refined simplicity and breathtaking craftsmanship, designers rode the crest of the 'economic miracle' that transformed Japan into an industrial superpower, punctuated by the 1964 Tokyo Olympics and Expo 70 in Osaka. Kuramata led the pack, steering in the direction of 'total design'.

His dream of becoming a designer dates back to the United States' occupation of Japan, which brought 'the good old days of America', in the form of big-band music and consumer goods, to the country and to the 12-year-old Kuramata. He was 'amazed' when he first saw a package of Lucky Strikes and a Studebaker, both of which were designed by Raymond Loewy. 'So he was cultivating a longing, an adoring for those things when he was around 16,' says Kuramata's interpreter. 'They were very beautiful and shocking to his youth. That's how he came to learn there is a so-called "designer" in society.'

Further evidence presented itself in 1949 in the form of a public telephone box lighted by a single red light bulb. 'At that time,' says Kuramata, 'there were no private telephones. Japan was still poor. In an emergency situation, people looked for a red roof—that was a telephone box. From that I learned how design is associated with society's needs. I found it meaningful.' Kuramata experienced these shocks while studying the art of lacquering in the woodcraft department of Tokyo Municipal Polytechnic High School. In 1954, he joined a furniture factory 'to practise'. He learned about the technical end of design, but felt 'there should be something else of the essence in designing.' This he sought at the Kuwazawa Design Institute, a Bauhaus-influenced school.

Kuramata's approach to design synthesizes school, or 'thinking', and factory: 'You have to have both.' He refers to his designs as 'collaborations with craftsmen', and regularly commutes to factories in a variety of countries. Within the last two years, furniture manufacturers in Japan, Italy, Switzerland, France, and the Netherlands have sought him out, and several of his proto-types from the 1970s have been put into production. He attributes this sudden surge of attention to the radical Italian design movements of the 1980s, Studio Alchimia and Memphis, which 'led to a boom in furniture and interior design'. Kuramata has exhibited with the Memphis collective since 1981, and the publicity hasn't hurt: 'Manufacturers took another interest' in his work. 'Ettore Sottsass is my maestro,' says Kuramata. 'It's very spiritual. I don't want to use the word "teacher", but he's a person who has been very stimulating, sort of inspiring to me. He makes me awaken and visualize things that are invisible.'

From the time he opened his office in 1965, Kuramata has been 'very much attracted' by the design of commercial space: 'Furniture is for myself, in one sense; interiors are for clients,' he says. He explains that a commercial design is 'very temporary. It will be extinguished in a certain period of time. It's totally the opposite of a monument, which stays forever.' In this sense, he continues, he's 'very Tokyo-like'. In Tokyo, he says, 'There's nothing concrete, nothing permanent. It just comes in and goes out. Commercial space could be representative of that Tokyo phenomenon.'

But there's no separating Kuramata's interiors from his furniture. In 1985, Kuramata took a bentwood chair designed by Josef Hoffmann and manufac-tured by Thonet, wrapped steel rods around it, welded them at the joints—

and then burned the chair. What was left was the glittering aura of a modernist icon, a burden violently dispatched. Kuramata called the work Homage to Hoffmann: Begin the Beguine (the name refers to the big-band music of Occupation days). How High the Moon, designed the following year, is a descendant of Begin the Beguine and marks the beginning of Kuramata's use of expanded metal. It is an armchair—a shimmering phantom of a chair, really. It's as though there was once a chair inside, and Kuramata took a torch to that, too. The Issey Miyake Men boutique for the Shibuya Seiku Department Store (1987) is a larger, darker, more heavily layered take on this idea—a barrel-vaulted cage within a cage within a bustling, brightly-lighted homage to shopping. Expanded metal appears again in the Lucchino Bar (1987), but in combination with neon, triple-layered glass (transparent, cracked, and etched), and the round acrylic table implanted with diodes. It is the dynamic orchestration of light, shape, and insubstantial substance, creating a shadowy, expectant, subterranean world, all mood and traces, nothing definite.

'I like expanded metal for its transparency,' says Kuramata, designer of the split second. 'It doesn't shut out the space of the world. It looks very light, and therefore, it looks as if it floats.' Of Sing, Sing, Sing (a song made famous by Benny Goodman), a chair of expanded metal with a chromium plate finish, he says, as he could say of his commercial environments: 'If you extinguish anything more, it won't work as a chair. This material is the last condition to complete the surface—the deadline, the very last minute to retain the surface. At that point, the material creates a tension because it's just at the point of disintegration.' As for the chrome plating: 'It's just very sexy and erotic. I am destroying and multiplying at the same time.'

— Tokyo, September 1988

John and Patricia Patkau

While big architectural outfits based in Ontario are no strangers to the corporate downtowns of western Canada, there are welcome signs of a reverse trend: smallish firms from the west are beginning to make their mark on the institutional landscape of Ontario. IKOY, a group of Winnipeg architects, were designers of the William G. Davis Computer Research Centre at the University of Waterloo. The job of creating a new Earth Sciences Building at Trent University just went to Richard Henriquez, of Vancouver. And Patkau Associates, likewise of Vancouver, were selected as architects of the Canadian Clay and Glass Museum in Kitchener, for which the financing will soon be announced and working drawings commenced.

Significantly, all three projects were awarded after nationwide searches—

two were design competitions—and in each case, Larry Richards, former director of the University of Waterloo architecture school, served as professional adviser to the selection committee. In that position, which is roughly the equivalent of talent scout, Richards is emerging as The Equalizer: someone who believes in giving fresh ideas and fresh faces a chance, regardless of place of origin. That may seem an obvious prerequisite for getting some good new architecture built, but it doesn't often coincide with the Canadian Way of Doing Things.

Of the three firms granted Ontario passports, the freshest faces belong to John and Patricia Patkau, a husband-and-wife team, both originally from Winnipeg. He has a degree from the University of Manitoba; she studied interior design there, but got her architectural training at Yale. So far, the Patkaus' work is comprised of houses, a couple of them in Victoria. Neither is typical of the domestic architecture of that city, which runs to rambling turn-of-the-century mansions in a Lutyens vein, mock-Tudor ranch houses, and what is referred to in real-estate listings as the traditional west-coast house: two-storey bungalows alternately faced in wood siding and stucco, the ground floor often half-buried in the ground.

The Patkau projects have both been inserted into Rockland, one of Victoria's oldest residential areas, which began as a three-hectare subdivision and, since the end of the Second World War, has been subdivided again and again. Lots are still being pinched off the steep, heavily treed grounds of large estates, and it is on two of these, both very different in character, that the Patkaus were invited to build. The houses, too, are very different, although they share a common vocabulary. In the context of Rockland, where anglicisms and ornateness are the rule, the first thing that hits you is that they're modern. Blank stucco walls and flowing white interiors in Victoria? You got it.

The Appleton residence, designed for a couple and their three children, is the homier of the two places. It's set on a flat, small, odd-shaped property that used to belong to a nursing home, on a short street surrounded on all sides by greenery and houses. Tight site—bold, simple gesture. From the street, it doesn't look like much—recessed doorway, garage, mute stucco face—but once inside, you're in a high, bright space, both elegant and relaxed, known as the 'great room'. It's living-room, dining-room, and kitchen combined, the spaces divided by a single, monumental white column that branches out at the top, like a tree, to engage with a skylight. The imagery is apt: every window offers an intense close-up of flora—and no view at all of neighbours.

The fireplace is another exaggerated gesture that gives the great room an aura of greatness. Its dimension is large, the mantel piece a long, steel ledge. Around the corner from the dining area, through an oversized pivoting door, lie the parents' quarters, a den and bedroom. Up the stairs at the other end of the giant room is a gallery leading to the children's rooms and a corner playroom. The interiors are white, as is all the furniture in the bedrooms, which is built-in. The plumbing is white. The tiles are white. And in the interests of preserving the feeling of white and bright, the house is full of decentralized storage. Everything that can be hidden away, including all appliances and electronic equipment, has been hidden away—in drawers, cupboards, free-standing cupboards, recessed cupboards.

Even the Appletons have been hidden away. The outdoor swimming pool is enclosed by a stucco wall that wraps around the master suite, giving privacy. From the swimming pool, which affords the best view of the house, you see a large, quiet sculpture, each volume indicating a different space behind, with the stucco planes tinted different colours for subtle emphasis. The Appleton residence has elements of Frank Gehry (the Danziger Studio, the Hollywood Library) and Luis Baragan—but we can't forget the Patkaus, who are very strong in the siting, colour, and texture departments. And the Patkaus understand that in a setting as ornamental as those supplied by nature on the west coast, an uninterrupted white interior is right.

In the Pyrch residence, which is slightly smaller but three times more expensive than the Appleton house, the Patkaus spread their wings and soared. The clients are a retired couple from Edmonton who acquired, in their own words, 'one of the great lots in Victoria'. Indeed. It looks innocent enough from the street, where it rises gently upwards. But at the top it's a piece of rock with a 12-metre drop to another street below—and a majestic view across the ocean to Mount Baker.

The Patkaus responded with a house that's slung high across the property in a wide-open V-shape. On the street you see only an expanse of silvery stucco and a domed tower clad in greening copper. The entrance is off to one side, up a long set of stone stairs. The door opens and you're in the lobby, a fulcrum space. To the right lies the living-room. That's the dome. Nice paintings on the walls, but the best painting of them all is ahead of you—a huge framed picture of water and mountains.

Angled off one side of this superb room is the master bedroom and bathroom, and off the other, the dining-room, kitchen, and den, one following the other. A door leading from the dining-room takes you outside to a terrace carved out of rock. A staircase in the den takes you down to the guest suite, which has its own rocky terrace attached. The place has a dynamic flow and rhythm. On the inside, with its shiny wooden floors, white walls, and expansive white detailing, the house gleams. From the outside, it looks like an extrusion from the rock.

The Patkaus aren't interested in aping details of surrounding architecture: they're modernists. But they're not denying the neighbourhood, either. Both of their houses fit, their forms and materials graciously in tune with landscape. Neither screams, and neither is afraid of being itself. They've just taken their rightful place on the street alongside everything else. That's fresh—now on to Kitchener.   — *September 1988*

Pyrch residence

John C. Parkin

John C. Parkin, who died in Toronto on Tuesday, will be remembered as a pioneer of the International Style in Canada, and a partner in what was, by the end of the 1950s, the country's largest and most powerful architectural firm.

For architects ambitious to practise modern architecture in Canada after the Second World War, there were only two offices to consider: John B. Parkin Associates, where John C. Parkin was in charge of design; or Page and Steele after Peter Dickinson, an Englishman, came on as chief designer. Both men were on a mission, and both had visions of becoming the Skidmore, Owings, and Merrill of the north. But the Parkin firm came closer to pulling it off. The company's achievement was to marry a strong design direction with an equally strong construction and engineering capacity. That's a powerful combination.

The history of the Parkin office is complicated and confusing, not least on account of surname. The principal founder of the firm was John B. Parkin, a graduate of the University of Toronto and eleven years John C.'s senior. They weren't related. They met in Toronto in 1944. John B. was becoming known for innovative school design, and John C., who had just graduated from the University of Manitoba, was working for Marani and Morris while making arrangements to study at Harvard. John C. worked briefly for John B. before his departure. The original partnership, formed in 1947, consisted of a trio of Parkins: John B. Parkin; his brother, Edmund T. Parkin, a landscape architect, and John C. Parkin. (Edmund retired in 1964; John B. moved to Los Angeles in 1969 and died there in 1975.)

It was a great match. John B., a Christadelphian, was an astute, aggressive businessman who dreamed of developing a strong industrial-design practice in the tradition of European modernists. John C., fresh from Harvard where he studied under Gropius, audited lectures by Alvar Aalto, chummed with classmate Paul Rudolph, dined with Le Corbusier, lunched with Pierre Trudeau and his brother Charles—John C. was ready to bring Bauhaus to our house.

'We were the missionaries,' says Jeanne Parkin, who met her future husband at Harvard, where she was studying art history at the Fogg Museum. 'These were the dreamers and the white knights. John talked about the furniture he would design, and how we would live. He and John B. were good together. John B. always seemed to be easy-going, the opposite of a heavy-handed manager, but he had very strong ideas about design. He was a purist.'

The firm took off. Between 1949 and 1951, Parkin Associates completed forty school projects in Ontario, and commissions continued to roll in: industrial buildings, office buildings, hospitals, warehouses. By 1962, a thousand commissions had been seen to fruition and the 180-strong staff were completing Terminal One at Pearson International Airport and working in joint venture with Viljo Revell to build Toronto City Hall. The same year an article summing up the first fifteen years of the practice reached the following conclusion. 'Their claim must rest . . . on the fact that they are doing something about the best ideas presented by the great law-givers and form-givers of the start of the modern movement. They are the expediters in the arts; the practical and sensitive rationalizers who have succeeded in bringing the basic stuff of the law-givers to reality in everyday buildings and everyday needs in construction.'

Says Parkin's lifelong friend and frequent client Douglas Crashley: 'John B. and John C. gave us the clean edge of the Bauhaus-Mies van der Rohe approach, which was absolutely new to the city. They believed this to be the way, and they were having a difficult time to persuade owners to follow this approach. It was a tough sell in the 1950s. And compared with Arthur Erickson and others, John reacted to budgetary constraints. Everything he built came in on budget. People didn't understand that side of John. He took his architecture very seriously.'

The first fifteen years were the heyday of John B. Parkin Associates. Highlights of the period include Ortho Pharmaceutical Ltd, the Ontario Association of Architects Headquarters, Parkin's own residence, and the airport Terminal One, all but the latter finished before 1960. 'I would always go to buildings as they were being built,' said Jeanne Parkin. 'The airport—that was so thrilling. I would go to these little schools and all those funny buildings out in the sticks. These were pioneering days. I'd go up to Aylmer and look at that lousy little school—the fact that John put the smoke-stack separate from the building, that was thrilling.'

Parkin did all the drawings for the OAA headquarters, inspired, he said, by Mies van der Rohe's Farnsworth House, in the early 1950s. And he undoubtedly designed his own house, now much altered, which he considered an act of daring. He counted 'less than 100 architects in the country who had the audacity to make that personal statement without having to blame everyone but themselves.' It stands on an inside property in the Bridle Path, and Jeanne Parkin once described it as 'a series of blockages'. It had a blank wall on the street, 'and then,' she continued, 'walled in, walled behind those walls, are two courtyards.' Inside the front door stood a long row of cupboards that had to be walked around to arrive at the living-room, its back wall entirely of glass. At first, the floors were all terrazzo—no carpets. Antiques were not allowed—Parkin hated eclecticism—and for a long time, paintings weren't, either. The architecture was everything. 'John did not believe in bringing the outside in,' said Jeanne. 'Only two kinds of plants were allowed: split-leaf philodendron or rubber plants. Those were his signature plants.' Flowers were not permitted outside, with the exception of a small patch dedicated to cutting varieties. Telephones were required to sit at right angles to the desk.

It was in this suave and disciplined, if impractical, house, that Parkin kept his Barcelona chairs; his autographed pictures of Parkin and Mies, Parkin and Le Corbusier, Parkin and Gropius, Parkin and Buckminster Fuller; his

Ortho Pharmaceutical Ltd

family coat of arms; a dictionary on a pedestal where, in his spare time, he'd stand and memorize words for his speeches; and the extensive library of books and periodicals he had started in Winnipeg—and it was here he sat, every Sunday night, going over drawings. For it wasn't long before Parkin left off designing to become 'the editor, and eventually, the publisher'.

The role of editor included that of promotion, at which he excelled; image meant a lot to him. He could spot talent, too. 'It was a question of how one could control,' he once said. 'Being reasonably pragmatic, I was trying to prove if it wasn't possible to control an even quality. You'd have to have awfully skilled designers around you, and be prepared to listen to them, and have critiques, and go to design seminars.' He put a premium on talent from Harvard and Yale—on such as Douglas Rowland, who joined the office in 1957. Rowland is now a principal of Neish Owen Rowland Roy (NORR), the firm that emerged, first under a different name, from John B. Parkin Associates in 1971, when John C. departed the company after a bitter power struggle and set up John C. Parkin, Architects Planners.

'He persuaded me to come to Toronto,' says Rowland. 'He was a creative person, not conceptually, but he had a lot of imagination. He had a remarkable touch in refining a project, and a lot of interests. He was probably better read than any architect I've ever met. He had taste. His own house epitomized what he could create in the way of a whole environment. The original house was a superb work. He refined, and refined, and refined.'

Two of the most talented architects that Parkin attracted were Macy DuBois, an American, and Australian John Andrews, both finalists in the Toronto City Hall competition. Parkin wined and dined them at the Imperial Room, and sold them on staying in Toronto. Says DuBois, who lasted only the year 1958-59: 'He made it very attractive. He gave me an opportunity. He said he wanted to get that input, the Corbusian background.' There were other things he was thinking of—he wanted to show he was a forward-looking firm bringing new talent in. 'He was remarkable. He structured a firm so as to keep a level of design that was identifiable and reproducible. It didn't work for me—it told me what I didn't want to do as an architect— I wasn't given the detailing of a toilet to do. I was given a broad scope.'

The 1970s and 1980s were definitely post-heyday for Parkin. He collected honours and medals aplenty, but his winning competition entry for the National Gallery in 1975 didn't get built, and what did get built lacked the sparkle and force of what came before, with the possible exception of the College of Nurses of Ontario, which opened in Toronto in 1982.

John and Jeanne Parkin were divorced a few years ago, and their house was sold. (It now belongs to the couturier Maggy Reeves.) Parkin moved into a penthouse condominium on Bloor Street, with his library, his photographs, his Miesian furniture, his family coat of arms.

In person, he could project self-confidence, vanity, unease, and rage, all in a single conversation. He made few public appearances over the last two

years, one being to attend the funeral of friend and colleague Ron Thom, and another to attend the opening of the National Gallery, in the end designed by Moshe Safdie with Parkin's firm serving as production house. His death brings to a close a roller-coaster chapter in the history of Canadian architecture, and a life, sometimes recklessly led, dedicated to urbanity and urbanism.
— *November 1988*

Peter Hamilton

Two buildings in downtown Toronto, both designed by Peter Hamilton, both nearing completion, are both worth waiting for. From Hamilton, savvy modernist, we have learned to expect handsome, flowing, light-filled spaces. Characteristically, his architecture leans toward simple forms, white interiors, and sophisticated use of industrial elements and materials: few can match his way with glass block. The combination is hardly revolutionary. What impresses is Hamilton's restraint and delicacy—his light touch. He's always understating the case. He understands amenity. He has a cultivated sense of when to stop.

Nothing's changed, but there's a freshness and cheek to the new work that show a different side to Hamilton. No stranger to leafy neighbourhoods, he's designed a mixed-use building on Cumberland Street, east of Avenue Road. Good address, incoherent context. Chalk that up to a 1970s predilection known as split-level, or front-split, retail. You know the stuff. Yorkville is full of it. One set of stairs leads up to a store, or group of stores; another leads down to a half-buried store, or row of stores. Sidewalk and door never meet.

Hamilton was required to fit his building between two mismatched neighbours. The building to one side meets the property line; the front-split special to the other side is recessed from the sidewalk, separated from the street by a pit. Although the Phase Three development contains upstairs-downstairs store space, the point being to maximize retail, as developers say, Hamilton insisted on putting the doors on street level, where he thinks they belong. In other words, instead of putting stairways outside a building, forcing it back from the street, he's put them inside. You'd never guess, walking past 136 Cumberland, that there was a store below grade. Maximum retail, no pits.

To belabour the point that you can walk straight into a building from the sidewalk seems ridiculous. It only shows how thoughtlessly streets—and street life—have been impaired. Front-split retail went too far. Nonetheless, Hamilton developed a strategy for dealing with it as both commercial reality and next-door neighbour. He's designed a prototype for Yorkville that repairs the streetscape. Without surrendering the street line, and by gently flaring and curving one side of the building, he makes it appear as though the façade of 136 Cumberland is flowing into the adjacent one. His wave has created an intriguing interior space as well. The building is polished and articulate, front, back, and side. A lot has been packed into a site that is only 30 feet wide. There are four stories in all, counting the downstairs. The ground floor is retail, and the second floor is retail at the front and offices behind. Above that is a combined office/apartment with mezzanine leading, via an internal bridge, to a huge patio overlooking Cumberland. Each space has its own identity, its own entrance, but the ensemble is rhythmic and unified in subtle ways.

The residence is recessed for privacy, the windows protected by perforated metal sun louvres, painted blue, yet the metal balcony in smart canary yellow protrudes slightly from the Cumberland façade. The big windows of the second-floor retail space are mullionless; they're set into a protruding steel channel. Three tiny wired mesh windows have even been set into the glass block wave so that shoppers can look east towards Bay. A matching pair of curved glass display bubbles is positioned between the concrete columns, each wrapped in blue perforated metal, that anchor building to sidewalk. The last time an architect tried to work with so many kinds of glass and window resulted in the embarrassment known as the Metro Toronto Police Headquarters. *Vive la différence.*

When an architect of Hamilton's talents works for one of the top graphic designers in the country, the results are bound to look good. Burton Kramer turned to Hamilton, an old friend, to re-renovate a narrow, three-storey house on Dupont Street into his offices. What he got was a three-dimensional billboard on the street—Hamilton gone Hollywood. And with reason. Not only is his client in the image business, but also his client's future office was leaning to one side, off plumb by a foot. The solution was to re-skin the front to make the building appear what it wasn't, namely straight.

Hamilton chose corrugated aluminum with an embossed finish to do the job. The roof of the building is flat, but he rounded the silver skin at the top, so we know it's a false front, and stepped the aluminum cladding around one side, filling in with green stucco. Since the building as found was wonky, Hamilton responded by going wonky too. He placed the front door to one side, on street level, and put a rectangular piece of glass block next to it to light the reception area. The second-floor window is off-centre; it looks like a bay window pressed through a wringer. The square window at the top is likewise asymmetrical. Triangle, square, rectangle, curve, wedge. Red, blue, yellow, green. Kramer's line of business is well represented.

The rooms inside are small but bright. Hamilton exposed the ductwork and designed the handrails and continuous lighting fixtures from standard parts. One wall of the conference room angles out as a lighthearted reminder of the building's original condition, and one handrail looks to be out of control. Shooting through the top two floors is a box made of wired mesh glass topped by a skylight that brings natural light into what would have been

Kramer Design Associates Ltd

the darkest rooms in the house. There's a big deck off the third floor, and an elaborate metal fire-escape stair painted turquoise that the staff uses to exit. The place is all sun and fun, and as eccentric as its occupants.

— *March 1989*

Prince Charles

Architects have been speculating about the downside of modernism for 25 years; writers, sociologists, and conservationists have analysed the damage wreaked by bulldozers and housing projects for at least as long; and neoclassicism has been promoted and institutionalized as a style since the early 1980s. But it wasn't until Prince Charles delivered his 'monstrous carbuncle' speech of 1984, wherein he attacked the arrogance of the architectural profession in general, and specifically the winning scheme for a high-tech extension to the National Gallery, that the common man was alerted to yesterday's news— and three disparate streams of theory were funnelled into a single set of influential opinions. The prince's views on architects, developers, and planners have provoked stormy debate in England and elsewhere; when a royal talks, the world listens. Charles talked non-stop for 75 minutes in a BBC documentary broadcast a year ago called *A Vision of Britain*, which he wrote and hosted. Now comes the book that will carry the royal message beyond the bedsits of the nation to plop it onto the global coffee table.

A Vision of Britain, the book, is laid out like a children's story. The print is large, the text consists of blocks of cautionary prose rarely exceeding three sentences in length, punctuation runs heavily to exclamation points and question marks, illustrations are profuse and colourful. Sketches and watercolours by the man who will be king have been included, some unsigned, others marked with a C. The first one to appear is accompanied by the coy directive: 'If you look carefully you will find other sketches by me throughout this book.' Has Charles been reading *Where's Waldo*?

The princely primer is more sophisticated and sophistic than its format suggests. Charles understands the power of persuasion; he's been using it regularly to kill or change building projects of which he disapproves, and he uses it to bring his points home. One 'monstrous carbuncle' from a silver-tongued prince is worth a thousand words. So, reproduced in the book, is a glowing panorama of the Thames painted by Canaletto, showing the dome of St Paul's Cathedral aloft over the eighteenth-century London skyline. The Canaletto crosses over into rhetoric by the addition of a translucent, made-to-measure insert printed with a photographic image of the same skyline updated to the present. In shades of grey it pictures the dome of St Paul's in mid-smothering by the towers of Canary Wharf, a huge Olympia and York development designed by Cesar Pelli.

Observe the golden eighteenth century through the murky scrim of the twentieth and you've got the prince's vision in half-a-nutshell: how we've gone wrong! Imagine the twentieth-century landscape in-filled with neo-Georgian architecture and you've got the other half: we can still get it right! Clever, this reference to tracing paper, a designer's aid, to attack the architectural profession—and not a bad marketing tool for a prince on a mission. Make no mistake, C is selling. He's taken his vision to the market-place. He's putting his mouth where his money is. So what's he looking at besides carbuncles and old paintings?

Plenty, actually. He's familiar with the splendid vernacular architecture of British town and countryside. He likes it and, not surprisingly, he likes neo-vernacular architecture, or new buildings that closely resemble the old. On his hate list are the council estates built to house low-income families after the war; the National Theatre, which he calls 'a nuclear power station in the middle of London'; the new British Library, of which he queries: 'How can you even tell that it *is* a library?'; and James Stirling's proposal for a commer-cial building on a historical site in the City, which elicits a comparison to 'an old thirties wireless'—and prompts the question: 'Is somebody proposing to dive from this tower?'

Town planning is as much a part of the princely vision as individual buildings, which are either complimented for looking 'traditional' or criticized as being 'egotistically "modern" or "revolutionary"'. It follows from the monarch-to-be's taste in architecture that he would like new chunks of city and town to have 'a modern, classical look' like Seaside, a planned community in Florida where, by decree, houses are pastel and have picket fences and porches. The prince is planning his own version of Seaside: he's hoping to create four new villages on 350 acres of his land in the Duchy of Cornwall to plans by Leon Krier, an influential theorist of the neoclassical revival.

Basic principles are of the essence if we're to get it right this time, he writes. So he has come up with a list of ten principles—ten command-ments—whereby his vision of a traditional future could become reality. In précis, they say that a building (or development) should blend with the landscape, display a legible hierarchy of parts and maintain a sense of civic hierarchy, defer to human proportions, harmonize with its neighbours, pro-vide a feeling of enclosure, be constructed of local materials, feature decora-tion, incorporate art commissions, stand free of banal logos and ugly signage, and encourage input from the community.

The positive aspect of the prince's platitudinous crusade is that it has made architecture a popular subject—no mean feat, unless you're Tom Wolfe. (Come to think of it, Wolfe and the prince have much in common: wit, chutzpah, and contempt for modern architecture.) The prince is no fool. He's got eyeballs, and he has a lot of things right. Yes, a great deal of contemporary architecture *is* menacing. No, it *isn't* easy, as noted in a paragraph on hospitals, 'to be healed in a soulless concrete box with characterless windows, inhospitable corridors, and purely functional wards.' Council estates *are* dreadful: they were built quickly, cheaply, and often thoughtlessly. Is there need for 'a far greater emphasis on art and design and drawing skills in our schools'? Probably. That Siena is a marvellous town goes without saying.

But eyeballs or no, the visionary has a blind spot. When it comes to modernism he can see only in black and white. The International Style comes in only two alliterative varieties: 'rising rot' and 'creeping cancer'. The 'argument between modernist and traditional architecture' comes down to 'the argument between the inhuman and the human.' (He phrases the argument elsewhere as one between function and aesthetics, which is equally uninformed.)

Prejudiced pronouncements such as these not only betray pitiful ignorance, they promise a realm in which entire avenues of imagination will be barred to traffic. But a man of influence must do his homework; someone who preaches modesty might realize he's not the first person to believe 'man is more, *much* more, than a mere mechanical object whose sole aim is to produce money'. Hateful modernists by the names of Le Corbusier and Mies van der Rohe were ahead in the queue. Thus does one visionary knock off the others.

'What we really need to do,' he writes, 'is to regain the humility to understand the lessons of the past: not just of classical architecture, but of Gothic and other traditions as well.' He can't admit that modernism, his leg to stand on, is one of those other traditions. Or that the best of today's British architects—Stirling, Norman Foster, Richard Rogers—have made good use of it. Charles doesn't get it, he *will not* get it: remember the ten commandments. Visionary with blinkers, humble and not-so-humble, man of the people, Moses surveying the Promised Land—in royal fashion, the prince is having his cake and eating it too.   *— September 1989*

Edward Jones

Edward Jones, designer of Mississauga City Hall, has kissed Toronto goodbye and returned to London whence he came. He's not the first architect to have landed here with great expectations, only to fall on hard times, but he's surely one of the most spirited. Jones gave it his best shot, but his career in Boomtown, Ontario, lasted all of six years. During that time he completed a half-dozen projects in the Toronto area and competed, unsuccessfully, for several more. Last July, fed up with also-running, he packed it in. He's back in England now, working on the extension of the Covent Garden Opera House with old friend and colleague Jeremy Dixon.

That's not what Jones had intended. In 1983, when he and then-partner Michael Kirkland were celebrating their victorious entry in the Mississauga City Hall competition over a champagne lunch at Fenton's, there was much talk about auspicious beginnings and ships coming in. At a leave-taking lunch in the same restaurant, weeks before weighing anchor, Jones's mood was, inevitably, retrospective: what happened, or more pertinently, what didn't?

A lissome man with a Beethoven hairdo and oodles of self-esteem, Jones also has wit, dash, and a talent for outspokenness. He came to Toronto 'with a real intention to have a North American life,' he began, speaking prunes-and-prisms English. 'It wasn't the hit-and-run. I hoped Mississauga would have produced other work, but it only produced lists of things.' Jones and Kirkland were listed for most important jobs recently awarded by competition, including the Ballet Opera House and the Art Gallery of Ontario addition and renovation. Moshe Safdie won the former, while the latter went to Barton Myers (in a joint venture with Kuwabara Payne McKenna Blumberg Architects). In either case, Jones and Kirkland didn't make the final cut.

'We thought we had a chance,' said Jones, who parted company with Kirkland, a transplanted American, in 1988 to go it alone. 'But the competition system that wants you on those lists has nothing to do with competitions at all. You're not competing about ideas, but about what other people think about you and your bank balance.' It's no secret that architects sometimes lose competitions (or aren't even considered eligible) because they can't pass the Wood Gundy test, or because they don't have the right chemistry with a jury, or the right connections. Whether Jones and Kirkland suffered on that score—'maybe I didn't spend enough energy ingratiating myself,' he said later on—or because of their ideas, however, is impossible to say. Jones, for one, has no doubts whatsoever. In Canada, he maintains, 'a proper competition is hard to find: Mississauga was one.' In other words, Mississauga was an open, anonymous design contest with a credible jury.

Mississauga, the building, proved a mixed blessing for Jones. It was the first big project he'd ever completed, and it became, internationally, and even in advance of competition, the most publicized and published building in recent Canadian history. But nearer at hand, opinion was divided. Mississauga's new landmark was a tough building to come to grips with. To many it seemed a composition of fragments of some imaginary European city of indeterminate age and classical pretensions that had been airfreighted to the suburbs for assembly. Deeply conservative in outlook and plan, the building had a lot of *noblesse oblige* about it. At the same time, it was bold, radical in aspiration, not just another pretty face. 'Mississauga scared a lot of people off,' in Jones's opinion. 'It was the toast of London, New York, and Paris, but in Toronto the jury was still out. Few things going on here have good press outside the country.'

Few architects, it should be said, work as hard as Jones and Kirkland did at promotion, but that's not what Jones had in mind. Lack of press is directly related to lack of strong designers, he said. Or, put another way, Canada has too few strong designers, and too many architectural brokers. Jones doesn't like brokers, by which he means architects who specialize in writing reports, acting as professional advisers to competition juries, organizing exhibitions, and writing catalogues—people who decide who's in and who's out, listmakers. 'There are very few full-blooded architects in this town,' he reiterated. 'There are a lot of brokers, but no strong professionals. Ron Thom was certainly one. Barton Myers is one, and he had to go, too.' (Myers, who made his reputation in Toronto in the 1970s, moved to Los Angeles a couple of years back for much the same reason Jones left: disappointment at losing competitions.)

There are good brokers and bad brokers, according to Jones. Philip Johnson, the powerful American architect who designed the AT&T building, is a good broker—because he's not exclusively a broker, said Jones. 'Philip Johnson also puts himself on the line,' he insists. 'Here, being a broker anaesthetizes you from doing anything else. There are no lions in this town.' There are, however, young architects and designers with lion potential—'an underbelly to Toronto that's brave, risky, talented', in Jones's words. Among them he counts Brian Boigon, John Shnier, Donald McKay, Stephen Teeple, Steven Fong, and Victor Jaunkalns. It seems Jones, too, has his lists.

In fact, had things turned out differently, Jones, always the roarer, would have become a broker himself. In 1987 he put his name forward for dean of the University of Toronto architecture school, but was passed over in favour of Anthony Eardley, a very dull choice for a school that lacks fire. 'I made it clear to the interviewing board that the school should have some control over the university plan—that it should become the voice of architecture in Toronto,' said Jones. 'It was an opportunity to influence results. I put my name on the line.' He claims to have had the support of students and younger staff, but none of senior staff, whom he categorizes, impatiently, as 'failed chairmen and deans'. Acknowledged both here and abroad as an excellent teacher and critic, he was offered positions at Princeton, Rice, and Cornell universities, but turned them down in favour of practising in London.

So what does any of this say about Toronto? 'It does seem to keep shooting itself in the foot,' replied Jones without hesitation, and he wasn't just alluding to being run out of town. 'In Canada, you get these symposia which are apparently publicly accessible, and it all goes dozy—amazing! We've been through the show of criticizing the ballet-opera competition, and they're getting on with that crummy corner building on Bay and Wellesley by Moshe Safdie. He can get the financing. Safdie's been hired as a broker. Toronto is a mercantile town. So to be an architect here, you have to be an urban guerrilla, pulling off things nobody can quite get at before they're done—because if they're done through a process that's legal, Bay Street can't argue.'

That situation isn't exclusive to Toronto, Jones noted, but at least in the US they also support the untried in a way Canada cannot because 'it's too cautious'. Mind you, Jones was untried when he and Kirkland were handed the opportunity to build Mississauga. The problem was that he wasn't tried more often, even if, as he insists, 'at the end of the day you want to do only a few buildings the best you can.' Ironically, that's exactly what happened. Jones built his few buildings in Toronto the best he could, and he got better as he went along. For structural engineer Morden Yolles, he designed a smart brick headquarters building with Art Deco ornament on Queen Street East. He built a wonderful glass-skinned addition to a 1950s plant in Scarborough for Charles Armstrong. Most recently, for art dealer Sandra Ainsley, he produced an elegant glass gallery in First Canadian Place—his swan song.

'There is a definite Toronto style, isn't there?' Jones said out of the blue. 'I see it in painting, in literature, and a bit in architecture. In a funny way, it's very public, very optimistic—extremely optimistic, I think—and it's urbane. There are damn good streets, restaurants, and a vibrant, causative youth. There's that ground from which something very good will come, but not in my lifetime.' And, hardly pausing: 'The outsider in Toronto has a bad time. In other cities that's not true. I felt a distinct fustiness from the profession when I came. It's as though I were a carpetbagger coming in and winning a competition—"I hope it fails! Oh dear!" There is a certain lack of tolerance shown to foreigners.'

He's a foreigner no longer, but he'll be remembered as the designer of a large foreign object known as Mississauga City Hall, of which he finally had this to say: 'It was a big building done at the beginning of maturity. It's an immensely fallible building. For that I have a tremendous love of it. It's tremendously gawky. Probably, in that moment of history, it was hard to build a consistent building.' It's an oddity of history, too, that Jones got his first crack at a monumental public building in Canada, and that as he got going on smaller projects, refining and loosening up, he couldn't muster enough support to keep him here. 'I would stay in Canada for the rest of my life if someone had given me work,' he said. 'I'm very grateful to Charles Armstrong, Mordy Yolles, and the Ainsleys for giving me public things after the rest of Toronto was sucking its teeth after the Mississauga thing. There are opportunities in England. I'm English, I'm not Canadian, and I'm going home.'   — *September 1989*

Russell Spanner

Russell Spanner throws a wrench into the idea that Canadians never designed stylish furniture. The first inklings of revisionism appeared a few years ago at The Art Gallery at Harbourfront, when Virginia Wright, an expert on the subject, curated 'Seduced and Abandoned', a ground-breaking survey of Canadian modern furniture manufactured between 1930 and 1980. Among the visitors to the show was Toronto artist Robert Fones. By his own account, he fell in love with two blond armchairs on display that were identified as the work of Russell Spanner.

What appealed to Fones about the chairs was their forward look and cartoon-like resemblance to the human body: in addition to arms and legs, they appeared to have neck and head. ('They've got everything,' he jokes.) At the same time, they were as simple and solidly built as the school-desks he remembered from his childhood. It wasn't long before Fones decided to hit the trail and find out everything he could about Russell Spanner and his designs.

The problem was there was no trail—no public collection of Canadian furniture for reference, no book on the history of Canadian industrial design. Fones turned to the telephone book instead. He started calling Spanners. Three years and a lot of legwork later, he had an exhibition for The Power Plant—an exhibition that amounts to an occasion. Call it a reunion with a little-known, long-lost relative—not the man, who died in 1974, but his aura and his accomplishments.

Spanner came to furniture via the battery box and wrestling mat. Wooden battery boxes were a specialty at Spanner Products, the family business that started in Toronto, in the early 1920s, in a downtown factory that is now the back end of The World's Biggest Bookstore. Spanner joined the works as foreman of the nightshift in 1941, by which time the company had diversified into pingpong tables and dinette suites. He was 25, and till then his success had been as a prize-winning amateur wrestler. His father wasn't impressed, nor did he take kindly, at the end of the war, to Russell's ideas for new furniture lines. Spanner was unschooled in industrial design, but he knew how to run a factory, he knew about joining pieces of wood, and he had stamina and an agile, competitive spirit that served him well in the marketplace.

It wasn't until his father was gone from the factory that Spanner bloomed. 'He'd been waiting for his chance, he got it—there was an explosion of design ideas,' said Fones. In 1950 came Ruspan Originals—tables, chairs, desks, buffets, and bookcases designed on a modular system to be mixed, matched, and variously combined. The wood is birch, the mood is modern, the look is unmistakably 1950s. (The name, incidentally, may have come from The Originals Club, a bar across the lane from the factory that Russell frequented.)

Of the thirty pieces in the exhibition, the majority are Ruspan Originals. (That may indicate availability rather than curatorial preference: Ruspan sold through Eaton's and Simpsons, and sold well.) The chair that inspired Fones's search makes several appearances, in different finishes, with and without arms. The spunky armchair says it all. Spanner curved the back, splayed and tapered the feet, and turned back the arms like fins. Interwoven canvas webbing makes the seat, which is boxy in shape, and reinforced at the corners with dowels.

Fones sees the influence of the battery box—and of furniture by Swedish designer Jens Risom and an American, Paul McCobb. But Spanner had a way of working all his own. Sketches and models were not his thing. He'd

Three-drawer desk

Ruspan Originals side-chair

Catalina side-chair

build a prototype, and then throw it around the workshop to see if it would break. You might say he wrestled his furniture into shape. He was also fond of standing on top of a little coffee table and jumping up and down to demonstrate that it would take a 250-pound weight.

Ruspan could withstand abuse, but how was it meant to be used? Fones consulted a photograph of a Spanner Products display for a trade show held at the Canadian National Exhibition in 1950. He created the room, which Spanner called Business Man's Apartment, down to the fabric panels on the wall (they were specially printed for this exhibition) and the magazines on the bookshelf. The only things missing are a cocktail shaker and a couple of martini glasses, but they were absent from the CNE display, too. Spirit is there, nonetheless. Spanner's aim was to create popular, serviceable, sturdy, affordable, youthful-looking furniture. Mission accomplished, and in a hurry.

Ruspan was followed, in 1952, by Catalina, a California-inspired line best represented by a side-chair with two necks, or splats, and a gracefully arched backrest shaped like a butterfly. The chair in the exhibition has a black lacquer finish and white vinyl seat—sharp! With Pasadena, a collection introduced in 1953, Spanner went tropical, if rather beefy. A table made of black lacquered wood with a cork top edged in blond wood is exceptional. That furniture designers don't bother with cork any longer is cause for regret.

Regrettable, too, is the fact that Spanner Products went into decline by the mid-1950s, and into receivership in 1959. Spanner joined another woodworking company, where he once again involved himself in production and factory management. His career as a designer was a closed chapter. Fones has reopened it, and with a precision and determination that Spanner might have admired. 'I don't want to say it's great furniture. I hope the exhibition will instill a sense of our design history and our local history—that people will say: "Hey, I got that chair!" or "It's part of my immediate experience." There's a tendency in Canada, I don't know why, for something like this to happen and sink back into the ooze.' —*January 1990*

Scott Burton

To say that Scott Burton was a man of heart and nimble intellect might not seem much of an obituary. Yet it's those qualities that made something special of even casual acquaintance. Alabama-born but based in New York, Burton was a sculptor who helped to re-invent public art, allowing that 'the whole field is completely muddy and contradictory and full of problematic difficulties'. He was a frequent visitor to Toronto from early in 1988, when he was chosen to design the plaza for BCE Place, an enormous downtown development. He died of AIDS-related causes two days before the New Year. He was 50.

The Toronto project will be realized by August, when phase one of BCE Place is scheduled for completion. It wasn't Burton's first plaza. He collaborated on the design of the waterfront plaza at Battery Park City in lower Manhattan with friend and colleague Siah Armajani—'we became activists in the trenches,' he said of that experience. In Toronto, however, he was on his own. The given was a 150-metre-long strip of great outdoors that runs north from Front Street into a cul de sac surrounded by buildings. Burton designed it as three parts: granite seating massed on the Front Street end, a landscaped area of water, rocks, and trees in the middle, and, up from that, a low set of stairs for use and performance. 'And I added a new element,' he said mischievously, 'a riddle for Canadians. I don't know if I should say more about it to the press.'

Chairs, even more than riddles, are a Burton trademark. 'My breakthrough is functional art,' he said. 'You start with use: where people like to sit, where the sun is. That's supposed to be what architects do, but they don't. Architects are busy being artists.'

Burton's first business as an artist was painting. (He studied with Leon Berkowitz and Hans Hofmann.) In his early twenties, he was a student of English literature. In his late twenties, he turned to conceptual art, presenting performance works that included furniture as means for exploring social behaviour. By 40, he was a known gallery artist who made chair sculptures that crossed—and questioned—minimalism and furniture production. 'I could go along as an art world artist quite happily,' he said. 'But there's a drive to be part of a world larger than the art world, as awful as that world is.'

The rise of public art in the 1980s presented an opportunity to satisfy that drive, whether through collaboration with the architects of commercial developments or through programs initiated by city authorities. Burton worked with Cesar Pelli at Battery Park City, with I.M. Pei at the arts and media technology building at the Massachusetts Institute of Technology, and with James Stirling at the Tate Gallery, Liverpool. Benches figured in each project. Indeed, there's nothing more essential to social life than a place to sit, unless it's a place to eat, and tables were another of Burton's passions.

One of his last exhibitions was 'Burton on Brancusi' (at the Museum of Modern Art), which he curated and installed, his personal contribution extending to the design of brochure holders, seating, and some new display bases. What fascinated Burton about Brancusi's sculptures was their bases. He considered them a specialized form of table: 'I think . . . that some of Brancusi's pedestal-tables are of the same conceptual order as any of his busts or torsos,' he wrote in the catalogue. 'His best pieces of furniture are not only functional objects but also representations of functional objects. We have here sculptures of tables, close in character to Brancusi's other sculptures. They are both object and subject.' He could as well be describing his own furniture, which is likewise 'a usable meditation on utilitarian form', to use another of his phrases.

Burton's usable meditations for BCE Place will be made of granite: 'solid, butt-jointed granite, not slab and veneer with cork joints, like architects do,' he said last spring. And not just any old granite, either. 'He was taking the whole idea of stone seats to its most radical,' says Peter Day, the consultant who ran the public art competition for the BCE Development Corp. 'Here, he's picked stones for seatability. They're very large. There's a one-seater, a loveseat, some where two people can sit on the same rock without intimacy, and others where people can lounge.' Burton deliberately chose heavily striated, water-washed granite from the Canadian Shield, to remind people of it, says Day, who accompanied Burton on 'expedition after expedition' to stone merchants in northern Ontario.

'I feel artists have to justify architectural art, not just to intellectuals but to the public,' Burton said. 'I feel people like me can help the art world. I'm not a Marxist, I'm not an intellectual, but I feel we are all part of our times. How do you take the optimism and failures of the sixties into the real world? There's got to be a resurgence of some belief that we can make changes.'

Burton wasn't hopeful of changing society; he described his work as 'a very modest kind of thing—maybe the more modest, the better.' Asked to enlarge on his hopes for the plaza, however, he quickly replied: 'That the trees should live! That it's successful as social space and artistic space. That in warm enough weather, people will have a pleasant lunch hour.'

— *February 1990*

Ada Louise Huxtable

'Watch an architectural landmark demolished piece by piece. Be present while a splendid building is reduced to rubble. See the wrecking bars gouge out the fine château-style stonework. Hear the gas-powered saws bite into the great beams and rafters. Thrill to destruction. Take home samples.'

— *Ada Louise Huxtable, in 1965*

'America the beautiful,/ Let me sing of thee,/ Burger King and Dairy Queen/ From sea to shining sea.' — *Ada Louise Huxtable, noting that a Dairy Queen drive-in would be built on the site of a historic building in Hudson, New York*

There's no one writing popular architecture criticism today who does not owe a debt to Ada Louise Huxtable. She was the first full-time writer on architecture for a daily American newspaper, *The New York Times*, where she spent nearly twenty years in passionate communication of her views. She invented a profession and cleared a space for those who would follow: a big space. She wrote about new buildings and old, styles and counter-styles, deals and double-dealing, cities and threats to cities, values and corruption: the way of the world. The voice could be calm, lyrical, cheeky, weary, or brittle with rage, depending on whether she had come to praise or bury; to report, admonish, or patiently explain.

She retired from the *Times* in 1982, having sat on the editorial board for eight years in addition to writing her column. Inching towards 70, spirited and *soignée*, with a significant body of work already behind her, she could be resting on reputation and laurels. Thirty professional awards and almost as many honorary degrees have been bestowed. Of these, the award she treasures most is the National Arts Club Medal for Literature, which she received in 1971. 'Saul Bellow was at my table—and *he* acted as though I was a writer!' she says, reaching for a gold disc big enough to serve sandwiches on. 'I am mad for writing!'

It shows, and so does Huxtable's quick-witted charm. She lives in a comfortable penthouse apartment on Park Avenue, alone since the death of her husband last June. Garth Huxtable was an industrial designer born in Nova Scotia, who was once industrial designer Norman Bel Geddes's right-hand man. Some of his work—a low marble-topped coffee-table, cube-shaped end tables, candelabra—furnish the space, along with a Bruno Mathsson dining table ('we had it a million years'), an eighteenth-century Venetian mirror, and Tiffany vases known as Favrile. 'One is always interested in preservation if one grows up in appreciation of fine old things,' says Huxtable. 'What I've always liked, of course, is the combination'—fine old things and fine new ones, buildings included.

Becoming an architecture critic was never on her wish list: 'It happened in a funny way, as these things always do. I had a mixed and crazy career from the beginning.' After graduating magna cum laude from Hunter College, she studied art and architectural history at New York's Institute of Fine Arts. Philip Johnson, who had just taken over the department of architecture and design at the Museum of Modern Art, came looking for an assistant curator. From 1946 to 1950, Huxtable filled the post. 'I was fresh out of school, and there I was exposed to an incredible mind, incredible tastes,' she remembers. But that didn't stop her from slamming Johnson's AT&T building twenty years later: 'I'm sure he was deeply hurt by it, but what can you do?'

In 1950, she was off to investigate contemporary Italian architecture ('a revelation'). On her return to New York, married, she started writing free-lance magazine articles about architecture and urban planning. She collaborated with her husband on the design of flatware for the Four Seasons Restaurant in the Seagram Building, 'but he was the designer, I was the critic.'

A Guggenheim Fellowship brought research into stylistic and technological advances in American architecture. Huxtable thought she'd be spending her life writing for scholarly journals.

She thought wrong. She wrote 'a letter as long as an article' to *The New York Times* on the subject of housing in Caracas, responding to an exhibition review, 'and they printed it!' Articles she wrote for the Sunday magazine section excited support from staff writers. Yet in 1963, when she was offered the new position of architecture critic, she said no. Content and in her forties, she was afraid it would change her life: 'I wasn't trained to think of my right to my own life and professional interests. I married young, I had a marvellous relationship, and I didn't want anything that was going to create demands that would lead to conflict and guilt I couldn't handle. Today you have to create some kind of eccentric persona and circulate it: I was known for my work.'

Moments after refusing, she accepted. She wasn't intending to set up a cause: 'I have an enormous belief that architecture is the mother of the arts, the inescapable art. That was my mission: to help people understand what it did in their cities and lives, what it was in art, the ways in which they were being cheated, which led to politics and sociology. Architecture is an enormous, exciting subject. I wanted people to know they have rights: we also have entitlements in this field. We can only get them if we understand it.'

Her life changed, 'completely, completely', but not her convictions: 'I had a profound and deep experience in architectural history. I've always been interested in innovation, standards or quality, in the excitement of people who devise new and remarkable ways of doing things in application to ourselves, our cities, our lives. On the level of art, architecture increases our dignity as human beings. I've always been this way. I'm not interested in superstars and public relations. I always throw press releases in the wastebasket. I'm not interested in celebrity.'

She is celebrated, however, for her fearlessness and nerve. She was writing for a powerful newspaper, in New York, city of Trumps and towers, kicking buildings right and left: weren't there complaints? Phone calls in the night? There was plenty of flak. The *Times* would hear it, she would hear it. 'There's a very simple bottom line. You're incorruptible, you don't care, and your paper backs you. I don't think there's a real estate man who thinks I don't have a price but just hasn't been able to find it. I am extremely vulnerable. It's very, very painful. That's why I've been reclusive in public. If you start thinking about who is going to think what about you, if it will be advantageous or disadvantageous if this person is your enemy, get out of the business!'

For years she went about hers 'in a deliberately blinkered way', doing what she believed in. When she got the Pulitzer Prize for distinguished criticism in 1970, the first time it was ever awarded, she 'could no longer escape that what I was doing had influence': she was sick for six months. 'I'm not hard-shelled, I don't want power, I'm the greatest no-sayer in the world,' she says.

'All that matters is the objectivity, thoroughness, and integrity of what I write.' Her way of looking at buildings 'is the only way to do it', she insists: 'It's not how it tickles my eye, or work that gives me a *frisson*. Architecture is a structural and programmatic art. I want to thoroughly understand the structure, the client's program, the architect's rationale. To that I bring what is essential to teach young architects: art and architectural history, so if you're talking about mannerism you really know what it is. There is no flawless building. That's why it's terribly important to understand more about a building than people think you ought to.'

For that reason, her writing became more oriented towards issues than individual buildings—among them, the so-called 'crisis' of modern architecture and rise of postmodernism. Huxtable has no patience with modernism-bashing, even when it comes from Prince Charles. She thinks it's time he stopped beating a dead horse and pressed on with the problems of inner cities: 'If you understand modernism as the aesthetic of the twentieth century, and we're not being judgemental now, in historical and cultural context it's one of the most fantastic periods in all of history. True, it ran down and was trivialized—it's all part of the history. But to pretend it never happened, how could you be so arrogant?'

Postmodernism happened too, and for good reason. Modernism became stagnant and it was 'perfectly natural' for something to take its place: 'When the ideology broke down, it opened a dangerous and desirable floodgate. The bad thing was postmodernism became a peculiar frosting that was supposed to make buildings look different. Accurately, there should be an evolution of modernism to something else.'

She has found that something else in the work of Frank Gehry and James Stirling above all: 'You're getting an enormous enrichment of Le Corbusier. It's hard to give it a name, it's so natural. It's another kind of architecture. It's modernism developing into whatever the next stage of the art of building will be. It's almost independent of polemic. It had to happen. Frank Gehry, James Stirling—they seem to need the polemics but they would have happened anyway. They're probably the two most important architects. They visualize the whole thing, three-dimensionally, in all this complexity.'

That's what Huxtable was doing, too, with abundant success. She left the *Times* not because she couldn't take the heat, but because she felt burned out: 'Working confrontationally, as you do in editorials, is very exhausting. Think what it was like on the editorial board. I thought it was a move into the policy-making area—a plum—but it's a confrontational position eight times out of ten.' She left having received a real plum, a McArthur Prize Fellowship, which she used to write *The Tall Building Artistically Reconsidered*, a history of skyscrapers. Currently she is updating a book called *Classic New York*, sitting on juries, writing, looking—steadfastly.

— *March 1990*

Ernest Cormier

The one thing generally known about Ernest Cormier is that he designed the austere and glamorous house on avenue des Pins that is currently owned and occupied by Pierre Trudeau. However, Cormier's claim to fame reaches farther and higher than that—in geographical measure, almost to the top of Mount Royal. For it was on the northwest slope of the mountain, between 1928 and 1943, that Cormier's monumental masterwork, the main pavilion of the Université de Montréal, was gradually realized. Its domed library tower, symbol of the secular aspirations of the Catholic educational establishment in the 1920s and 1930s, is a landmark that is visible for miles. Yet Cormier, the man and the architect, has gone largely unnoticed.

He finally comes into view in a remarkable exhibition organized by the Canadian Centre for Architecture. 'Ernest Cormier and the Université de Montréal' renders tribute to the premier public architect of his time and place, and with an elegance of presentation that rivals Cormier's own. The CCA is richly equipped to mount this show. In the six years following Cormier's death in 1980, at 94, the museum and study centre acquired from his widow an extraordinary number and variety of artifacts and papers—'leavings of an architect', as CCA director Phyllis Lambert calls them.

The CCA's Cormier Archive spans 100 architectural projects ranging from intimate to colossal. It contains nearly 30,000 drawings; 14,000 photographs; close to 100 metres of textual documents; 3,500 books on subjects including architecture, engineering, print-making, photography, ceramics, sculpture, music, medicine, gynaecology, and gardening. There are, as well, drawing tables, easels, cameras, maquettes, tools for bookbinding and bookstamping, plaster casts of bas-reliefs, snapshots, medals, press clippings, samples of materials, appointment books, postcards, even Cormier's passport and painted glass shingle. (Presumably, Mme Cormier held on to the cigarette case and ashtrays.)

Needless to say, Cormier was exceptional in the breadth of his knowledge, interests, and accomplishments: he was a man of expansive consciousness and great discipline. Born in Montreal in 1885, he studied civil engineering at the Ecole Polytechnique, after which he worked as design engineer for the Dominion Bridge Company. He spent the years 1908 to 1918 in Europe, mostly at the Ecole des Beaux-Arts in Paris but also in Rome, on a scholarship awarded by the Royal Institute of British Architects. He ended his sojourn abroad working in Paris as an engineer designing reinforced concrete structures.

Internationalist by choice, cosmopolitan by nature, Cormier returned to Montreal with a formidable arsenal of skills. He drew with exquisite precision, painted in watercolours, sculpted. He designed furniture. He had absorbed both the technical innovations of the European avant-garde and the ornate spatial traditions of the Beaux Arts. These two streams of thought and

Rear view of the main pavilion, showing (from left to right), the chapel and west wing, the auditorium (with tower above), and the east wing, Université de Montréal

practice, the one tending to abstraction, the other to ritual and ceremony, each allowing for boldness of expression and emotional intensity, fed into Cormier's conception of the main pavilion of the Université de Montréal. But there's nothing to account for the originality of Cormier's vision. Who, even knowing of classicism and Le Corbusier, could have predicted the stepped pyramid that tops the amphitheatre wing? (Eat your heart out, Michael Graves.) Who would have envisioned such a scale of operation?

The Cormier exhibition offers surprises of its own. Curated by Phyllis Lambert and Isabelle Gournay, herself a graduate of the Ecole des Beaux-Arts in Paris, the show (and accompanying book, which Gournay edited) explains, with lucidity and imagination, the complicated history of the design and construction of Cormier's buff-brick behemoth. You see Cormier's design unfurling from tiny but authoritative sketches on tracing paper into huge, intricately detailed drawings. You learn about his clients, who were determined to do for the image of French Canadians what McGill University had done for Montreal's anglophone community. You follow the evolution of Cormier's career from its beginnings through to his later major commissions, the Supreme Court of Canada, the National Printing Bureau in Hull, the sculpted doors of the United Nations General Assembly building in New York.

You get a feeling for the moment, and for the man—from the drawings and photographs of the house he designed for himself on avenue des Pins, from snapshots of dinners and picnics with his friends, and from the large plaster casting of a frieze showing a young male being initiated into the mysteries of Eleusis that greets you, front and centre, as you enter the series of galleries at the CCA. (Cormier had two of these castings, one in his studio, the other at home.)

It's one thing to hang a lot of drawings on the wall, and quite another to design an exhibition that conveys the feeling of a grand building and a sense of *un grand personnage*. The designers are Luc Laporte, a Montreal architect best known for his cafés (Lux, L'Express, Le Sam), and his assistant, Luce Lafontaine. They've interpreted the idea of passage, which was key to Cormier, to mean the subtle orchestration of colour, for one, and the deft focusing on each separate room by a specially designed piece that either takes its cue from objects designed by Cormier, or incorporates them. Thus there is some painted metal grillwork that refers to Cormier's work in metal; a delicately fashioned metal stand that holds Cormier's medals; an enormous free-standing frame that contains the full-size maquette of the United Nations doors. The thinking seems to be that one good sequence deserves another, and that Cormier's passion for objects bears accent. That's a terrific way to layer.

The first room, intended to create the atmosphere of a man working, has been painted a shade of green peculiar to the Université de Montréal—a green so clear and subtle as to suggest a calyx in spring. Hanging symmetrically to either side of the doorway, three shelves of books. Over here, a work table of Cormier's design; over there, a piece of sculpture. Inside a glass case, examples of Cormier's bookbinding, photographs, and memorabilia. It would hardly be surprising if Cormier were to walk in for a look, fedora cocked, rakish bow-tie at his neck, pince-nez in place, cigarette dangling from the left side of his mouth.

Leave that room for another, and the walls are a paler shade of green; in the next one, green has modulated into yellow. Balancing that progression, in the CCA's Octagonal Gallery across the way, a sequence of yet another kind: 22 resplendent colour photographs of Cormier's university building by Gabor Szilsi: panoramic views, details; inside, outside; sensuous, rigorous; continuous, fractured: wonderful. Even more delicious is the way the separate parts of the exhibition interact dialectically, objects with drawings, one project with another, reason and passion. Cormier's work, as the curators specifically note, *was* dialectical, his poles of vision being modernist and traditional, European and North American, French Catholic and English Protestant.

That this mode of thought comes through so strongly in the show can only be attributed to Lambert's way of thinking, which informs the CCA. In view of the tensions that exist between anglophones and francophones in the Canada of this moment, this celebration of a French-Canadian architect by an institution dedicated to the art and culture of architecture, founded by a woman of awareness, is nothing short of healing. The Cormier show will go down as one of the CCA's finest moments.   — *May 1990*

SITES AND ISSUES

Goodwin/Lemyre Apartment, Montreal

'All great, simple images reveal a psychic state. The house, even more than the landscape, is a psychic state, and even when reproduced as it appears from the outside, it bespeaks intimacy.'
— *Gaston Bachelard,* The Poetics of Space.

For two years Montreal artists Betty Goodwin and Marcel Lemyre have been respectfully altering the space in a rented 90-year-old apartment at 4005 Mentana Street, in the old francophone section of Montreal. The rooms are temporarily open to the public, after which the apartment will be put up for rent again. Spaces should be experienced, not talked about—but basically the two artists have claimed the rooms as their own by exposing and expanding what was there, and embedding their own personal histories into the apartment's history.

The given: you push through the door on Mentana Street and enter a long hallway covered with its original yellow wallpaper. To the right is (or was) a double room divided by an arch; to the left is (or was) another double room divided by an arch. Behind them a back room with a window and an open area that was once a dining-room. Matter has soul: the spaces resonate with the spirit of their former inhabitants—as all rooms do. Time has become as palpable as space.

The transformations: Goodwin began in the back room, working intuitively. She peeled off the wallpaper with gesso and then created her own wallpaper by pencilling over all the walls using a repeated gesture. The pencilled design resembles a fresco; the delicate markings have transformed space into time by recording the pulse of the room and of the light streaming in through the window. Against one wall stands a painted white totem, sealed and inviolate as a tomb. It focuses a certain kind of spiritual energy in the room and introduces another reality: eternal time as opposed to diurnal.

This transformation completed, Goodwin felt the need to project outward. She sliced off a third of the closet door: an act of violation and decision. Beginning at this junction of desire and intent she then built a long skinny corridor that pushes right through the middle of one of the front rooms. Walking down the corridor you feel both protected by it and received into another space. It's a combination birth canal and coffin. You feel grateful for the light at the end of the tunnel.

You emerge from the darkened corridor. Turning around, you see, on either side of the corridor, the walls of the room as Goodwin found them— covered in their original ornate red and gold wallpaper and divided in half by the tunnel. One room has become three. Goodwin has painted the outside walls of the corridor with gold leaf, which has its own kind of light built into it. The gold leaf plays a visual duet with the gold on the adjacent wall paper. One kind of light interacts with another, enacting the relationship between individual thoughts or feelings. She has even painted over a bit of the paper—gold leaf on gold—to show the interaction between handiwork and machine-produced paper and to show that she was there.

There was only one room remaining after Goodwin built her tunnel— the front half of the original double room. Inside that space she built yet another room—a little sanctum open at the top made of thick heavy beams stacked horizontally and covered with lime. Bright and monastic, it corresponds to one of those recesses of the mind marked 'private'. Inside the little chamber your senses concentrate and intensify: you are alone with yourself. When you view it from the outside, the room no longer encloses: it functions as a physical barrier. You are confronted by sheer mass—stubborn white walls revealing all the labour that went into their construction the same way that peeling off the layers of wallpaper—or history—in the back room revealed the way the apartment was constructed. In fact, wherever you are the elements of the given refuse to go away: you look up and see carved

Goodwin/Lemyre apartment, corridor

Goodwin/Lemyre apartment

lintels and bits of moulded ceiling; you look through the window and see Mentana Street. The new spaces reveal the old.

Goodwin has taken the existing elements of her rooms and pushed them to their limits. Her theme is continuity: deciding what to leave was as important as deciding what to change. Her work is not concerned with rupture, but rather with evolution. One space leads to another just as one mood or state of consciousness leads to the next. The passage from the back of the house to the front resembles the passage through life's mysterious corridors, each lit by a different light, all connected in surprising ways and all reflecting unconscious drives and conscious design.

Lemyre has chosen to work with reflections and illusions—the surface of the mind. In his double room, opposite the hallway from Goodwin's, he built a second window over the wallpaper at a right angle to the street window. The fake window reflects the street window, which in turn reflects everything on the street in an infinite series—a variation on Goodwin's room-within-a-room idea. Then he painted the closet door in the adjoining room the same floral design as the original wallpaper. The new *trompe l'oeil* window and the old door masquerading as wallpaper set up a system of opposites: real and fake; added and subtracted; illusion and reality. Finally, in the former dining room Lemyre has drawn over a section of the original wallpaper with its repeating tree pattern, creating a soft Oriental revery full of willows and watery reflections.

Lemyre's rooms interact with Goodwin's: and both interact with the reality of a 90-year-old house on Mentana Street. Architecture is a potent form of poetry. I left 4005 Mentana with a new set of blueprints stored in my mind. Our memories are lodged in the rooms we have inhabited; our personalities are linked to certain spaces. Outer architecture corresponds to inner architecture, or in Bachelard's words: 'A house that has been experienced is not an inert box.' Inhabited space transcends geometrical space. Goodwin and Lemyre rented an apartment full of ghosts and created a new set of spaces for them to wander in.   —*January 1980*

Cormier House, Montreal

Given the placid architecture of the surrounding neighbourhood, and the dumpy brick apartment house next door, the Art Deco palace on the slopes of Mount Royal looks more like a film set than a building. (Enter Greta Garbo, stage left. Miss Garbo materializes in the Italian marble vestibule and winds her way down the nickel-and-steel staircase to the library. Meanwhile, a bevy of butlers with marcelled hair drift from the catering kitchen, bearing trays of cocktails. In the background float strains of Bach.)

Like most fantasies, this scenario happens to be based on the truth. Every Saturday night in decades gone by, Ernest Cormier—the architect who built the stucco-and-concrete residence on Pine Avenue—would preside over his salon. The music would play, the waiters weave, the guests make cultured conversation. When Cormier died last January at the age of 94, an era of grace and refined eccentricity—a time when gentlemen grew mushrooms in the basement and constructed follies in the garden—went with him.

In recent months the Cormier house, dignified on the outside, delirious on the inside, has become a conversation piece once again. Cormier's obituary in *The Globe and Mail* ended with the report that Prime Minister Pierre Elliott Trudeau was negotiating to buy the house (estimated value: $300,000) from its present owner, Jacques Beyderwellen. With that announcement, the thick patina of glamour covering the Cormier house shone even brighter. Recently, *Vogue* magazine had its cameras and models at the mansion. The Society for the Study of Architecture in Canada, not to be outdone, scheduled a tour of Cormierland and an illustrated talk about the house, both conducted by MFA student Sarah McCutcheon, during its recent annual conference.

As both McCutcheon and Beyderwellen point out, it's useless to discuss Cormier's work without referring to his life and lifestyle. The house on Pine Avenue is like a swirling stone shell built up granule by granule, by Cormier's many talents and preoccupations. He graduated with an engineering degree from the Ecole Polytechnique in 1906 and, encouraged by relatives and friends, headed for Paris, where he studied at the Ecole des Beaux-Arts. In Paris he met the architects and designers who would evolve the Art Deco style: Ruhlmann, Edgar Brandt, Sue et Mare, and others. In 1912 he worked on the decoration of a transatlantic liner with Pierre Patout, designer of the *France*. Four years later he studied military construction, which introduced him to the potential of reinforced concrete, particularly in the area of acoustics. When Cormier returned to Montreal in 1918, it was with exceptional qualifications for his profession.

For Cormier, living was an art. He had, argues McCutcheon, 'a passion for everything'. He was a bibliophile, an expert bookbinder, a sculptor, photographer, watercolourist, ceramicist, flautist, furniture designer, and *bon vivant*. When it came to designing buildings, every facet of his personality came into play. Always there is a sense of solid monumentality, the legacy of his Beaux-Arts training, but always it is fused with an abiding joy in sensuality. The sheen of marble, the polish of rare woods, the dense mystery of velour—these join with Cormier's pursuit of permanence to make up his rather daunting personal style.

Cormier designed and built a number of buildings, including the Palais de Justice (now the Ministry of Cultural Affairs) in Old Montreal, with its splendid brass and glass lamps; the Supreme Court of Canada in Ottawa; St Michael's College in Toronto; the Queen's Printer building in Hull; the Grand Séminaire in Quebec. He is perhaps best known for the main building

Cormier house

and chapel of the University of Montreal. The central tower, empty since its construction, is visible from everywhere in the city.

It was while construction was beginning on the University of Montreal, in the late 1920s, that Cormier began working on his house. Often he would order one extra of something that was to go into the university for the residence, which accounts for the similarity of materials in both projects. But while the university buildings were moulded to other people's specifications, Cormier's four-tiered house was his castle. He was the architect, the contractor, the designer, and the client. He personally took care of every detail: the light and light fixtures, the patterned stone and terracotta salon floor, the garden, the furniture, the acoustics. In everything he insisted on the best materials—solid walnut, teak, burled walnut, marble—and honesty of function; the radiators, in high-tech fashion, are always exposed.

The Cormier house was finished in 1931 and sold to Beyderwellen 44 years later. Every room is special, but two are extremely special. There's the 25-foot-high salon on the ground floor, papered in peach-coloured, wood-veneered Japanese wallpaper stained with beeswax and mahogany dye. You don't walk into the salon—you're wafted into it on waves of light that flow through the tall, narrow, metal-framed windows and skylight. Anchoring the vast amount of empty space is a black marble table with squat legs, an imposing marble fireplace—and virtually nothing else. From the adjoining balcony you look down on the stone pigeon house, whose spiral staircase connects the garden with Redpath Street, 50 feet below.

The stairway leading down from the main floor marks the transition between public and private. At the bottom lies the direct antithesis to the salon: the study. No windows here, just a lot of wood-veneer panelling and gloom. The entrance is presided over by four columns painted in gold leaf; the main article of furniture is Cormier's marble-topped desk. Over the fireplace is a frieze showing a young male being initiated into the mysteries of Eleusis by Demeter and her daughter—a reference, Beyderwellen suggests, to Cormier's relationship with his grandmother.

All in all, it's a sumptuous house, a regal house—but not a house for the meek or cowardly. There is a quality of Egyptian tomb about it. In 1975, the house, its furnishings and garden were all listed as historical monuments by the Quebec Cultural Properties Commission, which guarantees its immortality even further. Trudeau has met his match.   —*June 1980*

Calgary, with Alan Singer

The sun is setting over Calgary and a futuristic film set materializes at Alan Singer's bare feet. The wood and glass house he built alongside his teepee on top of a scrubby hill, empty except for his toys, records, and a dining table fit for a hidalgo, turns into an observation deck. The eye sweeps over an electrically-wired valley shaped like a jumbo oyster-shell, only to stop, with the shock of an immutable force meeting an unforgettable object, at a scene de Chirico might have painted. Ringed in mist and framed by the Rockies floats a mass of blinding flood-lit towers—oil into gold into the landscape of a dream.

Calgary. Population in 1975: 400,000. Population in 1982: 605,000. Population projected for 1990: one million. City or chimera? Singer, 35, a post-1960s developer whose name, haircut (James Taylor, circa 1970) and taste in sweaters (funky) found their way into Peter C. Newman's catalogue of the nouveaux riches, *The Acquisitors,* is noncommittal. He's here, he could have been elsewhere, he's having fun. He's no stranger to departure lounges, however. The family company, United Management, owns real estate in Calgary, Edmonton, and Winnipeg, and arranges development deals in Canada, California, Arizona, and Texas. 'I've travelled with Alan a lot and wherever he goes, it's like he's been there before,' marvelled a friend. 'I hate leaving Calgary,' said Singer, as if to set the record straight.

Still, after graduating in psychology from UCLA in the mid-1960s he hadn't the least intention of returning to a city all his friends were in the habit of leaving. What changed his mind? The clothing business, which he fell into 'accidentally' and exchanged ten years later for real estate. Simple as that, at least for Singer, whose chief vice is modesty, followed closely by understatement.

His friends are more than willing to compensate for his reticence. 'That acquisitor stuff is ridiculous—Alan's a bohemian,' a vivacious woman with a beaded headband whispered in my ear seconds after we'd been introduced. The number of whispers on these lines I heard within thirty-six hours would fill a canyon. Instant city, instant mythology. Charisma, in its benign form, is the power of receptivity to invite projection. Calgary, city of reflecting mirrors, feeds on it. Singer's got it in spades. He's one of a strange post-1960s hybrid—groovy consciousness, conservative politics. 'He's probably one of the best persons I've ever met. You bet. No doubt about it,' said a friend in cowboy gear, just returned from an oil-rigging gig in Billings, Montana, who arrived at my hotel with his dog at 2 A.M. to talk Calgary. 'Alberta basically boomed seven years ago—bango, Alan just happened to have the right properties when it hit. His retail business, the Strawberry Experiment, hit at the right time, too. Scott McKenzie was singing "If You're Going to San Francisco", and everybody wanted to be cute. He hired girls from Toronto as buyers and managers but the whole operation was Alan's personality. When he had to go away nobody could handle it. It was wild. He did a helluva number.'

At the Ranchman's bar, where the hit tune is 'Okie from Muskogee', a criminal lawyer in a natty three-piece suit grabbed my arm: 'Calgary is the

North America of tomorrow—and this punk knows it. That guy's a wizard but I bet he won't tell you anything about himself—right? It's guys like that who are moving everything, but he never takes a bath and he's the biggest chintz around.' This unscheduled version of the Calgary Stampede lasted till the next afternoon. 'I've got no values anymore,' confessed a fellow developer with the nonchalance of someone who's just renounced blue pyjamas. He was offering himself up as a sacrifice: 'Alan's spartan. He's a man of reason, he should be a judge.'

Singer is spartan. He drives a Volkswagen Bug with a rainbow decal on the windshield, but after lunch at 4th St Rose, notable for its skylights, plants, and stuffed mushrooms, he opted for the comfort of his father's Cadillac Eldorado. (The father is Jack Singer, flamboyant investor in Francis Coppola's *One From the Heart.*) At the restaurant, he murmured his prologue: 'Calgary's real dynamic, a real young city. People come here with the expectations of making it. People here are real friendly. You can break into any group here, whereas in Toronto you have the established families. Here the established families are of the ranching nature with some in oil. Calgary's been real positive for years now, especially with the oil thing. All the head offices are locating here. There's no city like it.'

And no city as sensitive to budgets and interest rates. Just before the oil price agreement was signed, Singer said, 'It was like the whole town was going to close up, everyone was going to leave and the buildings would be half-finished. It was really strange. The budget was kind of a follow-up whammy out here. It was the first time pessimism really crept in and people became negative and scared. The worst things about Calgary are the traffic and Ottawa.'

The best thing was watching Singer stage-manage his tour, always melting into the wings but somehow always occupying centre stage—the axis around which others naturally revolve. After driving through the exclusive district of Mount Royal, where American oil companies station their executives, we stopped at 'a little shopping thing'—Mount Royal Village, built by Webb Zerafa Menkes Housden, the Toronto architectural firm responsible for Yorkville's Hazelton Lanes and, incidentally, a firm that Singer employs. The Village has little to say about Calgary other than that it wants and gets what Toronto wanted and got.

The Michael Richard Gallery, on the other hand, is 'a new concept for Calgary', according to Singer, who wafted through the door in clogs, no socks, as though expecting a chinook to blow in at any moment. The gallery, located just around the corner from the Village, is an altar to American painter and printmaker LeRoy Neiman, who churns out lithographs of sports figures such as Wayne Gretzky (edition: 300; price $3,800). The back wall of the gallery is covered with photographs of Neiman, all hat and moustache, with assorted celebrities; on a table sits a videocassette machine rolling bits and pieces of Neiman's television appearances. Art meets *People* magazine.

Enough of retail. Time to search out the hiding places of real power. First stop is the Ranchmen's Club, an Edwardian mansion built by Ross E. Hayes, behind which the ranchmen are now sticking a condominium. Scaffolding surrounds the carved granite entrance and inside; the place is deserted except for a contractor marching through the denuded rooms with a roll of renovation plans. Just as well, since women aren't usually allowed over the holy threshold. Singer is disappointed; for some reason, he'd expected the club to be grander.

We were soon approaching Mecca. Over every intersection gawked a crane. The silver trains of the new above-ground LRT (Light Rail Transit) system flashed overhead. 'I haven't met anybody who's been on it yet,' Singer commented, but he likes it anyway because it means Calgary's 'thinking into the future'. He waved in the direction of the massive indoor shopping centres connected by overpasses cum commercial malls at the fifteenth and twentieth storeys—part of the plan to revive the downtown core.

'There are two centres in Calgary,' he continued, sucking on a Bangalore Ganesh Beedie. 'Traditionally, it was the Hudson Bay Company, but now the power centre is The Petroleum Club. Every new company in town tries to locate near it.' He parked in front of a totally undistinguished grey mole-hill faced with metal trim. We walked in, listened to the Muzak and inspected a cowboy painting. Five minutes later, we were spotted, questioned and thrown out.

Our tour of Calgary architecture ended here. Although Singer had made much of the glittering bank buildings—Petro-Canada, Nova, the Bank of Montreal, Esso Plaza—he didn't think to take me through them. It's enough that they are there, beaming out the Calgary dream, luring fortune-seekers from far and wide to scale the heights of the future tense (at their peril) so that millionaires in boots and jean jackets can go about their business incognito. No matter that this showbiz architecture originates across the border— all the better, really. 'Local architects are not of the size to handle big buildings,' Singer explained. His own method of choosing architects is simple. He sees something he likes and picks up the receiver.

Sunrise, sunset—and Singer was concerned he (or I) hadn't done a proper job. 'It's very important people get a good impression of Calgary,' he said over the phone, and arranged to meet for lunch at a deli called My Marvin's. He produced a sheaf of handwritten notes and went down the list, feature by feature. Sunny climate and optimism of the people. Proximity to the mountains. Low crime rate, although increasing. City revolves around people's houses. The mayor, Ralph Kline ('a people's guy'), always accessible. Lots of big parks in the inner city. Phase One of the Eau Claire Estates on the banks of the Bow River, the largest mixed-use development in North America (44 acres; $1.25-billion) almost finished. Ground already broken on a 640-acre site on the west side of the city for Trimedia, the only major movie studio in Canada. The 1988 Olympics to take place in Calgary. A $75-

million centre for the performing arts to rise on the five-block site of the new City Hall in the east. High suicide rate, attributable to the anxiousness of expectations.

Still Singer wasn't satisfied. For dessert, he unleashed a real live exemplar of the spirit of Calgary in the person of Billy Yarrow. In a previous life, Yarrow was in the garment business in Montreal. Six years ago, he lost his shirt, arrived in Calgary, consulted Singer, and founded Royal Bison Investment and Resources. He now describes himself as a 'born-again Calgarian'—one of a new breed of pioneers fleeing Quebec and Ontario for the 'bastion of free enterprise on all levels'. It's not unusual for members of the new breed to hold down two or three jobs at once because 'the pie is getting bigger, while in the east, the pie is always the same. The statistics are always outdated. Easterners are welcome here so it's becoming a cosmopolitan city.' (Singer, enjoying his reflection's performance, interjects: 'A lot of people don't know how good they have it here—they're too busy enjoying and living their lives.')

Yarrow, whose house has become a resettlement centre for eastern fugitives, hit the myth on the head, just as Singer knew he would. 'Everyone here has APT—auto-positive thinking. There are no racial problems. Look around the restaurant—there are no two people over 45. There's no establishment because nobody's from here. I'm against the government of Canada— I'd rather fight for Alberta. In the garment business in Montreal, people would kill for a quarter—here I'm doing big real estate deals with a handshake. It's Starting Over. "Here's an empty blackboard—write anything you want on it." '
— *February 1982*

St John's, with Christopher Pratt

Christopher Pratt, tightening his cap against the wind, is standing on Signal Hill, the scarred stone cliff overhanging the entry to St John's Harbour. Intoxicated with the salt air, he points a small gloved finger across the water at a natural cubist painting—hundreds of flat-topped buildings pitched on the winding terraces of a steep hill. As the bashful March sun reaches through the clouds, the cubes flash turquoise, green, orange, yellow. If it weren't for the absence of palm trees, you'd swear you were in the Mediterranean.

Look again. This is St John's, the easternmost edge of the continent, England's first overseas possession, the harbour with the longest history of continuous use in North America. It was here, against a backdrop of water and fog and lumpy glacial residue, that French and English soldiers fought local extensions of European wars; here on Signal Hill that Marconi received the first transatlantic telegraph (in 1901); and here that young Christopher

Pratt, not yet one of Canada's leading realist painters, used to watch American warships passing through the narrows.

'When I was a kid, I thought of the whole world as being out through the narrows,' Pratt booms, scanning the waves with practised eyes. 'Absolutely everything was out through that gap through the rocks—Toronto, New York, London.' But when he left Newfoundland for the first time in 1953, at the age of 17, he headed in the opposite direction—art school in New Brunswick.

Before that, he only ventured out of St John's on trout-fishing expeditions or monthly visits to Bay Roberts, where his mother's family has been since at least the early 1700s. The waves beckoned, but there wasn't even a main road across Newfoundland. To go to Canada, says Pratt, as though describing a space shuttle to the moon, meant a 600-mile train journey to Port aux Basques, a ferry crossing to North Sydney, and another train to the mainland. There was a regular steamer service to Halifax and Boston in one direction, and Liverpool in the other. Catch 22—the train or the narrows.

The narrows—the archetype of the birth canal through which you pass, with shocking suddenness, from the primal ocean into the child-like world of clapboard cubes. The image is so immediate that Pratt returns to it again and again, trying to convey its drama in words. 'Right here at the narrows you can see where the city ends—bang, there's the Atlantic. There isn't an immense no-man's land between them, no coastal suburbia as there is in Halifax. It's not an indefinite thing: it's a precise thing—and I like that.'

Pratt, 46, is a definite man with definite eyebrows who paints precise pictures, azure crystallizations of his memories, archetypes of feelings and associations buried in the subterranean reaches of his mind. 'My painting about St John's tends to relate to recollections of rooms, especially interiors and environments that stuck in my craw when I was a kid. I rarely know this at the time I'm working on a painting. When I'm nearly finished it, I think to myself—hey, that's such and such a place.'

The layering of memory finds its perfect analogue in the layering of St John's. Four times in the nineteenth century, its clapboard buildings were swept by fire, the major ones occurring in 1846 and 1892. Some mid-century buildings escaped the last fire, others were rebuilt on the ashes of their doomed ancestors. Yet the pattern of the city, its fabric, has remained. The roads still twist, the hill still slopes, the clapboard cubes still huddle together for protection.

And now, says Pratt, great-grandson of a Methodist clergyman, St John's is being destroyed again, 'except in this instance it's not a three-night conflagration which engulfs all. It's three houses this month, five the next winter.' Right on the water's edge, in defiance of St John's stunning human scale, are some examples of beauty become beast—unsightly ten-storey brick buildings and a parking garage.

Newfoundland—highest unemployment in Canada, highest provincial income tax, highest cost of living, highest sales tax, and lowest per capita income. 'Newfoundlanders are so terrorized by the economy, they're afraid of any regulation that might lose six jobs,' explains Pratt. 'To be the head of the planning department in the municipal government of St John's must be as frustrating as being the ecumenical chaplain in hell.'

Christopher Pratt is driving through St John's looking for traces of his childhood. It's almost twenty years since he's lived here. From 1961 to 1963, he taught in the fine arts department of Memorial University; he and his wife, painter Mary Pratt, lived in a 'typical CMHC house', near the university, that almost drove him mad.

'That was my ultimate crisis with St John's,' he says of the suburbs constructed with complete disregard for the ebb and flow of the landscape. He and Mary escaped to St Mary's Bay to live and paint. This summer, they finally built themselves a townhouse in St John's, a townhouse designed by Pratt's architect brother Philip. There, with their four children, they are slowly adjusting to the city again.

So much has changed in the meantime. The wharves that used to jut into the sea like fingers have been filled in, and a concrete road runs along the harbour. A 'colossal explosion' of civil servants has helped to triple the population to 100,000 since Pratt was a boy watching the schooners sailing through the narrows.

Yet there are still places that 'ring the bells'. We're on Waterford Bridge Road, site of Pratt's new townhouse. Coincidentally (perhaps), his family once lived on the same street. Down the way is Littledale, a convent school where Roman Catholic girls from all over Newfoundland boarded. It's a shallow stone building with a turret at one end. Scattered around the grounds are clumps of deciduous trees that have been shamefully treated by the wind.

Round and round the convent we drive, slowing down to take a close look at the weather-stained façade, the arched windows, the dormer windows. Pratt is a connoisseur of windows. It's not that he has a Protestant's macabre suspicion about what might possibly be going on in the cloisters, he jokes. 'It's just a fascination with that total preoccupation, the total commitment that's required for that kind of life.'

As he roams through his past, Pratt reveals himself. He is fascinated with monastic things. His taste in music runs to plainsong; and in art, to Piero della Francesca, Fra Angelico, Giotto. He also admits to a 'particular feeling' for yellow houses, old churches, rectories, and schools. (Pubs, of which St John's has an abundance, are not on his list of preoccupations—he's a teetotaller.)

Yellow houses. On Lemarchant Road, he parks in front of a large yellow building. He lived in the basement of that building until he was 7. He remembers looking out the window through the metal picket fence (he touches the pickets) at some lilac trees and seeing people pushing perambulators along the sidewalk. Those associations, coupled with memories of family

Easters at Bay Roberts, are jostling inside his head. He wants to do a painting called Easter Sunday.

Churches. Pratt lingers near the Anglican Cathedral ('it's got the European monastic thing about it'), built in 1846 by George Gilbert Scott in the Gothic Revival style. It was burned in 1892 and rebuilt by Scott's son, but there was not enough money to replace the steeple. 'If I were really wealthy,' says Pratt, listening to the peal of church bells, 'I'd put a spire on that church.' Hard by is St Andrew's Presbyterian Church, known as The Kirk, built in 1894, which Pratt started attending when he was in grade four to catch a glimpse of one Burdina Forbes who wore a little purple hat.

Schools. Holloway School, an imposing red brick building near the Kirk, where Pratt was a student. 'A very special place,' he calls it, and now it's boarded up and scheduled for demolition. Another painting is surfacing in Pratt's 'vegetable soup of recollections'. Before we drive by more churches, more yellow houses, and a rectory or two, Pratt makes a confession: 'The strange thing about me and St John's is I always wanted to be somewhere else. When I moved into Waterford Bridge Road [at the age of 7], I used to tell friends I lived in Topsail, in Conception Bay. Looking through the narrows, the last thing I saw was Canada.'

Yet here he stays, anchored to his memories. He's been in and out of the narrows many times, but he's never escaped St John's.   *— March 1982*

College of Physicians and Surgeons of Ontario, Toronto

The College of Physicians and Surgeons of Ontario marks a puzzling departure for Eberhard Zeidler, the architect best known in Toronto for the design of Ontario Place, much of the Eaton Centre, and, most recently, Queen's Quay Terminal, the mammoth warehouse renovation at Harbourfront. In all three landmark projects, Zeidler has shown a flair for handling public spaces on a grand scale, endowing them with a combination of elegance and splash that has made them the architectural equivalents of instant bestsellers.

The College of Physicians and Surgeons is a much smaller job—a six-storey building for MDS, the developer, to house the disciplinary body of the medical profession—and it's as though Zeidler has tried to cram all of the architecture of the Western world into a closet. The building attempts to be a grand and dignified statement honouring an august body of self-governing professionals. But the image it conveys from the outside, where images reside, is one of confusion—an assortment of random and sometimes conflicting ideas that defy resolution.

'They were looking for a building they would feel comfortable in, that had a feeling of tradition,' Zeidler says of the building's tenants. (The college occupies the first three floors; the top three will be leased as office space pending the college's need for expansion.) In addition, he says, 'they wanted an important entrance, and they had an extremely limited budget.'

The doctors got their important entrance: a bulging, free-standing brick screen that incorporates an archway, a concrete keystone, and five windows, and rises three storeys into the air. Three storeys above, where the building and sky meet, stands another concrete keystone. (Putting an arch with a keystone on top of a building is like putting a pair of shoes on your head.) The entire extravaganza is recessed from the corner of College and Elizabeth streets, allowing room for a small paved plaza.

Keystones signify only one thing nowadays: the revival of classical forms for purposes of decoration and the remembrance of things past generally known as postmodernism. 'I wholeheartedly embrace postmodernism, but not on its own,' Zeidler says. 'It allows us to use forms which are part of our heritage without feeling embarrassment. This structure is a bluntly straightforward frame building clad in brick. The only thing that has been done in the building is a certain amount of carving and moulding—a play with details.'

But if details are applied to a brick box only as rhetoric, playing with them is like playing with matches. In addition to being twice-borrowed—once from the Romans and once from Michael Graves, the principal agent of its revival—the keystone doesn't say much about doctors other than that they've been sold last year's suit. Even in terms of urban design, the grandiose entrance isn't convincing; does the corner of College and Elizabeth, by no means a major intersection, warrant such a dramatic gesture?

Still, Zeidler's entrance might have worked were it not in competition with the rest of the exterior. Appended to the College Street façade is a window waterfall—a symmetrical orchestration of greenhouse windows—fitted between three-storey brick columns. The columns support the projection of the top three floors of office space, which have their own separate entrance and lobby on College.

One problem: the columns are the same height as the fancy bowed entranceway, throwing the façade as a whole off scale. Another problem: the window waterfall is a form of modernist appliqué that doesn't have much in common with keystones. (Zeidler used greenhouse windows and postmodernist details at Queen's Quay Terminal, but there the enormity of the box he was working with absorbed their collision.)

Then there are the Elizabeth Street and Bay Street façades, which Zeidler refers to as 'the developer sides', meaning that there he bowed to expediency. These feature yet another variety of window—the punched kind—and provide more proof of the adage that if you try to please everyone, you end up pleasing no one in particular. The redeeming features of the tacky façade are its height, a good fit with the surrounding buildings, and the warm red colour of the brick.

Given the overwrought exterior, the prevailing sense of order and graciousness inside the College of Physicians and Surgeons comes as a pleasant surprise. Everything has been kept simple and graciously ordered. The central spiral staircase behind the window waterfall is paved in rose-coloured terrazzo and landscaped all around. The lobby and waiting room are warmly lit and comfortably furnished. Particular attention has been bestowed on the third-floor council room, the setting for disciplinary hearings: its interior is responsive to both the austerity and the compassion of the law.

As a member of one self-governing profession to those of another, Zeidler had a feeling for the quality of space and amenities the doctors and their staff were seeking. But if a building can be judged by its cover—and it can—he was confused about the image his clients should project to the public. Maybe that's why he gave them a choice of four or five—and left it at that.

— October 1983

ManuLife Head Offices, Toronto

Manufacturers Life is the second largest life insurance company in the country, but the new $40-million, 435,000-square-foot addition to its Toronto headquarters on Bloor Street East is in a class of its own. The North Tower, as the structure is known, is the second major addition to the head office, originally a handsomely detailed limestone building in the Georgian style completed in 1924. In 1952 came a sensitive 11-storey limestone addition to the north. Now the firm of Clifford Lawrie Bolton Ritchie Architects has extended the complex as far as it can go without toppling into the Rosedale Valley ravine.

The same architects designed the ManuLife Centre at Bloor and Bay—a disaster from many points of view, but especially that of urban design. (It is currently undergoing renovations.) This time they seem to have tried harder for ManuLife's head office and its beautiful grounds. In fact, ManuLife is the only corporation in sight with a resident gardener and a greenhouse. The gardens, which have been extended, will soon reopen to the public.

Instead of going the well-worn atrium route, the architects joined the new and the old on two levels with a free-standing copper-domed rotunda. (It's invisible from Bloor, but there's a great view from the Carman Lamanna Gallery on Yonge.) The rotunda is entered from St Paul's Square on the west or from a curving pathway through the grounds to the east. Both entrances are glassed in and set into porches defined by square concrete columns. They pick up the colour and the limestone detailing of the original buildings and provide a visual link to the North Tower, a bold interplay of concrete and gold-tinted glass that rises 13 storeys above ground, and terraces down toward the ravine. The glass is of the wavy variety and smacks of cliché—that is, until you compare it to Bregman and Hamann's new glass box for Crown Life across St Paul's Square. I rest my case.

The rotunda isn't exactly neoclassical, and it's too dignified to be considered postmodernist. According to Peter Ferguson, who designed most of it, the dome has always been associated with funerary monuments and hence made sense for an insurance company: 'It's a monument to people who died at the proper time.' In any case, it's not the only thing that ensures the continuity between 1924 and 1983. There's the suave marble floor that's been installed from one end of the complex to the other, the imaginative integration of the windows and doors that once formed the back of the 1952 addition (one door was closed off to form a niche for the bust of Sir John A. Macdonald, president of ManuLife from 1887 to 1891), the duplication of light fixtures, and the pervasive atmosphere of solid comfort commonly associated with wealth.

The entire North Tower speaks of ManuLife's success and its policy to making office life enjoyable, if not downright luxurious, for its employees. These are abundantly obvious in the ubiquitous niched cherrywood panelling—even the Mitsubishi elevators are lined with it—the limestone fountain in the rotunda, the marble-floored, staff dining-room, and the voluptuous circular cherrywood staircase between the top two floors, where the top brass disport themselves in the style to which they're obviously accustomed.

The presidential suite has a shower. There are four dining-rooms stuffed with expensive furniture, a lounge with a limestone fireplace and a bar, open-air terraces through the doors, and an oval boardroom that's actually an enormous cherrywood sculpture. Add to that an extravagantly endowed fitness centre, office floors organized at staff and management's request into 'neighbourhoods' instead of seas of desks, and the gardens—and it's hard to see how any of the 1,500 occupants of the building will go wanting.

Much of the credit goes to Don Bolton, who oversaw the design of the addition and is responsible for much of the detailing. Bolton, a University of Toronto graduate, worked in Marcel Breuer's New York office for three years, and it shows. He hasn't got the chandelier in the rotunda or the executive lounge right, and there's a ring of stained glass at the top of the dome that is a shade too funerary. For all the attention he has given the interior design of the top two floors, the rooms are still of the stilted hotel variety: orchestrating sofas and tables isn't something architects excel at, even though they argue to the contrary. Quibbles aside, the North Tower is a resounding success, and proof that governments don't hold a monopoly on good architecture.

— December 1983

Peace Garden, Toronto

It didn't take a crystal ball to know that the Peace Garden on Nathan Phillips Square would end up as yet another illustration of the pathetic standards of public sculpture in Toronto. As early as December, just after Mayor Art Eggleton had succeeded in getting all twenty-two aldermen to approve the project before it came up to City Council, architects and landscape architects began voicing doubts about the design and location of the first major intervention on the plaza since its construction in 1957. In retrospect, every one of them was correct. In retrospect, they were all too kind.

Now that the Pope has set the eternal flame going with a taper lit from the embers of the eternal flame at Hiroshima; now that he's poured water from the rivers that flow through Nagasaki into the reflecting pool, it might be possible to survey the Peace Garden without being accused of standing in the way of world harmony. It was designed, at Eggleton's invitation, by Ken Greenberg, head of the Urban Design Group, and its most controversial and dominant feature is a cube-shaped limestone pavilion—or the ruins thereof—which has been elevated from the pavement in the manner of a villa overlooking its gardens. The structure is represented by three columns at the corners—the fourth one is missing. There are two complete arches forming a corner, two gaping half arches with jagged edges, and a pitched wooden roof that seems badly in need of repair.

The crumbling walls enclose the shallow reflecting pool on which flickers the eternal flame, set into a metal container and positioned in the exact spot where the fourth column of the pavilion would have been. Surrounding the tottering temple is a controlled mishmash of trees, bushes, flowers, grassed terraces, stone benches, paving stones, stairs, inscriptions, a ramp, and a sundial.

As a piece of sculpture, the Peace Garden is a pimple on the plaza. The impression is of an overwrought picturesque folly that has been dropped onto a large expanse of concrete. It's no wonder the people who were suntanning in the garden or sketching the pavilion, or photographing it, or staring at it, hadn't the foggiest notion of what it is meant to symbolize.

'It's a current trendy thing called postmodern design,' said one. 'The water is eroding the architecture. It's an architectural statement, isn't it, but I don't know what it's supposed to mean. It's cute, that's all.'

'That flame is a fire hazard,' said another. Since, for some reason, symbolism dictated that it stand for the missing fourth column, it flickers dangerously close to the edge of the pool. Anyone who loses his balance while tossing a coin into the water is in danger of immolation.

The most telling criticism came from a young man pushing a baby carriage: 'They're going to have to put up a board to explain everything.' Little did he know that in June, City Council refused to endorse an explanatory plaque because the text submitted by Greenberg was considered long, trite, and ungrammatical. Alderman Anthony O'Donohue suggested that all the long sentences could be reduced to a single word—peace—in as many languages as there are ethnic groups in Toronto. Failing that, he suggested the inscription: 'This here Peace Garden was built after many acrimonious debates at City Council.'

The pavilion is supposed to represent the fragility of civilization and the destructiveness of war; the landscaping to stand for the life forces of the earth. The reflecting pool is eternity, perhaps, and the eternal flame, hope—but the relationship among all the elements is far too complex to express a concept that means so many things to so many people.

Depending on where you're coming from, peace could mean the absence of war, the absence of noise, a state of mind, a political strategy, holiness, cleanliness, privacy, freedom from want, community, misanthropy, oneness with nature. The symbol of the dove is simple enough to absorb a multiplicity of meanings—the Peace Garden is not. A single tree would have sufficed.

The Peace Garden is small and exposed, and it fights with the bold elements of Viljo Revell's architecture. Because of its location, the garden has entered into a lasting relationship with Revell's sweeping vision of modernity. Symbolically, it suggests that the modern world is not what it's cracked up to be, but Revell's City Hall, sure and serene, puts the lie to Greenberg's monument.

The juxtaposition of the garden and the skating rink is a mistake, too. The garden is, or should be, a contemplative element, while the skating rink is for recreation. A more fitting position for the Peace Garden would have been the gardens on the west side of the square. As it is, it is in need of protection. The grass has been trampled to the point where it had to be sealed off from the public by ugly metal barriers. The barriers will doubtless have to go up whenever crowds of people visit the garden.

There is nothing wrong with representational public art. There's nothing wrong with the concept of a peace garden. But there is something wrong when a piece of public art of less than high quality is put in the wrong place. Mayor Eggleton's mistake was not in proposing a Peace Garden, but in choosing to discount a competition or, barring that, an intensive review of the proposed design. He has chosen to dismiss the criticisms of the garden as subjective whinings—a matter of taste.

Too bad he wasn't on the square when a city employee with a fishnet arrived at the Peace Garden to fish for the coins—they couldn't have amounted to a dollar—that had been tossed into the reflecting pool. The pool was too shallow for a net, so the maintenance man took off his shoes and socks and waded in to snaffle up the pennies in his hands. Did he do this every day? Yes. And why was he engaged in this unseemly behaviour? 'The bums get 'em,' he snarled. At least a new job has been created: the prevention of indecorous elements from diving for coins in the middle of Nathan Phillips Square.   — *September 1984*

Metropolitan Central YMCA, Toronto

Even if Toronto's downtown core weren't filling up with depressing junk, the new Metropolitan Central YMCA on Grosvenor Street would stand out. A building of this quality has become such a rare thing (and what does it say about a city when a gymnasium is so superior to the public library?), it's difficult to restrain the hand from dipping into a dusty bag of superlatives.

The new 'Y' treats people like people instead of mechanical toys designed for the sport of architects. It makes no attempt to belittle the intelligence by pummelling it with ideology or cute tricks. There are no clever allusions to medieval clock-towers (*sans* clocks), no interior streets dotted with straggling excuses for trees, no reflective glass—no exercises in fake grandeur compensating for the alleged paucity of the present. To its everlasting credit, the new 'Y' doesn't cheat. It's hard to come up with another institutional building so lacking in hammer-to-head institutional charm. That might not have topped the list for the architects, A.J. Diamond Associates (fulfilling the program did), but it's a by-product of the thoughtfulness and imagination of Donald Schmitt, head of the design team.

The $13-million, 150,000-square-foot YMCA headquarters is really made up of five different buildings, each with its own shape, structure, and function. (In current architectural lingo, this kind of plan is called Neo-Rat, short for Neo-Rationalist, signifying a composition of a limited number of geometrical forms.) There's a huge drum or cylinder made of poured concrete that runs the full height of the interconnected complex, containing a two-storey circular public auditorium and, above that, the mechanical and electrical systems. The auditorium has two banks of upholstered bleachers that can be lowered for concerts or meetings, a sprung wooden floor for sports or dancing, and three large, curved oak doors that roll open to reveal a restaurant, servery, kitchen, and lounge space (with windows that overlook the pool, gym, and city).

The gymnasium building, topped by a walled outdoor courtyard and track, is a rectangle with a steel skeleton; the pool building is a skinnier but awesome rectangle with a wooden structure, flanked on one side by a sundeck and on the other by enclosed loggia. To the southwest of the main entrance, across from the gym, is a smaller rectangular building—Schmitt calls it an 'egg-crate'—holding stacked courts where members play squash and racquetball. To the east, across from the pool, is another little building containing a day-care centre, offices, and the administration area—roughly square-shaped, but curving back from the street to form the rear entrance.

The architects may have read their Euclid, but the 'Y' is more than the sum of its cerebral underpinnings. The parts of the whole, which present an intricate but unaggressive roofline to the street, are unified in a number of ways. On the outside, continuous horizontal bandings of red brick and terracotta-coloured Angel stone—the first time this material has been used

Metropolitan Central YMCA, staircase

on the exterior of a big building—wrap around the façade. The bandings emphasize both the single identity of the complex and the separate identity of each piece, while de-emphasizing bulk.

The 'Y' can be read as a series of buildings, but it can also be seen as a ceremonial set of rooms in a stately urban dwelling. Passing from one room to the next is an occasion, not a chore. The most sensational space in the entire place is a staircase—a four-flight athlete's stair topped by a skylight that links (and divides) gym and egg-crate. ('The Roman baths of Caracalla were very much on our minds,' says Schmitt.) The athlete's stair is basically the way to the exercise and work-out rooms, but it's wide enough to stop and chat on, tall enough to inspire heavenly thoughts, and open to the gym to allow for an acute sensory experience. It combines the informality of an old-fashioned high school with the formality of a great procession. The stair is a place all its own.

But the 'Y' is full of pleasurable things. There's a public circular staircase paved in a terrazzo that enhances the sensation of walking. The walls are finished in either rosy stucco or concrete, and even the concrete seems warm by osmosis. The furniture, selected or designed by interior decorator Murray Oliver, is colourful and faintly hip. The lockers in the women's health club— so much nicer than Twenty-One McGill—are encased in oak. Stainless steel baseboards make a nice transition from rough stucco to polished terrazzo or carpet.

Every room has a distinctive ceiling hiding (or sometimes exposing) electricals and mechanicals: of how many buildings can it be said that the structural systems are an immediate source of enchantment? (Morden Yolles was the consulting engineer.)

Special mention must be made of the lighting, because the sight (and aura) of so many incandescent light bulbs is an event. Even when fluorescent lighting is used, examples of Edison's invention are nearby to offset the glare. The architects have also paid homage to an even more elementary discovery, the window. There may not be too many on the outside, for programmatic reasons, but there are so many on the inside that the sight of a jogger or a swimmer is never more than a glance away.

There are a few disappointments, but the architects are disappointed too. Because the president of the 'Y' insisted on a 40-seat boardroom in the office building, desk space is cramped—and the cumbersome work stations turn their backs to the windows. At the insistence of city planners, the small plaza in front of the main entrance has been stepped instead of being left level according to original plan—and because of that rise, the city then asked for railings and large croquet hoops to keep people from falling. In every other respect, though, the YMCA is all elegance, comfort, and heart.

— March 1985

Eaton Centre

The television commercial is familiar. A dashing-looking couple tangos through the Eaton Centre leering at the hotdogs, the pastry, and the strawberries. He winks, she holds a rose between her teeth, and together they arrive at the climactic chorus: 'My city, my centre, yum . . .' A catchy ad—but members of the Retail, Wholesale, and Department Store Union wonder why it isn't their city and their centre, too.

The union has lodged a complaint with the Ontario Labour Relations Board alleging that Eaton's and Cadillac Fairview Corp.—major tenant and developer-manager-majority owner of the centre, respectively—are engaging in unfair labour practices. Since last September, the Dundas Mall area has been declared off-limits to both union reps and anti-union employees who congregated there before and after closing time to solicit staff for (and against) the union.

At issue here, among many other things, is the nature of the space known as the Eaton Centre: public amenity or private property? Since the acreage given over to what's now known as 'mass private space' is expanding with every jerk of the crane-lift, it's as well we find out what's implied by the term before somebody rings for the security guards.

For the union, the message is loud and clear: people are required to check their constitutional rights at the revolving door before being allowed to enter the Eaton Centre. In a submission to the city's neighbourhoods committee last November, Alan Borovoy, general counsel for the Canadian Civil Liberties Association, noted that 'the peculiar character' of the Eaton Centre makes it impossible for people to exercise their basic right to freedom of association and to join a union, which both depend on opportunities for open discussion. Usually, Borovoy points out, such discussions take place at business entrances before and after the working day. But most Eaton's workers arrive and depart via the subway, the subway exits feed into the mall, and the mall is managed by Cadillac Fairview. 'If the union supporters may not assemble in the mall,' he concludes, 'freedom of association for the people at issue will have to be facilitated through telepathic communication.'

For Cadillac Fairview, mass private space isn't 'peculiar'—it's simply private. In the words of centre manager John Dennis, who was asked before the labour board last week to account for the letter of 28 September barring the union supporters (and their opponents) from congregating or assembling in the Dundas Mall area: 'We sent the letter because we wanted to reinforce our private property rights, and make it clear to all parties who owned that private property and who controlled it.' Asked whether there was a single location in the Eaton Centre where the trade unionists would be granted access to solicitation, he replied: 'Probably not.'

Whose rights are right? For those who couldn't care less about Eaton's or about unions, it may not matter; for those who care about the city, it should.

For one thing, the proliferation of people-sandwiches known as multi-use buildings—retail below, offices above, condos way above, security guards everywhere—is shrinking the public domain in the interests of real estate. The fact that a half-dozen lawyers are wrangling over the interpretation of such terms as public and private is a sign that the words have lost any meaning in this context.

What's private about a place that purports to be our city, our centre? What's public about a place that edits community involvement to allow the Canadian Great Lakes Cat Fanciers to have a booth, but not to let men and women greet employees near subway exits? ('It's Babbitt gone bananas, the way the place is run,' says union lawyer Jim Hayes, referring to Cadillac Fairview's allocation of community service booths. 'Anyone the slightest bit different is intolerable.')

The creation of 'peculiar space' is not what the city had in mind when it envisioned the Eaton Centre back in the early 1970s. It was meant to contain the widest possible range of activities and to appeal to people of different ages, incomes, and tastes. The chief planner hoped it would include a major library, theatres, skating, cafés, housing (for example, for old people), learning facilities, galleries—as well as meeting places and open spaces 'which invite people to sit, eat, and meet'.

The word 'public' appears again and again in early planning documents. The project was supposed to 'emphasize the concept that these places belong to the public and are not simply an adjunct of a commercial operation.' As Borovoy notes, the basic idea behind the planning reports was 'to render the mall areas, as far as possible, an indoor counterpart of streets and parks.'

Fifteen years later, the reports seem hopelessly naïve. The Eaton Centre is painted as Oxbridge, Baycrest, and Queen Street West all rolled into one. It was assumed private developers would rally to the spirit of the project without notions like public and private having to be spelled out and discussed at length, and in public, by all interested parties. No mention was made of union soliciting, drunks looking for shelter, or other forms of human behaviour that take place in public places. Now that mass private space, or peculiar space, has become a matter for the courts, the city has an obligation to define the new usage instead of allowing corporations to rewrite the dictionary.

—April 1985

Toronto, with Michael Hough

Just as there is (or was) an international style of architecture that produced the same building everywhere, there's an international style of landscape architecture that produced the same green still-lifes everywhere. It's no news that architects have declared war on the flat-topped box, but with far less hoopla, landscape architects are taking a hammer to the flower box.

At least that's true of Michael Hough, of Hough Stansbury Associates in Toronto. Hough has just seen the North American launching of *City Form and Natural Process*, in which he offers his extensive research into the urban landscape in the hope landscape architecture will change course. His basic point is that 'the traditional design values that have shaped the physical landscape of our cities have contributed little to their environmental health, or to their success as civilizing, enriching places to live.'

Hough is no murderer of tulips. There's a place for the horticultural set pieces known as pedigree landscapes, he believes, as long as it's clear they are wasteful of energy and resources, oblivious to where they are, boring if taken to extremes, and, above all, immune to the complexities of life and nature. His book is an argument for alternatives and diversity on the assumption that 'the city that has places for foxes and owls, natural woodlands, trout lilies, marshes and field, cultivated landscapes and formal gardens, old as well as new buildings, busy and quiet urban spaces, is a more pleasant and interesting place to live in.'

Hough finds inspiration in sewage lagoons, garbage dumps, and back alleys—secret places where nature and culture flourish under threat of rehabilitation. He usually does his research on bicycle, but last week he gave a guided tour of Toronto's unofficial landscape by car, showing only moderate interest in the conventions of driving. In other respects he seems entirely proper. He hails from southern England, and wears the tweeds and brogues to prove it. His beard is as neatly shaved as the polite landscapes he loves to hate.

'My book deals with the cultural vernacular in the broad sense,' he says, pointing the car in the direction of Kensington Market. 'In all my travels through the city I notice places responding to necessity, which makes their design diverse and wonderful. The fundamental aspect of environmental and social health in a city is diversity—lots of things happening. In this particular case there's a cultural context in which hundreds of things are going on, just as in plant systems, and an in-built aesthetic comes out of it. There's no such thing as aesthetic motivation in nature. I'm interested in natural systems that occur in the absence of tidy-minded people and aesthetic doctrine.'

The car stops on Lippincott in front of a red brick house that could pass for derelict but is actually a Chicago 58 food factory. 'It's views like this I find absolutely stunning,' Hough says, darting through an alleyway and up a flight of metal steps. Hough has reached his Everest, a second-storey rooftop overlooking a jumble of sheds, fences, wires, laundry lines, and tangles of vines in bud. Behind him is the ceremonial entrance to an apartment over the salami shop. It has an aluminum door with a St Francis of Assisi motif, a garden consisting of odd containers planted with marigolds, clothes-lines attached to a workshop horse, and a couple of sheets of plywood in lieu of grass.

Says Hough: 'All the backgrounds have an absolutely functional purpose. The vines provide shade, and are also productive. This is an urban aesthetic that comes out of functional necessity. Compare this with a typical suburban garden and front lawn where everybody is conforming and which produces the most simplistic and sterile environment. It's strange that our profession is dedicated to enriching the urban environment, but in fact it does the opposite in environmental and social terms, or in terms of natural diversity. We're so immersed in doctrine we forget the fundamentals. What we're seeing here is common usage usurping planning—super!'

Hough rushes down the stairs and past some men in blood-stained coveralls. Soon he's standing in front of an Angel-bricked house on Bellevue he's always admired. 'She's got everything,' Hough says of the owner, meaning flowers, vegetables, an elaborate hand-made icon including dove, and a fountain made from a washbasin and light bulbs. 'There are very important design lessons to learn here,' Hough says, closing the residential part of the tour. It's time to inspect another set of conditions around Sherbourne and Jarvis where 'mini-urban forests are occurring in back places—wonderful street tree plantings that are absolutely natural.'

The trees are mostly iolanthus. They grow six to eight feet a year, withstand salt and solid rock, and provide wonderful shade. The illegal immigrants of the plant world, these so-called weed trees come from warmer climates and settle wherever they find suitable conditions for growth. 'The point I'm making about plants,' Hough says, stopping before a row of iolanthus clinging to a wall on Britain Street, 'is urban design treats the urban landscape as though it were perfectly static and made of plastic—the fixed picture. But these trees have adapted to the city.'

Official policy is dedicated to the planting of exotics or slow-growing trees, Hough says, but that shouldn't be the case. 'The Chinese and Dutch plant fast-growing stuff first, and slower-growing associated species concurrently. One comes up under the shade of the other so you have this constant cycle. That's the idea of process—what you start off with isn't what you end up with. We keep on planting slow-growing stuff that doesn't stand a chance against salt and terrible soil. You get a designer to do something like this and he'd plant polite trees that will do in fifty years what the iolanthus has done in five. The problem is we think engineering and horticulture, not ecology.'

The car whizzes along George, Richmond, Jarvis, and Sherbourne, pausing in front of vacant lots and burned-out mansions where the naturalized environment has taken root. 'The disadvantaged part of town gets the best deal,' Hough says, 'as long as designers keep out of the way. Of course, I'm as much to blame as anybody. That's a nice little row, isn't it?' Now he's headed for the lakeshore to show off his final set of conditions, this one dealing with another process, namely water, and another type of environment, namely industrial.

On Commissioners Row near Cherry Street, the car stops at an abandoned industrial site that was once occupied by oil storage tanks. When the tanks were sheared from their bases, drainwater normally collected into sewers was impounded by default to create an extraordinary wetland. Hough clambers through a hole in a fence and beams at a sea of bullrushes alive with movement and birdsong. 'There are nesting birds and muskrats in here, all in a couple of acres,' he says. 'It's like a small example of the Leslie Street spit. Over the next few years we're going to get a complete new forest where the oil tanks used to be, and marshland all around. It's an absolutely self-perpetuating ecosystem made out of neglect. Oh yes, there's a Canada goose.'

The ecosystem will disappear when the site is redeveloped, and Hough will be its chief mourner. He's the first to admit that the lessons to be learned from natural processes don't translate literally into design, but they point the way to a vibrant conception of urban landscape that is neither tedious nor cosmetic. Hired to mask the oil tanks at the Clarkson Refinery in Mississauga, Hough applied the principles he studied on Commissioners Row, and foxes, muskrat, and pheasants promptly came to settle. On behalf of the National Capital Commission in Ottawa, he's undertaken urban reforestation on the fast-and-slow principle. Where the ethnic vernacular of Kensington Market will take him is anyone's guess—but then, he's already there.

— May 1985

Toronto City Hall

Toronto's City Hall celebrates its twentieth birthday today. It has weathered the years with serenity, but it's never been content to be just a building: it's a place, a landmark, and, on occasion, a three-ring circus. If Toronto may be said to have a heart, and hearts are in scant supply in big North American cities, then Viljo Revell's sweeping vision of modernity is undoubtedly one of its ventricles.

Although bold and monumental, expressing the optimism and confidence of days gone by, City Hall is remarkably relaxed inside. It is still a pleasure to grab onto a sculptured wooden door-handle and walk into the lobby, spacious and imposing without being oppressive. In part, this is a comment on the simple, curvaceous detailing that follows the flow of the twin concrete forms that immediately became identified as the city's logo. The flared, illuminated column supporting the council chamber like a Saarinen pedestal is proof that City Hall is no spring chicken, but it remains, as intended, an uplifting element.

Toronto City Hall

The council chamber itself, which looks as drab as drizzle on television, is similarly restrained. Shaped like an amphitheatre, it feels more like a living-room. The colours are muted, the detailing refined. Separating public from public servants are ropes laden with copper rings. Separating the chamber from the aldermen's lounge, a casual museum of period artifacts overlooking Nathan Phillips Square, are a couple of undulating metal gates of superior design. The chairs and tables designed by Warren Planter are a good fit, even if Revell went into a modernist rage when he learned he wasn't to choose the furniture.

None of this came about without a struggle. City Hall was a controversial project from the beginning. In 1946, when council approved funds for the acquisition of the site, there was a furious debate about the demolition of two important landmarks—Shea's Hippodrome, a former vaudeville house on Bay Street, and the neo-classical Registry Building at Albert and Chestnut. Other shocks followed. In 1955, an $18-million proposal by three local architectural firms was nixed by public referendum because of cost. (City Hall eventually cost $30-million.) The next year, architectural activist Eric Arthur talked then-mayor Nathan Phillips into holding an international competition for the design of City Hall: insult added to injury, the home-growns cried.

The competition, a first for Toronto, attracted 520 entries from 44 countries. An eight-member jury chaired by Arthur and composed of architects from Canada, the United States, England, and Italy, awarded the job to Revell, a Finn, associated with John B. Parkin Associates. (Revell died in 1964, before the job was finished.) After 1958, the year of the competition, there was much ado about rising construction costs and the price of furniture. In 1966, Phil Givens said he lost his job as mayor because he backed the purchase of Henry Moore's sculpture *The Archer* for Nathan Phillips Square.

With or without *The Archer*, Toronto's one and only square would have flourished. The plaza is a startlingly generous gesture in a city that, contrary to Arthur's view, can be mean. Over the years it's seen practically everything in the way of concerts, celebrations, and political protests. (The Pope and Platinum Blonde appeared on the square in the same month.) It has also been subjected to a questionable intrusion, the Peace Garden. This land-scaped mock ruin does nothing for Revell's architecture except to diminish its power. And, unlike the process that led to the rise of City Hall, the insertion of the Garden, which was initiated by Mayor Art Eggleton, was an autocratic gesture.

The City Hall interiors have fared better. The Parkin Partnership has recently carried out the first phase of renovations to the first two floors. Aldermen have now been supplied with lovely new offices in keeping with Revell's spirit. (Room was created for the offices when the Registry Office vacated the premises in December, freeing 80,000 square feet.) Further changes are planned for the main floor over the next decade, so that much-used departments like permit parking and zoning information will be more conveniently located.

By today's standards, or even by yesterday's, City Hall is not perfect architecture. It turns its shapely back on three sides. Office space is cramped and frequently windowless. In the words of one city official, City Hall is 'indifferently laid out, but we've learned to use it.' In terms of its symbolic value, however, it can't be faulted. It gave Toronto a centre, a forward-looking identity, and a sunny place to eat a sandwich at lunchtime.

'You've got a headmarker for a grave, and future generations will look at it and say: "This marks the spot where Toronto fell," ' said Frank Lloyd Wright of Revell's design. The last laugh is on Frank.   — *September 1985*

Bloor Street

Stand at the corner of Yonge and Bloor for fifteen minutes or so, and more than likely you'll see someone you know, or once knew, or never wanted to know. It's that kind of corner. It was the corner in the 1960s, when the Village of Yorkville was still boho and Rochdale College a Shopper's Drug Mart, when the huge neon sign of The Pilot Tavern flashed like a beacon and you could count on seeing the whole neighbourhood at Pickering Farms on a Saturday afternoon. Bloor Street was, if not *the* street, that honour falling to Yonge, at least enough of a street to walk along and feel you were on the border of a bubbling quartier where the astonishing and unexpected could happen, and often did.

Stand at the corner of Yonge and Bloor today, and you'll see the odd ghost of a subculture so vibrant it was ordered back into the basement and a streetscape gone to the hounds. One by one the landmarks that made Bloor Street a synonym for fashion, meaning they set a tone people could hum to, are being made to disappear under either the wrecker's ball or tonnes of marble.

The Park Plaza has been saved from demolition, for which Toronto must be grateful. However, the University Theatre, the best moderne theatre in the city, stands blind and handcuffed, with Famous Players hell-bent on playing executioner. The Lothian Mews, where the well-heeled and down-at-the-heel used to meet over cappuccino, the open courtyard once a well-trod passageway from Bloor Street to Cumberland Avenue, was mercilessly and unsuccessfully remodelled in 1980. The smell of coffeebeans ceased to waft there: the corridor to Cumberland was sealed inside the marble walls of a restaurant that failed. Moreover, the city's first complex to consist of shops around a courtyard has had its eyes put out. Once again, Famous Players is fighting over the corpse.

If this isn't reason enough for a good weep, think about the buildings on Bloor, between Avenue Road and Church Street, that are being provided with appendages by way of bringing them closer to the sidewalk, emphasizing their doorways, adding more retail space—generally speaking, making them friendlier. Good intentions are hard to argue against. There's nothing like being able to spot a front door. But why the doorways of modern buildings need to take the form of triumphal arches and keystones is quite another matter. Modern architecture had its flaws, but postmodern droppings aren't necessarily the answer. The ManuLife Centre set a new standard in this category. To combat its unfortunate cliffhanging tendencies, the architects tacked a lumbering pomo portal over the entrance. The ManuLife, alas, only became uglier.

But there's no end to the varieties of cosmetic surgery being performed on Bloor Street's architecture. The Air Canada Building has been the recipient of a large granite lip with lots of circles on it. Stollery's, on the southwest corner of Yonge and Bloor, a charming building ornamented with Art Deco bas-reliefs, now has hideous 'sunglasses' grafted onto its skull. The CIBC tower on the northeast corner of Yonge and Bloor is having its bottom reclad and the colour of its eyes changed from bronze to something lighter. The once elegant Crown Life insurance building at Bloor and Park Road, designed by Marani and Morris in 1956, has sprouted stainless steel eyebrows all over the place, and the owners have seen fit to remove a row of beautiful box trees out front and replace them with a few straggling twigs. Has the world suddenly gone mad?

There is, of course, something to be learned from all of this. One lesson might be that modern architects didn't give enough attention to the street and street life. How else to account for The Bay building in all its blank horror, its long dull façade serving only to announce that real life belongs inside and down in the subway-station malls? Another is that planners have failed us—how else to explain why the street line was never defined, and grown men weren't required to meet it? For thirds, the assumption that new is improved is a mistake. Fourth, that the plastic surgeons at work on Bloor are only vulgarizing the street and its architecture, shedding their critical role for that of purveyors of imagery for consumption.

Bloor Street, for all its spiffy new torchères and marble highlights, has become decidedly unfashionable. It has turned into a dumping ground for neoclassical fripperies that are already dated and meaningless decorative gestures. While some of the street's strengths are still visible—the walkways through, the charming remnants of the early part of the century—the Bloor Street we came to love is being drowned in a tide of kitsch. It will survive. It is one of those avenues whose aura transcends its design. But let's not kid ourselves. If it were to be renamed Anti-Bloor Street, no one would raise a stainless-steel eyebrow in surprise.

—January 1987

Goodgoll Office

The advertising agency of Lowe Marschalk Goodgoll, better known to the public as the minds who hit on pink flamingos to sell pink insulation, will be holding a housewarming party next Thursday night in their new offices in the Confederation Life building. In part, they'll be celebrating one of the finest works to date by the brothers Aldo and Francesco Piccaluga, two of Toronto's most fastidious and imaginative designers.

In the past, the Piccalugas' eagle-eye detailing has sometimes verged on overkill, as though by focusing so intensely on the veins of a leaf, they lost sight of the forest. With this project, the givens being 11,000 square feet of empty space with 18-foot-high ceilings on the top floor of Confederation Life, and a mandate to create a plant-filled, joyful office environment, they had a terrific excuse to loosen up. The detailing is as tightly tuned as ever, but not at the expense of the scenario.

The idea was to build a city within a big space, completely independent of the existing structure. Not a new idea, to be sure, but one the Piccalugas haven't tested before. It made sense because of 'the problem of the high ceiling and the need for separate offices', says Francesco Piccaluga, and also because of the nature of the advertising company: 'If you see these guys work, the way they run around, it's like a real city.' To go further, the heightened sense of theatre, while never indulged to the point of hysteria or syrup, seems just the things for people in the illusion business.

The Piccalugas' $500,000 'city' is mainly constructed of drywall, a material for which they affect no admiration. To enliven the dead stuff, they've used colour as a material—thirty-one colours of paint, to be precise—and exploited it as a reflector of light. Natural light penetrates the prestige offices, which have views onto Queen Street. But even the spaces farthest back from the street have openings straining for the sun, the windows lined up to afford generous glimpses or, at the very least, sensations of the outside world. The main source of illumination, however, is a large trough—metaphorically, an aqueduct—running the length of the boardroom roof. It bounces brilliant halogen light off the 18-foot ceiling and back into the offices through skylights, windows, and the openings in drywall colonnades.

The 'city' is organized, roughly, in a continuous loop around the elevator shafts. Stepping out of the elevator, you're on a white marble 'path' edged in stripes of 'grass'—doormat brush. The path leads into the reception area, a pristine landscape whose focal point is a terraced marble promontory serving as both a reception desk and a rockery. (This inspired organic exercise has to be seen to be believed.) To the right and left of the reception area there's a streetscape, each office a different colour and shape, no two carpeted or finished alike. However, almost all have roofs and the roofs all have skylights.

A guide to Adville would also note the following: a couple of plazas, a pergola (seating area), a bunker with a self-contained foyer that overflows

Goodgoll office

with greenery (the boardroom), a tunnel (around the back where the bathrooms are), a row of smokestacks (tall banded columns), a one-way street lined with tall octagonal planters made of sheet metal (designed by the Piccalugas), and even, it would appear, a red-light district (a row of four offices for secretaries under a long peaked skylight, painted crimson).

One of the virtues of the project, however, is that it can be seen and enjoyed without having to think about streets and neighbourhoods. The urban metaphor may have helped the architects to form a concept of the space, but in a way, it's a conceit. What is really impressive is the way the Piccalugas formulated a number of principles and executed them with precision. One of these principles may be abbreviated as lighting. Another is the rule that nothing of the new physically touches anything of the existing: there are even little colonnades running inside the walls of the offices on the perimeter of the floor to separate them from the walls of Confederation Life.

And the Piccalugas have a professional rule that they apply to every project: to expend as much design capability per square inch as is humanly possible. As much thought has gone into the door jambs as into the stunning blackpainted steel staircase leading up to the financial department. (Black, according to the collective sense of humour of the Piccalugas, signifies money matters.) Wandering through the agency, what you feel most is the exuberance of designers doing what they do best. City or no city, it's the dignity of space that is really on show at the top of Confederation Life.

— February 1987

Montreal Museum of Decorative Arts

While Toronto continues to dicker about a design centre, the Montreal Museum of Decorative Arts has been stealthily collecting and showing modern design since 1980. Housed in the Château Dufresne, a circa-1914 residence in the Beaux Arts style hard by Olympic Stadium, the museum officially opened to the public in 1979 as a restored historical monument. It was saved from demolition by the City of Montreal in the 1960s and revived and refurbished through the efforts of the late tobacco tycoon and history buff David Macdonald Stewart. (The property is leased from the City of Montreal by the Macdonald Stewart Foundation for $1 per annum.)

A year later, Stewart and his wife, Liliane, began an international collection of furniture, ceramics, glass, metalware, and textiles created between 1935 and 1960 that has since grown to around 500 objects. Present and accounted for are many of the artists and designers that contributed to the exciting, inconclusive battle of styles that makes the period just behind our backs so difficult to put into perspective—people like Arne Jacobsen, Alvar Aalto,

Marcel Breuer, Harry Bertoia, Kem Weber, Charles and Ray Eames, Isamu Noguchi, Eero Saarinen, Frank Lloyd Wright, George Nelson, Tapio Wirkkala, Jack Lenor Larsen, Picasso, Matisse.

Collecting and exhibiting went together. The museum has played host to an impressive number of travelling shows, subjects including furniture by Breuer, Aalto, and Gaetano Pesce, Sèvres porcelain, Larsen textiles, Swedish glass, Frank Lloyd Wright—and currently, gold jewellery from the Cleto Munari collection. The first exhibition it organized and set out on its own was on Hungarian-born ceramicist Eva Zeisel; preparations are underway to tour the collection in North America beginning in 1990. Contracts have not been signed yet, but don't be surprised if a show called Masters of Modern Design 1935-1960: Selections from the Liliane and David M. Stewart Collection turns up at the Walker Art Centre in Minneapolis and the Art Institute in Chicago.

'It started with an empty house, broken glass, disaster. I think it has done very well in six years,' says Liliane Stewart, modestly. With her longish curled hair and plucked eyebrows, she looks the spirit of the 1950s, her appearance nicely in keeping with the collection. Mrs Stewart is the president of the Château Dufresne, the director is Luc d'Iberville-Moreau. An architect by training, with a doctorate in architectural history from the Courtauld Institute under his belt, Moreau was chief curator at the Montreal Museum of Fine Arts in the 1970s. It wasn't until he met David Stewart, however, that he found the perfect opportunity to 'bring air from the outside' into an old house and a receptive city.

The two agree they started the collection at the right time. 'Give it a few years, then our period will only be for rich collectors,' says Moreau, an outgoing person given to broad smiles. 'Think of the 1930s—you have to be very rich to make a collection with a big C.' Mrs Stewart: 'The first two years were marvellous.' Moreau: 'We're very lucky to have wonderful designers who give gifts to the museum. We're lucky to know about the American Friends of Canada [a foundation offering tax breaks for gifts to Canadian museums from Americans with business investments in Canada]—it's not being used in Toronto.' Mrs Stewart clinches it: 'We are lucky we're in the period.'

In other words, the collection has been built carefully and with a sharp eye to cost. The acquisitions budget is modest—$250,000 for five years, including the salary of David Hanks, the museum's permanent consultant in New York. That budget comes from the Macdonald Stewart Foundation. The province of Quebec gives an annual operating grant of $100,000. The city keeps up the grounds. Last year, according to Moreau, half the museum's acquisitions came through the American Friends of Canada. 'I want the Château Dufresne to be a metropolitan museum,' says Moreau. 'I would be more demanding if I had the power to be more demanding.' But he's been demanding enough to set an example for any design centre that cares to follow.   *— February 1987*

Mississauga City Hall and Civic Square

Mississauga City Hall opens today, with the Duke and Duchess of York doing the honours. Rarely has any building in Canada attracted so much debate and advance publicity. From the time Edward Jones and Michael Kirkland, neither then a figure in Canadian architecture, won the 1982 national competition to design a heart for a city anxious to shed its suburban image, Mississauga City Hall became another word for the cutting edge of contemporary architectural thought. One prediction has already been fulfilled: Mississauga City Hall has made international news. It will be featured on the August cover of *Progressive Architecture*.

Edward Jones was born in England, and wasn't even resident in Canada before the competition. Kirkland, an American, taught at the University of Toronto, ran a small office, and was a partner in the urban design firm of Coombes Kirkland Berridge, since disbanded. The two men formed a partnership in 1983 to build their winning competition entry. In short, Mississauga City Hall is the *raison d'être* of their firm, and the first building they have designed and built together.

So it's impossible to take the pulse of Mississauga City Hall by charting it against earlier buildings by Jones and Kirkland. Visible from all surrounding roads, the city hall, on Burnhamthorpe Road, is from a distance a sight out of a storybook. It rises into view as a bold but restrained complex of partly-joined forms, fashioned of beautiful buff brick, which, as you come nearer, sort themselves out into a long, shallow south-facing façade with symmetrically sloping gables, a cylindrical drum, a clock-tower, an office building, and a square defined by arcades and pavilions, the whole raised a metre and a half above grade and walled to distinguish it from its surroundings.

The ensemble, despite its size, has a toytown charm. By their very simplicity, the forms are suggestive, sometime to the point of allegory. Much has been made, with the encouragement of Jones and Kirkland, of the analogy between the city hall and typical Ontario farm clusters—clock-tower equals windmill, sloped building equals barn, office building equals farmhouse, cylindrical council chamber equals silo—but this is to be overly literal. Equally, if not more, it appears as a composition of classical fragments and types air-freighted from Europe to the centre of Mississauga, where it looms as a lesson in how cities should be made, public buildings should be designed, and civilization should unfold. Descended from the theoretical projects and

Mississauga City Hall and Civic Square

attitudes of Leon Krier, indebted to Aldo Rossi in its detailing, it places a premium on clearly established hierarchies, order, proportion, solidity, and durability.

There are several doors into Mississauga City Hall, some barely visible. The 'front entrance' off the square, nearly hidden by a fat, centrally positioned column, will be used only for civic events, such as today's royal visit. Other visitors may enter through doors at either side. The 'main entrance' at the north, on an axis with the 'front entrance' and announced by a peaked glass and metal canopy, is for anyone attending to city hall business. The idea is to allow penetration of the building from different points, as a city does. The joke, as your tour guide may point out, is that there's no back door. What's not so funny is that a grand house has been denied a fitting entrance from its front yard.

The interior is organized around three formal set pieces, the Great Hall, the Grand Stair, and the Council Chamber. The Great Hall, hub and symbolic crossroads, hits you between the eyes. The spare, abstract shapes seen from the square promise a sparse interior. What you get is a deluge of Deco—green marble and stainless steel lettering with the works. The Great Hall is empty, and doesn't invite habitation. Conceived as an indoor square, ceremoniously sunken, it has now been roped off to prevent people from tripping. It will be used for receptions and rented out for shoots and distinguished events. The Grand Stair is another exercise in overkill, a steep, tapering black-and-white affair that leads to nothing more than a corridor lounge and fitness centre. The link between these two pieces is low and dark, a break in rhythm.

Of the three major pieces, the domed, circular council chamber is the most successful. It is light in mood and touch, and the interior design isn't fighting with the architecture. Another success story is the cafeteria on the twelfth floor of the office building, which has wraparound views of Mississauga. It has been treated sparingly. The intelligence evident here is what makes the whole building worthwhile. At its best, the city hall shows a very sophisticated handling of scale and proportion—big windows and little windows, big columns and little columns, big extroverted spaces and private introverted spaces, all working in harmony.

But it also has its share of mean spaces. The enclosed conservatory, located to the south end of the Great Hall, just inside the 'front entrance', is almost completely filled by six large sphagnum moss columns on which plants are beginning to grow. Open the door and chin meets moss. The conservatory was a novel feature of the program, and it seems a shame it wasn't allowed to flow into the Great Hall. Of the wedding chapel, sombre as a funeral parlour, the less said the better. Surely the pews made of chairs lashed together with black webbing were a miscalculation. The charming wooden chairs and benches on the plaza and in the conservatory (also designed by Edward Jones) were not.

What you think of Mississauga City Hall may depend as much on your politics as on matters of taste. This is, after all, an institution of government. The theme of the building is the power of the state and individual pleasure. Its view of society is that of an aggregation of atoms. Doors are to be entered one at a time. Places for public assembly are small and peripheral—the 300-seat amphitheatre on the east side of the square, the formal garden to the west, the conservatory. (Even in the cafeteria, the centre is occupied by a large cylinder containing the kitchen equipment, the tables around the edges never affording a view of the crowd.) Should the citizens of Mississauga attempt to exercise collective political action on the plaza, they will have to form ranks around the centrally placed reflecting pool and four parterres. High above them, the mayor may come out on her balcony, of which there's another version inside, overlooking the Great Hall. She will find herself addressing her image in the water. The iconography of split square, central column, and elevated look-out sends out a message: Mississauga City Hall is anticipating the most submissive of all possible worlds.   —*July 1987*

The Calgary Olympics

A mighty publicity campaign has been mounted around the Winter Olympics opening next month in Calgary, but the architecture commissioned for the games hasn't even rated a mention in a press release. Why OCO (Olympiques Calgary Olympics, the organizing committee) is downplaying the design profession is debatable. Nevertheless, a cowboy-hatted OCO guide spewing out facts and figures during a day-long tour of Olympic sites couldn't produce the name of a single architect who had contributed to their creation. (Short of knowing their names, she was far better informed about the 500 pigeons in training for a special event: the first three homers to make it back to headquarters will be awarded Olympic medals.) But then, OCO has made sure there's very little of architectural merit on the sites—or 'venues', as they're known—to promote. It seems never to have occurred to the steering committee that hosting the Olympics is a made-in-heaven opportunity to showcase the art of architecture. Beyond physical skill, the Olympics celebrate internationalism, competition, and spirit triumphant. Appropriately, the city of Barcelona, which will host the 1992 Summer Olympics, has commissioned buildings and projects from Arata Isozaki (the stadium), Gae Aulenti, Richard Meier, Ricardo Bofill, Vittorio Gregotti, and Hans Hollein, among others, all timed for completion by opening-day ceremonies.

More than an ocean separates Barcelona and Calgary, where, except for the Olympic Plaza, not a single mega-commission was awarded by competition—even a local one—or solicited from a firm outside Alberta: they all went quietly to big Calgary firms. A national contest was conducted for the design and construction of three Olympic arches—those by Barton Myers Associates, A.J. Diamond, and Barry Johns were selected, although the latter's arch wasn't built—but that competition was envisioned and organized by a subcommittee of the Olympics Arts Festival in charge of visual-arts programming. Had the Olympic 'venues' been subject to the same criteria as the arches, Calgary—and Canada—might have benefited.

Of course, nowhere is it written that boosterism inevitably leads to bad architecture, or that competitions necessarily produce the great kind. But the fact remains that Calgary has only added more mediocre stuff to its already substantial inventory. Clark James Coupland's lodge at the Canmore Nordic Centre, site of cross-country skiing events and the biathlon, is an uninspired architectural non-entity harbouring a pedestrian cafeteria. More typical of the shouting approach favoured by Calgary's architecture is the lumpy lodge at Nakiska, set aside for downhill skiing events, which was designed by the Cohos Evany Partnership in a style best referred to as Chalet Kitsch.

Other projects are of more consequence. The Olympic Oval, designed by Graham McCourt for hockey, figure-skating, and speed-skating, is an enormous covered arena on the University of Calgary campus; it is attached on one side to a new physical education building. A lot of thought has gone into making this a top-notch facility with clear circulation and nice orientation to its surroundings. But the postmodernist entrance lobby that links the Oval to its neighbour is completely out of scale with either building, a dwarf among giants. (A huge red metal sculpture has been plopped opposite the entrance as though to compensate for its lack of stature.) More attention might have been paid to the public open space around and between the buildings: it is unnecessarily bleak.

Fred Valentine, of Cook Culhan Pedersen Valentine, was put in charge of laying out Canada Olympic Park, where events such as bobsledding, luge, and ski-jumping will unfold, as well as designing most of the buildings (day lodge, Hall of Fame, refrigeration plant) on the dramatic 200-acre site. As his model Valentine took clusters of farm buildings in the foothills, his versions being eye-catching, smartly detailed barn and shed updates, promising on the outside but otherwise humdrum. In fact, the permanent architecture of the Olympics is continually upstaged by the temporary media buildings (clean-cut, well-proportioned, and beautifully sited) designed by Ken Doyle and David Price, who are engineers.

The most alarming missed opportunity of them all is Olympic Plaza, a block-large public space smack in the middle of downtown, across from the glass hulk known as Calgary City Hall. It is on the plaza that medal presentations will take place. Paul Friedberg and Partners of New York, a landscape architecture firm, won a limited competition for the job, in association with the Gibbs Gage Partnership. The instant popularity of the plaza is proof that it was desperately needed in a city centre chocked with corporate towers. It can't have much to do with design. The plaza is a visual horror.

The appointments of the plaza include a neon-striped colonnade, a cumbersome row of Egyptoid arches, and a massive, free-standing iron gate that has been bolted open. These may look suitably festive on television. But Calgarians will have to live with this vastly inferior rendition of Charles Moore's 10-year-old Piazza d'Italia long after Olympic banners have ceased to flutter. They will use it, as they will use all the Olympic sites that OCO persists in touting as a 'legacy'—a euphemism for more than $500-million spent on capital works without quality control. But many already suspect that what has been handed down from Olympian heights falls short of divine. *—January 1988*

Vaughan, Ontario: Urban Sprawl

You don't have to be a nose-in-the-air urbanite to mistrust what's happening in Vaughan: a hatred of control will do. Vaughan calls itself a town on its way to becoming a city: it could as easily be certified a planet. On the dark side of Canada's Wonderland is to be found a mushrooming collection of look-alike, low-density subdivisions, strip malls, shopping centres, and commercial blocks—a 1950s landscape shaped by market surveys and traffic engineers. The assumption is that people crave privacy, security, amenity, and status; and that they were willing to pay, on average, $264,000 to live in peace with their cars, their kids, and their kind, on squiggly streets and cul-de-sacs enclosed by thick brick walls.

Drive through the gates of a new walled subdivision in 'Canada's fastest-growing municipality with a population of over 25,000', and you're in one-note country. The map says Woodbridge; the landscape tells more. The street line, curvy or straight, is formed by two- and three-car brick garages, many equipped with Georgian-style windows, pitched roofs, and coach lamps. Behind them stand matching two-storey brick houses in mock-traditional styles, which with minor variations are identical. Sometimes it's hard to tell which is the house and which the garage.

No telephone wires, hydro poles, pedestrians, or bus stops. No trees, stoops, or decks. No back lanes (maintenance would be too high and real estate is too valuable), no cars on the street (street parking is illegal). No visible idiosyncrasies of any kind. It's as if someone had come along with a giant can of hair spray and varnished everything into a still life. Drive out through the gates and you're on Highway 400, where traffic rushes; you wonder where on earth you've just been.

What goes on behind the doors on Nimbus Place, Wiffle Tree Court, Romeo Crescent, and Rocco Way is anyone's guess. Presumably the citizens of Vaughan eat, sleep, and watch *The Journal* like everyone else. What else is there to do in Vaughan, a city-to-be without a dance company, a live theatre, a string quartet, or an El Mocambo—much less a corner store or a coffee shop? This is no city, town, or country estate: it's a place people go after work. It's not just the prissy monotony of Vaughan's 'neighbourhoods' that offends, nor its single-family-or-nothing approach to housing—Vaughan has very few apartments, a total of eight non-profit-housing developments, and not a single senior-citizens unit—but, as far as the eye can see, the absence of a public realm—of social space.

To which John Sewell, chairman of the Metro Toronto Housing Authority, responds: 'There's no public realm because there's no private realm. Everybody is so separate, no one can touch anybody else.' In other words, end-to-end 50-foot lots will never produce the contact and clash essential to personal growth and city life. For now, crudely put, Vaughan is a 100-square-mile developer's paradise. 'This is where you used to be able to buy great tomatoes, where there were pick-your-own fields,' says urban-design planning consultant Joe Berridge. 'What you have now is a higher-order cash crop.'

Once upon a time Vaughan was a few far-flung villages: Maple, Woodbridge, Kleinburg, Thornhill (Thornhill straddles Vaughan and Markham). The boom began five or six years ago with the completion of the York Durham Servicing Scheme, or trunk sewer—a costly public-works project put in place by the Davis government to expand the tax base. 'Sewage capacity is quite a thing in Vaughan with all the developers,' explains Bill Prager, editor of *The Vaughan Weekly*. 'If you're on sewage, you can have smaller properties than if you're on a septic tank—and who needs a septic tank in a backyard you can't build a swimming pool on? You can't build on a 30-foot property if you're on a septic tank: you need 100 feet minimum. North of Vaughan, in King Township, you don't have sewers—so the lots are bigger, and there's less pressure from development.'

Half of Vaughan's current population of 80,000-plus followed the trunk sewer into town. 'There's clearly been a pent-up demand,' says architect Ken Viljoen, a specialist in subdivision planning and design. 'A lot of small industry moved in very quickly; then the housing was necessary.' How does Viljoen work? 'You start with the number of lots. Fifty-foot lots are becoming scarce now. Up in Vaughan a few weeks ago, a front-foot lot was valued at $3,300. Multiply that by 50 feet, and a lot costs $150,000—so a house would cost around $300,000. And Vaughan has just discontinued 30-foot lots because they create a huge parking problem. Right now we're doing 35- and 45-foot lots. The houses will cost $200,000 and up. The biggest cost of housing is the cost of services, and we have excellent services.'

Viljoen works closely with marketing people from the outset. 'We categorize the market as either first-time buyers, moving from an apartment into a town-house; move-ups, looking for their first house; move-ups, looking for their first single; and third-time buyers in the mid- to late forties, who are very sophisticated. It takes around two years to build a subdivision. In our recent market, within a half year the profile of the buyer could go through all three spectrums. If the market starts changing, within a few months you start getting an improvement in the quality of the houses—the bells and whistles inside. Usually we offer five types of floor plans and two elevations. When we put houses on lots, we're left with, essentially, the sizes and proportions of the windows, the roof, and the nature of materials to play with. They call it curb appeal.'

Viljoen used to work for Jack Diamond and Barton Myers in the late 1960s. A fancy design firm wasn't for him; designing a house for an individual client is, he says, 'a complete pain in the butt'. He enjoys working in suburbia 'because the people that are involved are really out to do things. You've got to call on everything you've got to produce what is needed and wanted.' Number-one need and want is a 'gourmet kitchen' on the island plan with a breakfast/eating area, followed by a master bedroom with en suite bathroom and sitting area, and an entrance that guarantees a certain feeling as you walk in the house.

Jews, gathered together in Thornhill, want large dining-rooms; Orthodox Jews want combined living- and dining-rooms for celebrating holy days and festivals, and kitchens with enough space for double dishwashers and double fridges (one of each for meat and milk). Italians, who are concentrated in Woodbridge, want 'a grand entrance hall, a beautiful staircase, and as much marble as they can get'—as well as large kitchens and high basements; 'They entertain a lot in their kitchens and in rec rooms.' Both groups want traditional elevations. Modern is a no-no. As for Viljoen's clients, developer/builders, they want profits—the quicker the better. Viljoen's 'turnaround'—the time it takes between getting a commission and going on the market—is six weeks, although he has done it in less. 'It's a very hairy business,' he says.

'Vaughan has to start looking at a city centre,' Viljoen continues. 'Now there are a number of separate communities that realize they must come together. It's a question of how to make them come together. That's political.' Says Vaughan planner John Stephens: 'Establishing a community identity for Vaughan as a whole has become a major task. Vaughan has always had a large industrial base; now it's office and service. Maybe eighty per cent of the community commutes to North York, Toronto, Markham, and Brampton. That may change when office development comes on stream. Thornhill will grow to 75,000 people, Woodbridge to 60,000, Maple to 20,000. Kleinburg will remain around 3,000. We have at the interchange of Highways 400 and 7—and the future 407—the potential for starting a business centre for the town. Substantial plans are in the works to utilize the area.' Will Vaughan become a city? 'Yeah. It undoubtedly will.' What will it look like? 'Trying to plan thirty years from now is beyond our framework.'

'What maddens me,' says Joe Berridge, consultant to Vaughan on the interchange of Weston Road and Highway 7, 'is that this tame little intersection will become the Yonge-and-Eglinton of thirty years hence. The real difficulty of this stuff is that it's utterly incapable of growing and maturing. The only way you can grow this into something like a city is by plowing it under again. That won't happen, so you're forcing yourself into permanent immaturity. North York's street-and-block landscape can grow into another level of city; this can't.

'All these curves are computer-generated to maximize frontage—you sell by the front foot—and minimize the run [the length of one straight row of houses], so people won't realize every house looks the same,' Berridge explains. 'Properties back onto main streets like Weston Road and Highway 7, separated by walls, so the street divides people instead of uniting them. The urban grain is frozen. This is a frozen set of planning values about the theoretical qualities of suburban life. People fled to avoid the problems of the city, but they're more exaggerated here. The traffic is horrendous. The only solution is transit. There's an emerging bus system, but if you build like this—low-density, twisting streets—there can be no good public transit. What could a bus do?'

What, for that matter, can Berridge do? 'I go out here, I don't have a clue.' The problem with 'post-growth Vaughan', as Stephens calls it, is that it's neither city nor town. It is an abstraction. Abstractions create their own reality—but is it really the kind of reality people want, need, or deserve?

— Spring 1988

Metropolitan Toronto Police Headquarters

'I am not sure what a police building should look like,' says Stephen Irwin, of the new $40-million Metro Police Headquarters on College just west of Yonge, designed by Shore Tilbe Henschel Irwin Peters. That confession could be an expression of an open mind, free of prejudice and preconception. But it also introduces a fundamental question about the granite-faced giant whose conspicuous blue headgear could teach the Queen Mother a thing or two: what is it?

Written off by the design community as a dog, the blatant beast is actually a mongrel. Glimpsed through the windshield as you drive south on Bay, the building offers the prospect of a condominium tower, a hotel, a bank, an insurance company, or maybe an office development with street-level retail.

But the big blue dome and eight-sided *chapeau* rising to a pyramid suggest aspirations beyond the everyday—and clients obsessed with the idea of image. The view from College, meanwhile, confirms that Irwin wasn't really sure what that image should be, other than non-institutional, attractive, and vaguely populist.

'I didn't want to do an ordinary office building,' he says, although the place consists mainly of offices and meeting rooms for police and Metro officials—no cells, no holding rooms. 'It has solidity and strength, and the important rooms express themselves as what they want to be. There was an opportunity of having windows and getting outside the building; you can see out, and people outside can see in. I was concerned with the overall character and presence, and that it should be good for people inside, and the public.' Colour, design, and profile were important considerations, too.

In short, justice must be done and must be seen to be done—and the men in blue must look out and be seen to be looking out. How odd, nevertheless, that this palace for police should have a profile but no face, and that an institution that stands for law and order should appear so undisciplined.

The view from College Street is a picture of chaos—chunks of building turned every which way; tiers of balconies that, come May when the building is inhabited, will be planted and furnished, with chairs if not barbecues; a pierced colonnade perpendicular to the entrance; a free-standing arch at street-edge. And if that's not enough, there are stretches of glass block, alternating stripes of polished and flamed granite, panels of sandblasted glass, sheets of plate glass behind which the police museum will be located, and a courtyard with stairs where it is hoped the well-mannered public will bring paper-bag lunches. But no façade. It's as if a heavy weight had fallen on the construction site but no one had bothered to rebuild the ruin. It's a fashionable ruin, to be sure, but it symbolizes indiscriminate use of power and money rather than any real desire on the part of the police to go public.

That said, the interior of the headquarters is clearly organized around an atrium and smartly detailed, decorative pointy arches. (This building has a lot to do with decoration: the dome is an excuse to conceal the elevator machinery; the pyramid shelters the mechanicals.) The lobby, which, like the floor above, is public and security-free, looks like a dozen other upscale office lobbies in town, except that it will have a waterway and bridge off the three-level museum space, as well as public washrooms and phones. Leading to the second floor, where the 911 room, press room, employment offices, and public meeting rooms (bookable at no charge) are located, is a broad-loomed staircase with a large landing to accommodate tours. (Tours!) The police commissioners' boardroom up near the top is emphasized by a larger balcony than the rest. The offices, corridors, cafeteria, and senior officers' room are fitted with concealed or incandescent lighting, painted in shades of plum, mauve, and police blue, and carpeted to match; as a work environment with reminiscences of den, living room, hospitality suite, and country club, it has comfort and good lighting going for it. If it helps in civilianizing the police force, so much the better.

As architecture, however, it belongs in the lost-opportunity file, which is growing fatter by the week. There was a time when Irwin knew what a police building should look like. In the 1970s, he designed the 52 Division building on Dundas Street, a smaller project than the headquarters, admittedly, but principles are principles. Fifty-two Division is a controlled piece of design, fresh for its time, that stands nicely back from the street and fits nicely into the neighbourhood. Pedestrians haven't been invited to lunch, but respectful distance is not to be underrated as a means of engendering trust.

Something has happened to Irwin since he designed 52 Division, and, it would appear, something has also happened to the police, who wished a palace. The freedom Irwin feels to use colour, experiment with form and try on historical references—old City Hall was an inspiration for the super-friendly new headquarters—has resulted in a stew on College Street, an aggressive stew at that. Is this the image the police really want to project?

—April 1988

National Gallery of Canada, Ottawa

The National Gallery of Canada has been reborn, and not a moment too soon. A new home for Canada's flagship museum was desperately needed. Since 1954 it had been housed in an eight-storey office building whose rate of deterioration was matched only by that of attendance; a mere 4 per cent of the collection could be displayed at one time. In 1983, when the Trudeau government announced its intention to build a new gallery (and a new Museum of Man, since renamed the Canadian Museum of Civilization), the staff were sceptical. Previous design competitions, held as recently as 1975, had counted for nothing.

Both museums were rushed and under-budgeted by the Trudeau government because a federal election was near. The idea was to get them in the ground in a hurry and work out the fine points—such as how they would be clad and finished—later. With Jean Sutherland Boggs at the helm, a Crown corporation was set up to choose sites and architects for the two buildings, and to oversee construction. (Boggs was fired in midstream, because the Mulroney government was convinced the projects had become far too elaborate and expensive; the Department of Public Works took over as clients and managers.)

The selection of architects was controversial. Twelve were invited to submit proposals, six for each building. Boggs wouldn't divulge their names publicly, nor would she ask a name architect to be part of her jury. (It did include two non-practising professionals, however.)

National Gallery of Canada, Great Hall

Moshe Safdie had been asked to submit for the Museum of Civilization; he was given the gallery instead. His competitors whimpered, but Safdie was an intriguing choice. He'd scarcely been heard from in Canada since 1967, when he grabbed international attention with Habitat, his modular, for-everyone-a-garden housing prototype at Expo. A new chapter was beginning for both the National Gallery and its architect.

Safdie rose to the opportunity with an instant landmark destined for popular success. The gallery is a 600,000-square-foot *beau geste* on the banks of the Ottawa River. It occupies a dramatic, historically charged site that plunges down to the water at a promontory, Nepean Point. Across an inlet, to the south, looms the late-Victorian, neo-Gothic splendour of Parliament Hill. The mansard-roofed Château Laurier hotel is visible in the distance, across a large, sloping park. Running parallel to the river is the street that gives the gallery its address, Sussex Drive, Ottawa's embassy row.

So what do we have? A low, L-shaped building linked by overhead bridge to a separate curatorial block, the whole a puzzling mosaic of splash and whispers, cellular and modular, shine and drab. Simply laid out along two converging main axes, conceived as a microcosm of the city, the gallery is neither easily legible nor city-like. From the outside, it presents itself as a large, granite-clad box with an overlay of vestigial historical references—a decorated shed that has too many accessories in some places, but is under-dressed in others.

Safdie made his big move on the south-facing façade, which extends from the public entrance off Sussex Drive down toward the river. The entrance lobby is an octagonal, glass-skinned pavilion angled into the southeast corner of the building, its faceted roof supported by a ring of concrete columns. Through it, you're led upward along a skylit, colonnaded ramp into a pavilion of glass pavilions—the Great Hall, whose main function is to overwhelm. Elevated and skewed for panoramic views of the nation's capital, its form echoing that of the parliamentary library across the water, the Great Hall is Safdie's signature space. It's part crystal cathedral, part airport lounge. Safdie calls it 'a giant candelabrum in the heart of the community'. (Although not part of the original program, it's slated for state dinners.)

The big gestures are there, but where's the art? Unhappily, a visitor could easily pass fifteen minutes circling the entrance pavilion, traversing the ramp and admiring the view from the Great Hall, before sighting, or sensing, a single painting or sculpture. The grand entry sequence, Great Hall included, might be peeled away from the rest of the building with no more harmful consequence than granting immediate recognition to being inside an art gallery, and not a giant light fixture. (Removing the gift wrap would, however, reveal the uninspired nature of the remaining elevations.)

To reach the contemporary wing of galleries, another hike awaits you from the Great Hall, this time along a vaulted galleria running at right angles to the ramp, pausing for breath when it reaches an octagonal, glassed-in rotunda at the hub of a restaurant (overlooking the river), a staircase (to the curatorial block) and, at last, a rectangular courtyard flanked by two floors of high, white, loft spaces accommodating modern works. The path to the stacked Canadian and European galleries is equally circuitous, and the doors hard to find, a deflating introduction to what are, after all, the nation's treasures.

If the circulation system is all jolts and delayed gratification, the rooms dedicated to Canadian and European art are about peace and quiet. Floored in wood, entered through wood-framed archways, they loop around a pair of double-height courtyards, one a landscaped sculpture court marked off by a free-standing colonnade and overlooked by a continuous, second-floor balcony off the galleries; the other a water court. The galleries are a combination of vaulted and half-vaulted, rectangular and square, large and small. Mirror-lined skylight shafts piercing the vaulted ceilings diffuse soft, natural light through both floors, the light deflected to the walls by hundreds of small prisms set into the shafts. (Photoelectric cells in the light shafts control motorized blinds that open and close to adjust the light level.)

There's no arguing with calm, but bland has its limitations. There are times when something rich and kinetic starts to happen in the galleries, when you find yourself looking directly through a porthole at the inside of a light shaft, or from a gallery through a half-gallery onto the ceremonial ramp. Layered experiences such as these are rare, however. Past the ramp and Great Hall, the architecture seems to run out of steam, inside and out.

The building wants to be fundamentalist and sublime—profoundly simple—but ends up, instead, feeling flat. An entire dimension of detailing seems to be missing. In the absence of follow-through, pragmatism may be the National Gallery's chief virtue. The building satisfies a long, complicated program that reflected the demands and ambitions of a great many masters, grandeur and imageability not least among them. (It was the federal Cabinet that selected the final 'extroverted scheme' over another Safdie had prepared, which had the ceremonial ramp functioning as a street flanked by galleries on either side.)

Safdie's responses were serious and sensible. For every gallery wing, a garden (or glass knob). For every curator, a window with a view. For every head of state, a candelabrum.

The problem is lack of coherence, the absence of an overall concept in control of the parts. Bold gestures notwithstanding, the National Gallery is a fence-sitter. It's neither urban and tight-to-the-street, nor resplendent on stately grounds: a car drop-off separates it from Sussex Drive, and the romantic garden to the south, designed by Cornelia Hahn Oberlander and based on the nothern landscapes of the Group of Seven, is a meagre patch of residual space.

The gallery's skylights, knobs, and ceremonial façade project the same sort of ambivalence, and can be seen as reluctant analogues to the Ottawa skyline. It's as though Safdie, a vociferous critic of postmodernism, couldn't bring himself to overt symbolism, resorting to coy figuration instead. That's why the Great Hall appears both bombastic and limp; there's not enough story to it. While Safdie, without question, is a general who can get a project moving and win the confidence of his clients, he's been outmanoeuvred by a splendid, textured site. — *May 1988*

Industrial Design

If plenitude and display were the measure of a successful exhibition, the Power Plant's recently inaugurated overview of industrial design, entitled 'Art in Everyday Life: Aspects of Canadian Design 1967-87', would rank as an unqualified success. Curated by Peter Day and Linda Lewis (he is an art consultant and broadcaster; she is a professor of design at Ryerson Polytechnical Institute), this inquiry into the health of product design between the Expos—Expo '67 in Montreal and Expo '86 in Vancouver—draws strength from numbers. There are nearly 120 objects, or families of objects, filed under thirteen categories and stretched over two floors. The pieces range from tiny to huge, familiar to obscure, and many are shown in multiples.

So instead of one red plastic briefcase from the office of Michel Dallaire, there's a flock of them, suspended, geese-like, from the skylight of the Fleck Clerestory. Not one rolling pin by Koen De Winter, but sixteen pins, four of each colour. Enlivening a corner, there's a shower of ski toques designed by Murray Merckley. Down the stairwell, a cascade of Hadajopo Jumbo Hinges, the work of Neville Green.

The Power Plant's installation officer, James Lahey, has made it appear as if half the population were busy designing products for industry, and the other half clamouring to buy them. First impressions are of bright colours, exuberance, and diversity. The show's inventory further reveals surveillance tools, computer equipment, protective hockey gear, a barbecue set, chairs, hospital furniture, office furniture, concrete outdoor products, telephones, electronic equipment, playground equipment, a portable sun-heated shower, a bomb disposal suit, dishes, board games, a scattering of glass and ceramics— and let's not overlook, in the toys and games department, a soft-plush stuffed animal known as Binkley Bunny. Lots of stuff, lots of fun, something of the flavour of a shopping mall.

Then why, given the density and abundance, does the show seem thin and incomplete? Why could a person leave the Power Plant feeling dissatisfied instead of full? Perhaps because neither the context of the show nor the criteria of selection of its parts are obvious from the installation: lots of categories, no apparent focus. Or, to answer a couple of rhetorical questions with a few more rhetorical questions: if the exhibition is intended as a survey of the last twenty years of industrial design, why do more than two-thirds of the displays date from the 1980s? If the country under examination is Canada, why do half the exhibits originate in Toronto and two-thirds in Ontario? If Expo '67 is the show's theoretical and chronological springboard, why no visual clues—a representative grouping of objects for orientation, perhaps? If the subject is industrial design, a term usually applied to the manufacture of machine-made products, why the traditional Inuit parka and the reference to its anonymous seamstress as a manufacturer?

But Lewis and Day did have selection criteria. Although prepared to make exceptions, they were looking for mass-produced items that combine 'functional quality, technical feasibility, and aesthetic quality', and that share certain characteristics. These they spell out in a catalogue introduction that reads like a high-school essay.

In brief, they describe Canada as a country without a tradition of craftsmanship and Canadian design as lacking in ornamentation (in the interests of 'financial and common sense'). They also conclude that Canadian design exhibits simple finishes ('cheaper in a society where labour is expensive'); tough finishes (in response to 'extreme weather variations'); horizontal slatting or banding ('the result, possibly, of the technology being based on traditional methods of boat-building, or . . . a reflection of a deeper condition—the strength of the horizontal in the Canadian geographic vista'); robustness; concern for safety; and a preference for knock-down modular components or systems design ('to facilitate shipping'). Moreover, they make much of the bullnose curve—a shape that derives from the moulding process for plastic or concrete. 'In an era of manufacturing liability it now makes financial sense to avoid sharp, bruising edges . . . The curve is safe.'

Bearing this set of general characteristics in mind, go back to the exhibition and count the bullnose curves, the modular seating and kitchen storage systems, the components of the No-Name identity program that are doubtless easy to ship. But this may still not prepare you for the climactic conclusion that 'If any one product symbolizes an era and issues in contemporary Canadian design, it is the Duraglide Slide.' The Duraglide Slide? It's a piece of playground equipment made of polyethylene structured foam, designed by Gerald Beekenkamp and manufactured in Paris, Ontario. For Lewis and Day, it's got everything: safety, durability, and compatible components that can be knocked down and shipped in cartons. A safe, orderly, practical piece of design for a safety-conscious, orderly, practical people.

Fortunately for Lewis and Day, who have adopted a position that could be described as anti-intellectual, a great many of the objects they've chosen to display are of high quality, imaginative flair, and conceptual rigour. This is particularly true of the furniture and sporting equipment, which are the show's real strength. But in their zeal to explain industrial design as the pure result of external forces, without allowing that it is an art—that's what they say, but they're prepared to take the opposite view for cover—they've had to resort to the sorts of judgements that not only preclude depth and discourse, but also reinforce the image of Canadians as orderly, cautious, pragmatic: mediocrity junkies.

The exhibition, as projected through the catalogue and far too many of the show's contents, is sending out a message to young designers to play it safe and avoid the experimental. It's also saying, but without intending to, that one of the great gaps in the system of design promotion in Canada is the lack of trained design curators stemming from a lack of institutional interest in design. Until this gap is filled, the province of design is that of well-intentioned amateurs, some more gifted, adventurous, and prepared to dig than others.

To give them credit, Lewis and Day have worked hard to put together an exhibition of enormous scope, despite its rough and fuzzy edges. Day contributed a tidy history of the ups and downs of the industrial-design profession to the catalogue, which also contains the welcome beginnings of a bibliography by Ken Chamberlain. But as for the theoretical framework of 'Art in Everyday Life', it's just a lot of bullnose.   —*June 1988*

Toronto Under Renovation

There's something unnerving about a demolition site. It's not just that a building you may, or may not, have known is being removed, sometimes offering glimpses of shorn walls and tattered wallpaper on its way down. The crumbling residue of human habitation may indeed be a sobering sight. It offers evidence, if not of the vulnerability of what was thought to be secure substance, then at least of the strong attachments we unconsciously make with the archetypal figures of house, room, doorway, stair, and window. When they go, it seems that some part of us goes too.

But no need to wax anthropomorphic: let's talk architecture. The most nervous-making aspect of a demolition site might well be the thought of what's going to fill that big hole next. Down went the buildings—the Pilot Tavern, a Darling and Pearson bank—that once made Yonge and Bloor such a civilized intersection: up rose a pair of corner-killers, a bank tower on either side of Yonge, each an exercise in dismal. Down came the old YMCA on College, which was by no means the equivalent of a breath of fresh air: but up went the leading candidate for Worst Building of 1988, the Metropolitan Toronto Police Headquarters.

It's because so much has been levelled for the sake of so little, each demolition urging us to distinguish between the lasting and the replaceable, that the bulldozer hasn't been taken seriously as an agent of progress since the mid-1960s, when the backlash against mega-project redevelopment began in earnest. Words like heritage, preservation, and contextualism have become common coin—a retrospective form of motherhood. And, inevitably, as urban theory and architectural practice have shifted to accommodate the presence of the past, styles of wrecking have changed, too. Watch a building being destroyed today, and chances are you'll see a chunk of it left standing— the red-brick church tower on the northwest corner of Bathurst and College, for example, which will become the beacon of a new condominium development. We've entered an age of hybrids and mutations.

'The sixties were a good period for us,' acknowledges Steve Teperman, who, along with his two younger brothers, Stuart and Sean, represents the fourth generation of Canada's oldest and most successful demolition dynasty. Teperman is only 32, but he knows which way the wrecker's ball is swinging. The demolition business, he says, is fairly consistent: 'The only difference is there's a change from actual demolition to the gutting out of the existing shell. A lot of our work has been shifted.' As examples he cites the following eviscerations: Queen's Quay Terminal (whereby a warehouse became one of Toronto's snazziest mixed-use developments), the Elgin and Winter Garden theatres, and the Royal Mint in Ottawa.

Big stuff—modest beginnings. Steve's great-grandfather, Samuel Teperman, a Polish immigrant, abandoned a successful career as a baker to start up the business that became Teperman and Sons just after the First World War. In those days, and up to around the mid-1950s, when Samuel's grandson and Steve's dad, Marvin, began to make his dent in the dynasty, you paid for the privilege of taking down a building, and made your money selling what you salvaged. But salvaging has become a luxury with rising labour costs and increased mechanization. Steve says Teperman now crunches more than it salvages: 'You take whatever comes off easily—toilets, sinks—whatever you can steal in ten minutes. Then the machines crunch it. We're heavy into machines now. You need to feed the machine.'

As Toronto grew, so grew Teperman. The company's heraldic colours of black and orange have marked the graves of some of the city's finest structures, including the Yonge Street Arcade, Loretto Abbey, the old Telegram building, the Kresge building, and the Temple Building for the Independent Order of Foresters, a prestige office building in the Romanesque Revival style that stood at the corner of Bay and Richmond from 1897 to 1970. 'In my time alone,' says Marvin Teperman, 'I wrecked enough buildings to build a city— and in the city you could have Orthodox churches, conservative churches, schools, separate schools, apartment buildings, office buildings. . . .' Of all the buildings in Marvin Teperman's ghost town, the only one he's sorry to have devastated is Chorley Park, the 57-room mansion built in Rosedale, in 1915, to house Ontario's lieutenant-governors (it went in 1969).

The Tepermans, while they don't have much to show for their accomplishments, nonetheless have tradition on their side. Says Marvin: 'My father demolished the corner of Bay and King, and I demolished the corner of

Bay and King. I demolished Eaton's for the Eaton Centre, and my father demolished the buildings that pre-existed Eaton's.' Says Steve, right on cue: 'By all rights, I should be wrecking the Eaton Centre.' If he does get to complete the circle, however, he may have to crunch the galleria and leave the façades—because that's where Toronto is headed.

Some very strange things are going on in the name of historical preservation right now. Old façades are being grafted onto new construction, often with a cavalier disregard for how what's behind, what's up front, and what's on top relate: see the Millichamp building at the southeast corner of Adelaide and Victoria streets. At Scotia Plaza, further west on Adelaide, another weird experiment in architectural genetics: the entire terracotta façade of the old Wood Gundy building was dismantled, put in storage for several years, removed from hiding, and finally glued onto one side of Toronto's tallest rose-granite box.

Preservationists have terms for the mutations we see, in increasing numbers and variations, around town: 'partial retention' is one; 'façadism' is another. Technically, if an owner decides to save the shell of a building and rebuilds the inside in accordance with its original floor levels, his project falls under the classification of partial retention. If it's a case of removing bits and pieces of an old building and sticking them onto the sides of a new one, or leaving a front façade standing on a street like a large sandwich board, then the perpetrator is guilty of façadism. According to the Toronto Historical Board, partial retention isn't the best of all possible scenarios—full retention is—but if that's all they can get, they'll settle for it. Façadism is an outright derogatory term—yet the board will settle for that, too, when its powers of persuasion fail.

Both partial retention and façadism are hot issues right now. Sometimes the protectors of the past even have trouble telling them apart. For instance, the mammoth BCE Place development downtown involves every kind of preservation strategy going. The Bank of Montreal at Yonge and Front will be saved whole, on its original site (full retention). The Victorian warehouses on Wellington and Yonge, which survived the great fire of 1904, are having their façades restored, their backs torn down, and their interiors rebuilt with matching floor levels and volumes that 'will feel the same' as the originals (partial retention). The Commercial Bank of the Midland District on Wellington, as well as a warehouse next door, are going to be moved (with the façade of the bank to be rebuilt, complete with new back) inside a glazed street in the vast lobby of a new office building (partial retention? façadism? interior decoration?). Says Marcia Cuthbert, of the Toronto Historical Board: 'BCE will be the premier project of its kind in Canada.'

Alec Keefer, president of the Toronto-region Architectural Conservancy, a citizens' group whose mandate is 'to save buildings of merit', isn't buying it. Says Keefer: 'If a property owner, a developer, and an architect decide they want to play around with parts of buildings and give us something new, that's up to them, and the law permits it. But if the professionals who sign an oath in blood to save buildings—Heritage Canada, the Heritage Foundation, the Toronto Historical Board—start having arguments, and helping to save some elements, that's beyond their mandate. They have recognized partial demolition. BCE is façading everything except the Bank of Montreal. Buildings express man's life. We are trying to document that. We do not do urban design.'

Confusing. And to add to the mishmash, consider Tower 5 at the Toronto-Dominion Centre. That's the name of the project that will see the old Stock Exchange on Bay Street topped by a brand-new Miesian black box, code-named Tower 5 because it will be the fifth black box on the TD site, and recycled into a design centre. The Historical Board, while not entirely thrilled with the plan, is pleased that the Stock Exchange will remain whole: full retention. The Architectural Conservancy is not amused, arguing that 'the six-storey dimensions of the exchange say how powerful Toronto was in 1930: it wasn't Wall Street.' In other words, once there's a tower on top of it, the exchange's social meaning disappears. To which an architecture critic might add: cover a 1937 building with a 1960s tower, and you're not doing either of them a favour. Besides, it will throw off the composition of the TD Centre.

It would be vain to argue against the fact that old buildings are being taken seriously: that's progress. But like all good ideas that become institutionalized, politicized, and the basis for a new jargon, preservation can sometimes seem tiresome. Partial retention, full retention, façadism: these have all become moves in a develop's game. Old buildings make nice pawns. Keep a historic building: get a density bonus. Restore a façade or stick an old piece onto a new building: maybe not a bonus, but chances are the planning department will look upon your development, and your next project, favourably.

The public can stand to be cynical—and perplexed. By design, a building can now have so many faces and parts that a viewer may be forgiven for coming away with two minds, maybe more: when architects start playing around with genetics, monsters are inevitable. It seems, too, that when the past comes to be viewed as a set of images to replicate, rather than a set of circumstances that are internalized, and reinterpreted, the world of possibility shrinks a little. But for the moment, mutations are the rule, options are being considered, less is being taken for granted. Best put a brave face on things— before someone else gets there first. — *Fall 1988*

Horne Residence, Claremont, Ontario

It was called 'a wild and wonderful house that soars' by *Canadian Homes and Gardens* in 1959—and thirty years later, the description still holds. So does the original enthusiasm of Toronto artists Cleeve and Jean Horne, who commissioned the weekend retreat near Claremont, Ontario, in 1957, five years after purchasing a 200-acre property with the intention of searching out someone 'who could build, *with total freedom*, an adventurous country residence and hopefully make a contribution to Canadian architecture and/ or engineering'.

They succeeded. The house is all 1950s optimism and expressive engineering. Its single most arresting feature is a swooping, self-supporting, double-curved, thin-shell concrete roof: technically, a hyperbolic paraboloid. Set inside a square frame of white-painted beams that are bolted into concrete buttresses at the two low corners, the shell creates the illusion of motion and a dynamic image. It juts six feet beyond the glass-edged living space it enfolds, as if poised for flight, the impression of its shape shifting dramatically according to your angle of vision. The shell eliminated the necessity for bearing walls, columns, or beams. There's nothing inside to impede the flow of space or the feeling of belonging to a glorious stretch of rolling landscape. Yet the place is heroic in a modest kind of way, relaxed to the point of understatement. The plan is a simple 42-foot square.

The Hornes' modernist marvel was jointly designed by architects Michael Clifford and Kenneth Lawrie, and structural engineer Morden Yolles, who were young and raring to go; the builder was Nils Eriksson. The tale of the house is an intriguing episode in the untold story of Canadian architecture.

'We have always liked challenges,' says Cleeve Horne, at ease in the country, warming to his subject. The first challenge was finding a site. Horne bought a topographical map of Toronto, hung it in his office, put a dot where his house in the city was, and drew a circle with a 30-mile radius around it. 'That was as far as we could drive with three boys before the fights started,' says Jean. A flat road to the site was a second requirement, a creek or pond, the third. The Hornes answered an ad and became the owners of a 200-acre farm complete with rundown house, barn, water, and valleys.

Finding an architect was the second challenge. 'I'm a frustrated architect, but I'm not a professional,' says Cleeve. 'I was concerned that architects were always making excuses for not doing an ideal job. I'd listened to this since 1936.' That's when he began doing consulting work with firms like Marani and Morris, Mathers and Haldenby, and Page and Steele. He advised them on the incorporation of murals in their buildings. When he mentioned to some of them that he was looking to build an experimental house in the Pickering Township for $20,000, they scoffed.

When he spoke out at the Arts and Letters Club, however, fellow member Eric Arthur, professor at the University of Toronto architecture school, jumped to his assistance. Arthur immediately offered to run a little competition on the Hornes' behalf, and invited six fledgling firms to enter. There was one $100 prize for the winner, who would be given a chance to design whatever he wished, provided it was fresh and bold. 'We wanted a 360-

Horne residence

degree view and something that would sleep five of us—period,' says Cleeve. The Hornes wouldn't permit any of the competitors to see where they lived in the city lest it prejudice the design process. Carmen Corneil, fresh out of university, won the prize, but not the job. The Hornes were drawn to a design that was rejected as too expensive to build. They visited the architects, Michael Clifford and Kenneth Lawrie, both Englishmen who had worked at Page and Steele, and offered them the commission.

Starting over, the architects approached Morden Yolles, whom they already knew: would he be interested in designing a concrete shell? Yolles was familiar with the work of Felix Candela, the Spanish-Mexican engineer who was experimenting with paraboloid roofs in thin-shell concrete and other projects in the hyperbolic paraboloid line.

'I was only too anxious to do a shell,' he says. 'My drive was to have an engineering that was expressive. It was a kind of an ego thing. The advantage to shells is they conserve materials, and you don't have the conventional sense of flat things supported by vertical things. The shell on the Hornes' house is only two inches thick. From the material point of view, that's cheap. But to form it up is expensive.' Nonetheless, thanks to Nils Eriksson, the house was finished for $22,000, the extra money going toward a terrazzo floor in the living-room. (Jean Horne finds it hard on the feet, but it makes a handsome anchoring material.)

The Hornes got a blast for their buck. The house is roughly divided in half: one part is a combined living-room, den, dining-room, and kitchen. The remaining space is partitioned into a master bedroom and children's bedroom, these separated by a brick core enclosing two bathrooms and a furnace room. The brick core and two mahogany storage walls, one opening to the master bedroom, are the only solid dividers in the house.

As noted before, the house is square. But it doesn't feel square. It has an irregular beat. The rhythm comes from the roof, which was the first thing to get built. It rises from a height of 9 feet at the centre of the house to 13 feet at the two high corners, dropping to just 18 inches above the ground at the two low corners. Effectively, too, for the orchestration of flow, the architects dropped the floor slightly in the den area and master bedroom. There was once a fireplace in the corner of the den, where the roof is lowest and most protective. But it didn't work properly and so was removed. Too bad. A low, sheltered hearth would have balanced the glassy openness of the living room, where the ceiling flies highest and the view is panoramic.

The Horne house is a showcase of nature and ideas, not a status symbol. It hasn't been decorated to death, and it's not afraid of showing its age. The furniture is vintage fifties, but not every piece is the height of fashion. However, there are some Eero Saarinen pieces, a couple of wonderful Italian armchairs dressed in black leather and, best of all, a pair of Tecno chairs, with well-worn upholstery, designed by Oswaldo Borsani, which have become very expensive and rare. They're not there to impress, but only to serve: the Hornes have never heard of Borsani.

In retrospect, the house didn't alter the course of Canadian architecture, as the Hornes hoped it might. Clifford and Lawrie went on to specialize in corporate architecture, with mixed results. Yolles's second go-around with hyperbolic paraboloids was the Metro Zoo, at the invitation of master-planner/architect Ron Thom, who wanted containers that didn't look like buildings. He hasn't done one since. But the partnership of client, architects, engineer, and builder did produce something very special. Says Cleeve Horne, who gives credit to everyone but himself: 'It's a very contemporary little place, still.'   — *October 1988*

CBC Broadcast Centre, Toronto

The CBC Broadcast Centre broke ground this week, thirty years after a new network headquarters for Toronto first became an issue, and ten years after the CBC purchased its choice 3.8-hectare site opposite the Metro Toronto Convention Centre. The $360-million building—the budget is exclusive of equipment—will not stand alone on the downtown block bounded by Front, Wellington, Simcoe, and John. It is the cornerstone of a huge, mixed-use development that will eventually include office, retail, residential, and entertainment space, a hotel, and a half-hectare park. It is also the first building in Canada designed by Philip Johnson and John Burgee, the pair who shaped the AT&T Corporate Headquarters in New York, and our first glimpse of what may or may not be called Deconstructivism, depending on what you want to make of the term.

Add that all up, and you've got the largest, priciest, and most visible of a new breed of public buildings that are being financed and built by private developers, in this case, the Cadillac Fairview Corporation. In the Expensive Eighties, even Canada's public broadcasting network requires a corporate sponsor: Cadillac Fairview Presents the CBC. The Crown corporation will retain ownership of the land, lease it to the developer who will construct the entire block, and then lease back the Broadcast Centre as major tenant.

That the shovel has finally struck earth verges on the miraculous. From March 1985, when the CBC's project planners, under the direction of Janet Dey, issued a pre-qualification call to developers, the Broadcast Centre was pronounced dead more often than the Canadian Football League. The project has survived vacillating political support in Ottawa and countless more hurdles raised by its scope, its cost, its location, and, on several occasions, its enemies. For the consolidation of the CBC's twenty-four scattered sites in Toronto to occur while a Tory government is in power is something few would have predicted. As it happens, they underestimated Janet Dey. A woman with an iron will to control and an intentionally low public profile, Dey protected the Broadcast Centre development as a hen her eggs. The measure of her political smarts is that she got the job done, and with a minimum of fuss.

Dey kept the design of the Broadcast Centre a closely guarded secret. True, she hauled the model to city hall committee rooms whenever necessary, and showed it to consultants for evaluation. But she refused to allow the circulation of any images, or to unveil the scheme at a press conference, before ground-breaking day. She attributes this unusual behaviour to 'pure circumstances and energy', adding, 'there just hasn't been time to do it all properly.' Better to call it fear of controversy, and leave it at that. If the invitations to the wedding are sent out after the marriage ceremony, no one can stand up to object.

What Dey was protecting from public scrutiny was a very small model of a very large building that was commissioned on the basis of financial arrangements, not design. Three developers were in the final running, each with its own architects in tow. The winner, Cadillac Fairview, had as designers the firm of John Burgee Architects, with Philip Johnson listed as consultant: their associated firms in Toronto are Bregman and Hamann and Scott Associates.

What they came up with is a glass-skinned, 10-storey colossus defined on all sides by a white 'super-grid' that, in turn, overlies a secondary red grid—and from which three big rectangular boxes appear to have effected a partial escape. The most prominent of these runaway pieces, all of which contain major television studios at rooftop level, is clad in blue reflecting glass and slices right through the Front Street façade at an angle, terminating on the sidewalk. To the east of it, a mirrored-glass cylinder marks the main entrance. Other entrances are indicated by projecting canopies, and just for good measure, two large patches of green reflective glass jut out from the grid on two sides, as if somehow unable to stick.

The point of all the skewing and jutting is, as architects say, to 'break down the mass'—or to somehow disguise its bulk. No two ways about it, this is a giant: 'the biggest building I've ever worked on,' says John Burgee, who's worked on some mighty big ones. Counting rooftop and below-grade levels, the Broadcast Centre is 160,000 square metres huge. Stretched vertically, it would compare in size with a World Trade Centre tower, says Burgee, meaning it could rise to 110 storeys, or nearly twice the height of Scotia Plaza, Toronto's tallest.

What does that make the Broadcast Centre? Burgee calls it 'a very visual thing, varied, not standard, not a symmetrical kind of thing. It's a rethinking of a civic building. It's a monument—at least I hope it is—and not a commercial building. Symmetry isn't necessary to be formal and civic.' And how does it suit the Toronto context? 'Here, we were a little bit free. There's only the Convention Centre across the street. To express this industry in semi-high-tech and be contextual, too, is a conflict. We've been given a break. This is a new city centre here.' Raj Ahuja, Burgee's partner-in-charge of the Broadcast Centre, has a different idea: 'What is it? It's a big factory.'

Semi-high-tech civic building or decorated factory? Ask a Toronto architect and you may get another answer. In the new issue of *Canadian Art*, Larry Richards writes about the recent Museum of Modern Art exhibition 'Deconstructivist Architecture', which was curated by Philip Johnson in celebration of an architecture of disharmony, discomfort, and skewed volumes. Richards argues that the show was, in part, 'Johnson's convenient setting up of a theoretical and promotional context for his own deconstructivist design for the proposed CBC headquarters in Toronto, a scheme which strongly resembles recent Peter Eisenman work.' In other words, Toronto has become the recipient of a twice-removed, half-baked set of ideas filtered through the ego of an architect that baseball broadcaster Jerry Howarth would describe as 'a wily old knuckleballer'.

If this is Deconstructivism, however, it's Deconstructivism at its emptiest—Corporate Deconstructivism. As architecture, it represents not a direction but the sleek packaging of a direction. To Johnson's and Burgee's credit, the Broadcast Centre is a resolved piece of design, an interesting object. But Burgee is mistaken in thinking there was no context to work with. Front Street is a very important street in Toronto, with a strong historical and cultural context. From Union Station west, it is a street of riches that encourages street life. In the area of the Broadcast Centre, it's dull and barren. There's not much about the Front Street façade of the Broadcast Centre that's going to change that.

Deconstructivist or not, the Broadcast Centre has a few problems relating to where it is. Its success will depend greatly on its detailing at street level— the synergy it can establish with the park adjacent and the north-south pedestrian walkway, an extension of Duncan Street, which divides it from the rest of the development. Until that's thought through, the Broadcast Centre will remain an imposing, irrelevant object lodged in the heart of Toronto, floating in an ocean of reflecting glass. — *October 1988*

University of Waterloo, William G. Davis Computer Research Centre

It is bold, brash, brilliant—and believe it or not, it's a building. While Toronto hasn't had much to cheer about in the way of architecture lately, the city of Waterloo can celebrate a winner: it's the William G. Davis Computer

Research Centre, on the University of Waterloo campus. The $27-million graduate facility was designed by IKOY, a Winnipeg firm, with Mathers and Haldenby of Toronto. Not only does it rank as one of the most exciting buildings to appear on the parched Canadian landscape in years, but it also represents a personal triumph for IKOY's resident philosopher and chief designer, Ron Keenberg.

By now Keenberg is well known as a High-Tech Man who specializes in a kit-of-parts approach to making architecture—standard parts, nothing covered, no mystique. Many Canadian architects have practised High Tech, but none with his rigour and persistence. In previous work, such as the Earth Sciences Building for the University of Manitoba and the Red River Community College Auto Diesel Shop, which won a Governor-General's Award, Keenberg developed a distinctive way of orchestrating pre-fabricated building components to create functional, economic, colourful, materially textured, visually stimulating, highly ordered, light-snaring space. Easy to do? Think about it. It's tough to design a well-proportioned room using nails and drywall, let alone induce flexes, trusses, feeder ducts, and pre-cast panels to sing in harmony.

With hindsight, it seems everything Keenberg has done up to now has been in preparation to design the Davis Centre. Like his other buildings, this one is a sleek, partly transparent, thin-skinned container filled with layer upon layer of component systems—a giant, streamlined appliance. But hardware doesn't often rise to this level of stateliness. In composition, the building is a long, low, stepped, rectangular mass that extends from one corner to form an L. Overhead bridges, supported on bright red steel columns and crossed by wind braces, link the centre to the chemistry and math/computer buildings, the whole arrangement establishing a courtyard, or quadrangle—the first at the university.

Dramatically, two half-vaulted gallerias run the length of the main building, meaning about 180 metres. They're an astonishing sight from the road, not only because they provide glimpses of brightly coloured objects inside, but chiefly because of the curved, blue-green bands that seem to be holding them down lest, like a pair of futuristic boxcars, they have a mind to pull out of the station. These, it turns out, are feeder ducts more than a metre in diameter, and by moving them outside, Keenberg left space inside the building for other things, such as breathing. ('The place would have been filled with ducts,' he says.)

One of the reasons Keenberg opted for a stretched office block and wing was to give nearly all the users of the building what they wanted—offices with a window to the outside. (There are 425 offices, each accommodating up to three graduate students or professors.) From outside, it's easy to tell the Davis Centre's private parts from its public spaces. The office blocks, as well as a separate piece containing a robotic centre, are encased in champagne-coloured, anodized aluminum panels less than one millimetre thick; the public areas are sheathed in curtain wall. You could just walk around the building without going in, and go home feeling satisfied—there's that much to see and sense: red metal canopies, lampposts fitted with airport runway lights, a couple of lecture halls pulled out from the big mass and hung on metal trusses, the play of light and shadow, sheen and shine, skin and scales.

But then, of course, you'd miss the pleasures waiting for you inside, which are much more intense. The longer you stand (or sit) in any one place—whether it's the Great Hall, a galleria, or the gutsy diner-style cafeteria—the greater the pay-off. You can focus on the colours, which come in three ranges: full-bodied (turquoise, grey/blue), chroma (strong red, yellow, green), and 'frozen' (popsicle pink). Or the materials: concrete, steel, plastic laminate, steel, glass. Or the hardware: steel flanges, airplane cables, warehouse lights, electrical panels, fire hoses, hanger rods. Or the shapes, shadows, sounds, and the way people move through the place. It's hard to put it all together, take it all in. The experience is very rich, but the building is very disciplined. (And no smoking.)

The Davis Centre has proved controversial, as well it should. Bad stuff is easily blocked, but you can't ignore the good stuff. The building works as a symbol of computer technology, a good citizen on campus, a flowing set of spaces, a vote of optimism for the future. It's object, cinema, workplace, meeting ground. Democratic in spirit, forthright in manner, cheeky, and fun, the Davis Centre is also Keenberg's way of saying he loves what he does—and does so well.   *— November 1988*

Maple Leaf Gardens, Toronto

Maple Leaf Gardens landed in the limelight last week with news that the Preservation Committee of the Toronto Historical Board has recommended it for designation under the Ontario Heritage Act. The Gardens has been on the board's inventory of buildings of architectural and historic importance since 1974, but it wasn't until last February, when shareholders began speculating aloud about redeveloping the site in the event of owner Harold Ballard's death, that designation became an issue. The board held off going to the city with their application for as long as Ballard lay ill. The request to designate is now slated for consideration by the neighbourhoods committee on 19 January.

The board's decision touched off a controversy that set a benchmark for boorishness. A revived Ballard and his backers took to the airwaves spewing insults. The Historical Board was denounced as 'a bunch of idiots' and 'a bunch of commies'—Reds under the Golds. Former shareholder Morton Shulman called the Gardens 'the ugliest building in Toronto' and, since it dates from the 1930s, hardly of an age to warrant preservation. 'In Europe,' he ad-glibbed, 'they'd be asking: "Is that the 1830s or the 1730s?" ' It's worth going to bat for the Historical Board if only to protest against a week-long assault upon human intelligence and civilized public discourse.

The fact that the Historical Board, merely by serving notice to designate a property, could inspire such reaction—the value of shares in the Gardens took an immediate tumble—may indicate that the conservationist movement is gaining ground. But more probably, and especially since the price of shares has now returned to normal, it simply indicates ignorance, belatedly corrected, of the board's powers. True, these have been increased. It used to be that the city, on the recommendation of the Historical Board, could stay a building's execution for 90 days after a demolition permit was requested. As of last year, however, by virtue of an amendment to the City of Toronto Act, a designated building cannot be altered or demolished without the owner's first acquiring a building permit. In other words, an owner or developer must have a set of plans drawn up, and city council must approve them within 90 days, before a demolition permit can be issued.

That's one way the city can buy time for a threatened building. In addition, once a building permit is granted, demolition can be further delayed 180 days under the present provision of the Ontario Heritage Act. In brief, the city has up to 270 days from Designation Day to pressure an owner into preserving a piece of the past. But if an owner is hellbent on demolition, even if it means risking political favour and public opinion, there's nothing to stop him short of deportation.

That said, and assuming the Gardens is indeed under the gun, who besides the Toronto Historical Board is going to man the barricades? Specifically, in keeping with the nature of this column, what is the design community thinking? 'I love Maple Leaf Gardens,' responds architectural journalist Patricia McHugh, author of *A City Guide*. 'Historically, it is important. It's played a fairly serious role in the sports life of the city, and now, the concerts—that sort of thing. It's not a great example of architecture of the period, but it's one of the few we have of that period. Along with the Ontario Hydro Building on University Avenue and Eaton's College Street, it serves to remind us of one period in Toronto's history when it was hoped College Street would become a major street. Then the Depression came along . . .'

Says architect Robert Hill, editor of the forthcoming *Biographical Dictionary of Architects in Canada: 1800-1950*: 'I've read a great deal recently about the significant structural achievements in spanning that large area. The roof was complex for its time. It was designed to expand and contract according to conditions of climate, One corner is pinned in place, and the other three corners are on metal rollers. That, in the late twenties, would have been a major achievement, as well as to accommodate 20,000 people in one place. The exterior is a rather spartan form of Art Deco—not as handsome or beautifully embellished as finer pieces of Deco you could find in New York or Miami.'

Architecturally, in Hill's view, a stronger case can be made for keeping the Hydro building or Eaton's College Street, 'which have richer and more meaningful embellishment on the exterior façade. But the Historical Board must place value on the Gardens' historic significance. It's the largest indoor assembly hall we've had in Toronto. Virtually every major entertainer has gone through that space—Elvis Presley, the Beatles, the Rolling Stones. I have good memories of the space and events, but from an architectural standpoint, I have no emotional attachment.'

Nor does engineer Morden Yolles, who also argues that 'there are not many wild, wonderful things about the structure' of the Gardens. 'I would say that Queen Street West, and King Street West, are far more important than Maple Leaf Gardens,' says Yolles—'and what about Philosopher's Walk? There's some proposal for developing it. Why wasn't there more fuss and bother about that? I go past Maple Leaf Gardens, and it doesn't make me feel particularly good. If there was nothing else to save, I'd look at that. But I'd like to see those energies going to things that are more subtle. And if you compare Maple Leaf Gardens to Union Station, what are you going to say? Union Station is a great piece of work.'

Architect and theoretician George Baird grants the Gardens is not a master-piece, but, he says: 'I still feel bad about the Bulova Tower. It wasn't on top of my list, either, but I began to feel guilty when it became a *cause célèbre* too late. My position on the Gardens would be similar. It's charming and atmospheric, and as a piece of architecture it's consequential. The big room has presence, and so does the perimeter façade, although slightly less than the Pyramids, I would agree. Those guys [the owners] are keeping their options open 105 per cent. If they're not going to use it as an arena, I get queasy. It's not as though it has a thousand re-use options. Keep the façade and put a tower through the middle? My heart starts sinking. But if the question is: is it worth designating?—I have no doubt about saying yes.'

Something like Baird's queasiness comes across in architect Ruth Cawker's remarks. 'What I think significant from an architectural point of view,' she says, 'is the Gardens is one of the few remaining examples of architecture between-the-wars in Toronto.' What Cawker finds disturbing is the thought of another glitzy office building replacing the Gardens: 'People have tried to sanforize the urban fabric. Everything's a condo or an office building. All the others—the University Theatre is another—are slowly and inevitably being mowed down. At least the Gardens has some kind of character beyond the usual speculative building.'

According to this small survey, then, Maple Leaf Gardens stays, although not necessarily for the obvious reason that for more than fifty years it has served as a container for collective experience and, therefore, of collective cultural memory. Hockey is culture, and besides hockey, the Gardens has been the scene of political rallies, circuses, opera, and a great deal else. (As a venue for popular music, it's pitiful—unbearably hot in summer, an acoustic nightmare always—but fans keep coming anyway, because they must.) The Historical Board reckons 100 million people have passed through the Gardens since 1931. Knock down the Gardens, put up a fancy mixed-use development, and you've demolished, along with a slice of Toronto, a chapter of the city's public life.   —*January 1989*

Novotel Hotel, Toronto

You can't miss the Novotel hotel and neighbouring condominium on the Esplanade, can you? They're the buildings that look as if they've been moved out of O'Keefe Centre after a Canadian Opera Company production— neoclassical scenery worthy of a mezzo-soprano's last grief-stricken aria before her ankles give way. In fact, they're a developer's dream and an architectural firm's ticket to more of the same, only bigger. Boomtown Toronto is producing architectural aberrations by the dozen—and firms such as Matsui Baer Vanstone, born-again classicists who authored Novotel and neighbour (for the Avro Group), have finally found their niche in the marketplace.

'We've become known for providing something people want. We're getting good response from developers, if not architects,' says John Vanstone, who happens to think 'most people prefer what the city was to what the city is.' Maybe yes, maybe no—but what's that got to do with Matsui Baer Vanstone's emergence as 'Paramount Studio' designers of the 1990s? What is it they're providing that people want? 'Buildings that have a historical and classical basis,' responds Vanstone. 'It isn't dated—and we're not on the postmodern bandwagon. We like to think our buildings last, and that they fit.'

Precisely how, and what, they fit is another matter. The Novotel is jammed up against one of the saddest buildings in the St Lawrence neighbourhood, across from a stretch of renovated Victorian warehouses and a parking lot. The replica colonnade and dormer windows that are its main features seem obtrusive, not because they're trying to be—far from it—but because the façade is oblivious to everything around it. The Novotel is the snob on the block—who would guess that its rates are competitive with those of a Holiday Inn? It's a castle in a back lane.

Sitting by the front window for a happy-hour drink is an intriguing experience. You feel very much apart from Toronto, and evidence to the contrary, you know deep down this isn't Paris or the south of France. Finally, it must be admitted you're in Nowhere, Ontario—a nice place to visit, and closer to the capital of Nowhere than, say, the Aeroquay at Terminal One, but where's the fit? 'It's more like fitting in to what was happening,' says Baer, neglecting to specify where, or when, or why.

The most successful part of the Avro development is the tall, sculptured shaft of the condominium, which doesn't evoke the past and which, by comparison with most Toronto condos and office towers, offers a powerful image, particularly from the expressway. But that isn't uppermost in Jim Baer's mind what he talks about the firm's work. 'Our concern,' he says, 'is buildings are being put up according to the fad of the day. Architecture is going all over the place. We've been making wild jabs and stabs and coming up dry every time. Each time any of us goes to Europe, we revel in the old things over there, and say: "Why can't we create something of beauty, where beauty is the reason?' That's something we're searching for—what was beautiful, what was lasting. This isn't tongue-in-cheek.'

The firm evolved from a previous partnership, Dunlop Wardell Matsui Aitken, in 1972. Baer worked on the Etobicoke Central Library, which won a Massey medal in 1966, and the Wallace Emerson Community Centre on Dufferin Street, neither of which foretold a neoclassical future. Even now, Matsui Baer Vanstone will do a glass box, if asked, and they're known as sensitive designers of non-profit housing developments. But with the Avro project, and its successor, for Rylar Developments, a $100-million, up-scale, housing-and-hotel/retail complex called Grand Harbour, which will rise on the Etobicoke Lakeshore, the firm has begun to fly its 'French-Georgian' flag proudly.

It would be nice if they didn't have to knock other architects on their way to mansard-roofed heaven. Says Baer: 'Architects today are designing for each other. It's a closed shop. We're trying to re-establish, for ourselves, that you can do something people—my mother, your mother—can understand and like. There's a big public out there that has been denied a part of what's happening in architecture for years and years. What we do has to sell—people have to like it. There is a response. Marketers publish our work in their newspapers. The public's interests are seen to be the developer's interests. What concerns me is: is it beautiful? It's not that we're anti-modern. We're adding fabric that has been lost. We've torn down so much we truly like. Now we're left with those few weeds. . . .'

There will be no weeds in evidence at Grand Harbour, which runs the gamut from single-family townhouses with Newport detailing on the water, to high-rise condominiums with mansion penthouse above—'a hillside town', in Baer's words. There will be grand arches, a Bernini colonnade, and peaked roofs aplenty. 'The whole thing will be a delight to walk through,' Baer promises. 'When I'm drawing it, I get goose bumps.' Their colleagues in the profession get them, too, but from horror. They regard the firm's foray into Ricardo Bofill territory as a money-making shtick, and giggle at their ads for designers with a commitment to the Beaux Arts.

But Matsui Baer Vanstone's work has to be seen in context. It's developer architecture, designed to sell, and it's got something going for it: namely boldness, and a feeling for form and juxtapositions of scale. But the rhetoric we can do without. Like it or not, and however serious their intentions may be, Baer and Co. are doing classical kitsch—figments of Eurograndeur for speculators and the magnificently obsessed. French-Georgian with the works? If Ma spoke French, she might respond: '*Très vulgaire, chéri, n'est-ce pas?*' — *February 1989*

Bain Avenue and Other Co-Ops

Let's get right to the marrow of the bone. The topic is co-op housing: what is it, and why do we need to know? 'What's interesting about co-op housing,' says Alexandra Wilson off the top, 'is it didn't exist, for all intents and purposes, fifteen years ago—and now it's something many people have heard of, even if they don't know what it is.' Wilson knows. She was there. In 1974, when she was 18, she was living in a run-down apartment house on Bain Avenue, one of a set of low-rise, brick buildings designed in the early 1900s by Eden Smith on the Garden City model, and built by the Toronto Housing Company through bond issues guaranteed by the city. Sometime in the 1960s Mark Tanz became the owner, and in 1974 he announced his intention of converting the 260 apartments into condominiums.

For Wilson, this was the last straw. She had already been evicted from two other places because of conversion: enough was enough. 'I had a network of friends living there,' she says of Bain Avenue, 'and there was a modest tenants' association. We had a meeting, and decided we were going to fight— this had to stop someplace—but what to do?' The group considered protest action, but realized that, in the end, it would prove futile. Then, the light bulb: if they couldn't persuade the province or city to stop conversions, why not buy the buildings and run them co-operatively?

As luck would have it, the previous year, in response to growing dissatisfaction with public housing projects, the Central Mortgage and Housing Corporation (CMHC) had amended the National Housing Act, opening the door to non-profit and co-op housing (co-ops are a species of non-profit) by providing financing that made it possible 'to initiate and renovate', in Wilson's words. The Bain Avenue tenants approached the CMHC, which expressed interest. So did the City of Toronto, then in the Crombie era and starting up Cityhome. The city purchased Bain Avenue through a new CMHC program with the intention of turning the building over to the tenants' co-operative. 'It took an age,' says Wilson—to the end of 1977, to be precise— for that to happen, but the short of it is the Bain Avenue apartments became, if not the first co-op in the country, among the first ten in Toronto in 1974, and the biggest rehabilitation project in Canada at the time.

Says Wilson, who now works for the Canadian Co-operative Association in Ottawa: 'It was the first instance, anywhere in Canada, of tenants taking over publicly owned housing and running it themselves. It was something significant and new on the housing scene—a response to a market that was changing rapidly, a market in which home ownership was out of reach of people with moderate incomes, a market in which rental units were becoming scarce, a market in which rents were starting to rise and people were becoming especially concerned about tenants' rights. As well, public housing, which was developed in the largest amounts in the late sixties and seventies, was disappointing people. It was thought of as ghettos for the poor.'

If such was the situation fifteen years ago, then how much more desperate it is now! Says architect Barry Sampson, who remembers Bain Avenue as 'a turning point': 'Why are co-ops interesting? Because the private rental sector is dead. The rental sector consists of controlled rental buildings—aging stock, usually. Then you have condos. Two groups buy them: speculators, who rent them out, and people who are planning to live in them at some point, and who rent them out in the meantime. I call that black-market rental. Developers are all building condos, not apartments, and some end up being rental units, but they're not rent-controlled. They form an invisible rental sector. Co-ops are the one group building real rental accommodation. People move into a building, pay a monthly charge to the co-op, and when they move out, that's it. They take nothing with them.' In the words of another co-op activist: 'It's more than rental, less than ownership.'

Besides forming the *de facto* rental sector, a significant aspect of co-ops is that they house people of mixed income, including candidates for public housing. As Sampson puts it, 'Co-ops produce a decentralized social housing component.' To this Richard Tyssen of the Co-operative Housing Federation of Toronto would add, 'One thing we emphasize, over and over again, is we want a reasonable mix: twenty-five per cent moderate, and fifty per cent who can afford market rent.' In other words, some co-op residents are subsidized, while others are not. 'We've taken flak on both sides,' continues Tyssen. 'Some people say this is public housing, while others say government money is going to middle-income people. But that's the point—a mix of incomes. That's how you build good communities.'

Middle, shmiddle—what does it matter? There are an awful lot of people in Toronto who can't afford a house or condo at today's aristocratic prices. In any case, if you've got the pocket to buy a house, co-op housing isn't for you. Like Sampson said, there's no personal equity to be had from a co-op: you leave naked as you came. But as Wilson points out, some sixty per cent of Metro residents don't own houses, while the rental market has become a jungle. So say you're open to the idea of co-op living. Now what?

'The kind of thing we did at Bain is terribly hard to do today without professional help,' says Wilson. 'Urban land development has become so complex it's beyond the ability of a few families or friends to do.' That's where resource groups come in. There are five non-profit resource groups in Toronto whose job is to help people get co-ops built and running. Built, because although rehabilitating old buildings used to be common, it is now cheaper, but not necessarily easier, to start from scratch. Not easier, because finding a site, getting approvals, arranging financing, selecting an architect, contracting, and putting up a building are never easy, particularly at a time of inflated land and construction prices.

'It's a true challenge to get something happening in this city,' says Mike Labbé, a planner with Lantana, a Toronto-based resource group that has been developing co-ops since 1977. 'We provide the expertise to take an empty lot through to a building, as well as providing management education to the co-op board.' So far, Lantana has developed 3,400 co-op units, including those under construction, which amounts to forty-five co-ops. Any seven people can incorporate into a co-op, but if a group of only seven approached Lantana for assistance, they'd be persuaded to get involved with a project that's already under way.

But let's say a church group wanted co-op housing for its members. 'We would talk to them,' says Labbé, 'and if the church had property, we'd be anxious to work with them. If not, we'd say: "Let's use the church's contacts to find some land." We'd reach an agreement, incorporate, sign a contract, and apply to the province for money—a supply subsidy—to get started. That's where resource groups get paid. We take a percentage of that money. The critical point is getting the federal or provincial government to guarantee the mortgage. Before they will guarantee it, you need to provide a tendered set of plans.' The government doesn't set the size of units, but it does set the maximum price, and it's not enough to build big, classy apartments. The co-op sector builds low-end-of-the-market housing, Typically, a one-bedroom unit is 620 square feet; a two-bedroom unit, the most popular, is 830 square feet; and a three-bedroom is 1,000 square feet.

On average it takes three years to get a co-op going. Sometimes a resource group will come across a piece of land and pull people together, and sometimes a private developer will build co-op units into a development because the city, or province, insists—these are called turnkey units—and resource groups will see that they're filled. Tenants pay a housing charge (co-op jargon for rent), which consists of a percentage of the mortgage plus maintenance costs. Since the co-op is owned and managed by the co-op corporation, and can't be sold, there is no personal equity. What compensates for equity is control over environment, security of tenure, a sense of community, and protection from an inflationary real estate market.

'You're controlling the future,' says architect Wilfrid Worland, whose firm, Oleson Worland Architects, designed an artists' co-op on McCaul Street. Or, in Wilson's words: 'Over time, in a market like Toronto, you'll save money if you hang on—maybe set some aside and eventually buy a house. The advantage of non-profit housing is, well, let's say your co-op is in a neighbourhood without good access to transportation, and they extend the subway to your area. Market rents automatically go up. If you live in a co-op, your rent won't go up.' This is one reason for the stability of co-op communities. Says Labbé, who lives in a co-op in the St Lawrence neighbourhood, where fully half the housing is co-operative: 'The lower the income, the more stable the co-op. People with higher income are more likely to have a job change. We started with a fifteen-per-cent turnover the first year, and now, five years later, it's down to approximately five per cent. That's low.'

Over the last fifteen years the number of co-ops in Canada has grown to 1,400: 52,000 units, of which 10,000 units are in Toronto, where they form just under two per cent of the rental sector. The co-op movement is still small, but it's expanding rapidly. Says Tyssen: 'Right now the province is looking to build approximately 55,000 units of non-profit housing over the next three to five years, and we're priming to develop one-third of them. We are emerging. The province has delivered a clear message to municipalities. They have to see that twenty-five per cent of what gets built must be affordable.'

Logical, maybe, but not necessarily easy to pull off. 'My job has always been a pleasure,' says Tyssen, 'except for two aspects. First, the non-profit sector is undercapitalized. We don't have enough money to compete with developers in buying land. Then there's the municipal approval process. People don't understand what we're doing, and they react negatively. Home-owners don't want "the riff-raff" going to their schools. They think their property values will go down. But once they've seen a co-op built, and a project moves in, it's fine.'

'The big problem now, in Toronto, is land,' says Wilson, echoing Tyssen, 'and the federal government doesn't allow enough money to build properly.' That is an understatement. The 110-unit Arcadia co-op at Harbourfront, one of the finest new co-ops in Toronto from an architectural point of view, was built on a peanuts budget of $40 per square foot. Says André Lessard, the project architect for A.J. Diamond and Partners: 'The budget was ridiculous, really obscene. From an urban point of view, we wanted a good-looking building. The CMHC doesn't want money spent on decoration. It makes it look bad, as though it's spending the taxpayers' money on frills. . . . The drawings had to be done overnight, but federal lobbying took six months. It's time-consuming for professionals to do a building that's competent and cheap. What's exciting is that here is one corner of the market where there's room for experimentation. You can really design to the group.'

'The fact is we were bloody lucky,' says Wilson, who was in charge of developing Arcadia for the Co-operative Housing Federation of Toronto. 'When we were designing the project, I was terrified we wouldn't be able to

Arcadia Co-operative

build it. We got extremely lucky. The market was depressed, and we got lucky with the builder, who was excellent. At Arcadia, we have broom closets. People still have brooms, you know. It's the attention to fine detail that can really make the difference. Part of the reason Arcadia turned out was we had a good architect. The best co-ops aren't accidents.'

Nonetheless, and numerous exceptions notwithstanding, co-ops are often dull, ugly, cheap-looking buildings. 'It's quite sad,' Wilson acknowledges. 'When we all went into this co-op housing business, it was partly in reaction to public housing. We thought the poor deserved something better. There have been good developments, but what has happened over time is the federal government has steadily tightened the screws, partly in response to the rising costs of land and development. The CMHC has never been prepared to raise the MUP to keep pace with land and construction. Often you get something smaller and worse than the year before. Some of my friends and colleagues feel so beleaguered by the government, they give up. They don't have the energy to fight. Not all architects are equal, and the money is so stingy it sometimes doesn't matter who you hire. But you can't lose sight of your mission. You try to make the best of what's available.'

As long as Wilson and her troops soldier on, the mission will continue. The co-op movement may still be beleaguered, but it is important, not only from a financial point of view but also, and equally, from a social and urbanistic perspective. 'We're building affordable housing, and we're build-ing communities,' says Tyssen. 'The co-op sector is democratically owned and managed. The people who live there manage the buildings, they get on committees, develop bonds. They aren't interested in property values—co-ops aren't sold—but in social values. Economic self-interest is defused in a co-op.' Needless to say, in the year of free trade co-ops are out-of-step with the times. For this reason alone they deserve to be nurtured—for fostering, if not always superior design, such old-fashioned virtues as political astuteness, social spirit, diversity, community, civic-mindedness, and grit.

— *March 1989*

Canadian Centre for Architecture, Montreal

With the official opening of new and permanent quarters for the Centre Canadien d'Architecture/Canadian Centre for Architecture (CCA), the spot-light turns full-blast on founder and director Phyllis Lambert; her architect, Peter Rose; and the building they designed in Montreal for the housing, display, and study of one of the most extensive collections anywhere of photographs, books, and drawings relating to architecture. Lambert's largesse in creating and endowing the CCA, both museum and study centre, built at a cost of $60-million, is unprecedented in this country (and most other countries). Drawing on formidable resources of vision, commitment, aggressive energy, and personal wealth, she has fashioned an institution that can't help affecting the way architecture is perceived and interpreted—and, with any luck, built.

Lambert's stated mission is 'to make a case for architecture', but last week, barely able to sit still, she was making a case for trees. It was neither an accident nor a coincidence that on Boulevard René-Lévesque, just outside the CCA, city employees were planting Norwegian maples. One of Lambert's design imperatives for the CCA was to 'heal the scars of traffic engineering', and with reason. The CCA site, which extends north and south of Boulevard René-Lévesque, is bounded on two sides by expressway ramps and traffic. Nature heals. Institutions have grounds. The CCA is not just a building, it's a building with park and gardens. Each has a different mood and purpose, and they all get equal time. Moreover, it mattered to Lambert and Rose that the park and gardens be meaningful as well as medicinal.

In pursuit of both objectives, Rose set the form of the landscape and landscape architects Diana Gerrard and Gunta Mackars developed a planting program based on the ecology of the area. They identified three historical periods, each associated with a vegetation type: native plants, plants introduced by European settlers, and genetically altered species. These they introduced into the CCA landscape, streets, sidewalks, and all, in consideration of microclimate, environmental stress, and specific designs for two parks. Rose was given responsibility for the entry garden; Melvin Charney is architect of the CCA Park across the boulevard. (Charney's park, the larger and wilder of the two, won't be finished for opening day.) So Lambert could be forgiven for cheering on the Norwegian maples. Along with an apple orchard, seedless green ash trees, English oaks, sugar maples, periwinkle, gayfeathers, loosestrife, roses, beard tongue, Narcissus Unsurpassable, and grasses galore, they're actors in a grand integrative, reparative, regenerative, rationalized, scripted, mixed-media performance called Making A Case For Architecture. So, of course, is the building, which focuses the theatre of operation. 'I'm interested in the idea of architecture as integration, as opposed to buildings as autonomous things,' says Rose. 'Integration is the first order of cities— pulling things together. That's civilization. That's one of the driving ideas of this building.'

One thing that's been pulled into the building, physically and symbolically, is the Shaughnessy House, an ornate, late-Victorian mansion that was once two houses with two entrances, separated by a party wall. (Significantly, the wall was built on the property line that bisected a traditional Montreal lot, or cadastre.) Lambert bought the house in 1974, to save it from demolition. Fed up by the bulldozing of Montreal's architectural heritage, she'd turned activist. Feeling her way towards an idea of a building to house the CCA staff

Canadian Centre for Architecture

and collections, she gradually came to the conclusion that the 1.2-hectare site on which the Shaughnessy House stood was the right place for it.

Peter Rose began the design of the CCA in 1983. The Shaughnessy House was a given. The mansion faces onto Boulevard René-Lévesque—formerly Boulevard Dorchester—but the city asked that the CCA entrance not go on the boulevard because of traffic. Rose designed the new building to wrap around the Shaughnessy House in the shape of a C. He placed the main entrance on Baile Street, which runs parallel to the boulevard, and north. One of the puzzling things about the CCA, as a consequence, is that it has two fronts—and no back.

Each front has been treated differently. Flanked by the auditorium wing of the new building on one side, and the Special Collections Study Room on the other, the Shaughnessy House becomes a piece of a repaired street-scape. In effect, the house has been given replacement neighbours to compensate for those torn down to make room for the expressway. So the south side of the site presents a lesson on urbanism. That the envelope of the new building is of Trenton Limestone, the greystone of nineteenth-century Montreal architecture, reinforces the fit. New is embedded in old. That it's been given an aluminum cornice says times have changed. New materials add life to old.

The Baile Street front, however, is long, smooth, and elegant—it's the CCA's institutional face. But it too is disposed to the Shaughnessy House. Old is embedded in new. The historically positioned party wall of the mansion reappears as a vertical seam dividing the Baile Street façade down the middle. The main entrance is off to one side, announced by double doors and a grand, projecting window. Balancing the formal entrance of the other side are the windows of the library reading room. Recall that the Shaughnessy House once had two separate entries, and you've got the genetic make-up of the new CCA. It's not every architect, or client, who would treat a decaying old house, or pair of houses, with such deference. But the CCA, in addition to being a set of public rooms and private spaces, is aiming to build dynamic relationships between past and present, light and shadow, building and landscape, city and institution, drawings and photographs. (It can also be read as Lambert's biography: modernist, preservationist, classicist, she's the daughter of Mies and Montreal.)

If the mansion is the set piece of the new building—a museum exhibition on its own—it's because of what it signifies as a surviving fragment of nineteenth-century urban fabric, and not because it's an architectural master-piece. To CCA members, it will also signify club. It's being restored, down to the last mahogany doorknob, as a place to eat, drink, talk, rest—a heart. Shaughnessy House seems to have rubbed off on the interior of the new CCA building, too. It feels like a spacious, comfortably furnished country house. In part that's because bits of the Shaughnessy come into view as you wander the building, so you're always conscious of it. And partly it's that the

CCA rooms—the galleries, auditorium, bookstore, library, offices—are small and discrete, verging on domestic scale. (Baile Park, the entry courtyard, is the front lawn; Charney's CCA Park will be the moors.)

In all, nothing flashy or in less than good taste. Conceived as a place for the quiet viewing of small precious objects, the CCA is, inside, dedicated to privacy, comfort, and light. Materials have been kept to a minimum and rigorously ordered. What you see and hear are disciplined variations on the theme of grey limestone, anodized aluminum, and maple panels. Peace and quiet, tough and warm. The CCA has been criticized for its miniaturized spaces, and it has a didactic quality that sometimes interferes with its charms. But Lambert is happy, and Rose keeps watching the play of light and shadow on greystone as if he's just learned to see.

'I think the building is more wonderful than I'd thought possible,' said Lambert. 'There's some spirit of the building. People come in and expand their chests. The variety and quality of those rooms are superb—the gentleness. There has been this kind of madness in France. The Beaubourg is very successful because it looks like a railway station. You can go in and chew gum. They're doing the same to the Musée d'Orsay, and they're doing the same to the Louvre. This place isn't made for mobs. It's a place where you can feel very comfortable and close to what's happening. You rush through the Louvre—you can spend a whole day here.

'I want people to understand what the possibilities are. I think the CCA will change the history of architecture in Canada. People will see that as a field to go into. I think this is the rich logic of opportunity. I'm excited about how this museum is going to change things. I think just to have a building that pronounces, and having it quite so wonderful, says something. And the programming, and people thinking about architecture—let's have this conversation in ten years.' Meanwhile, let's expand our chests. Lambert and Rose have done us proud.   — *May 1989*

Canadian Museum of Civilization, Hull, Quebec

When the Canadian Museum of Civilization officially opens, the inventory of great Canadian rooms will have been increased. To be standing inside the Great Hall of the museum, looking across the Ottawa River, is a magical, liberating experience. The shape of the hall is made by two arcs, suggesting a canoe of magnificent proportions. The wall of window curving out towards the river is marked off by slender stone columns, flaring as they rise: a ripple of oars. Alternating strips of polished and unpolished granite band the floor: shoreline. To the back, a stage detailed to resemble a dock. Behind that, a row of Northwest Coast Indian houses built and decorated to traditional designs by native craftsmen. Towering over the houses, totem poles from the museum's permanent collection.

You're standing not only in a splendid space, but also within one of the great myths of European culture: discovering America, as retold by a spokesman for another, less understood, tradition of myth-making, Métis architect Douglas Cardinal. The primal scene of Canadian history—First Contact—is familiar from countless paintings of explorers landing on Canadian shores, but here the point of view is innocent, and you're in the picture. The architecture is more emotional, narrative and naturalistic than some people would feel comfortable with. It's cool, and not so cool. It's Douglas Cardinal of Red Deer, Alberta, taking the big risk and managing, in many ways, to pull it off.

Like the Great Hall, the design of the museum as a whole is grounded in legend. To Cardinal's thinking, the origin of architecture lies in the beating of wave upon rock, and the formative action of glaciers. It's an expression of prehistoric, natural theatre. This myth informed his entry to the competition for the museum in 1983, and it inspired the forms of the building, which is all curves, swirls, and topographical surfaces. The wave action can be dizzying. Cladding is of crushed and sawn stone, and Manitoba limestone patterned with fossils.

This is less a building than an idealized, built landscape, and it puts forward a different idea of monumentality than the one we're used to. It's nature and process that are perceived as monumental, rather than architecture as isolated incident. One of the most successful aspects of the museum is the way it frames, ennobles and defers to the monumental feature of the Ottawa landscape, the Ottawa River.

Consider the plazas that flow between the two main blocks, each low and sinuous, one dedicated to performance and exhibitions of ethnographic, archaeological, and historical artifacts, and the other to curatorial, storage, and conservation functions. The upper plaza neighbours on Hull, and has been treated as a formal space equipped with stone seating and reflecting pools. The lower plaza steps down to an amphitheatre that looks across to Parliament Hill. When complete, it will be ringed by a sidewalk café and washed by a waterfall emptying into the river. Cardinal had 27 acres at his disposal, and he's made the most of them.

He also had a 1-million-square-foot building crammed with technology to design, and a program to follow. In and behind the plaster swirls and carved ceilings, hidden away in the Imax/Omnimax theatre and the 500-seat performance theatre, buried in the columns and under domes, are no fewer than 100 miles of coaxial cable, more than 415 miles of fibre-optic cable, and some 830 miles of twisted-pair cable. These will support 25 communications systems ranging from basic telephone service to remote viewing of the

Canadian Museum of Civilization

museum's 3.5 million artifacts, from multi-channel television to two-way video linkups. The Canadian Museum of Civilization may well be the most intelligent building in the world, as well as one of the weirdest.

Some architects would have exposed the technology, or used it as a point of departure for design. Not Cardinal, who was the first Canadian architect to embrace computer-aided design in a big way. He couldn't bear to have ducts and wires get in the way of his forms. He couldn't even stand to have a single lighting fixture show itself. All light sources are concealed behind coffered ceilings or plaster clouds, with the result that the museum sometimes feels too chic, like a sprawling condominium lobby. It may be that no architect has yet designed the light of the moon, stars, and sun. Still, you wish Cardinal hadn't reneged on fashioning a single lamp. The museum has heart. It could have used a hearth.

In one blatant instance, Cardinal's fears of seeing his architecture smothered have been realized. The third floor of the exhibition block is dedicated to history, which has been interpreted to mean a winding network of streets lined by meticulously detailed replicas of period houses and shops: a house in Old Quebec, a nineteenth-century Toronto house, and so on—things you can still see by drawing the living-room curtains. The effect is nauseating, and not just because Cardinal's vaults and domes have been hidden from view. The idea behind the ersatz townscape is that artifacts, to be understood, must be placed in their correct historical settings. That's the equivalent of saying that a Group of Seven painting can't be appreciated unless hung in a room full of moss and maples.

In fact, the museum's decision to go for replica trivializes history and limits historical consciousness. History isn't tidy, selective, prissy, or picturesque. Even the Northwest Coast houses in the Great Hall shouldn't be there. Cardinal's room is itself a transformation of an Indian house, and as such, it would have been more powerful left alone with the totem poles. The history floor is even in contradiction with the museum's electronic capabilities. What point sawing and hammering when projections could have done the job more suggestively and, in some senses, more accurately? It's a sad day for museums when a director gets up, as CMC director George MacDonald frequently does, and announces he's in competition with Epcot Centre. Cardinal didn't set exhibition policy. He was asked to satisfy the museum's programmatic and symbolic requirements in a manner consistent with his talents. The weakest part of his scheme is the office block, the first thing he worked on. From a distance, it could be mistaken for a parkade. The snaking corridors throughout are conducive of vertigo. But the museum has too many good things about it to dismiss Cardinal's predilection for the round and wavy as indulgence. Deeply felt, generously given, hopeful of communication, the building is Cardinal's gift of vision. That's what civilization is about.

—*June 1989*

Trent University,
Environmental Sciences Centre

Construction will soon begin on a $12-million Environmental Sciences Centre at Trent University in Peterborough, Ontario. The centre will house the university's departments of biology, geography, environmental and resource studies, and watershed ecosystems. Vancouver architect Richard Henriquez won a limited competition to design the centre just over a year ago. It will be built in joint venture with Laszlo Nemeth Associates of Toronto.

Henriquez presented the Trent scheme at the University of Waterloo, where he delivered one of the 1989 Arriscraft lectures. The context was previous work in Vancouver, which includes the Sylvia Hotel addition, the Sinclair Centre, Gaslight Square, and False Creek housing. The projects share more than location. Henriquez's architecture draws on his lifelong fascination with biography, archaeology, and history. He delights in peeling back the layers of a site and incorporating pieces and remnants into new structures, either actually or symbolically. Closely linked to desire for continuity is an aversion to wastefulness, an attitude he traces to having grown up in Jamaica. In this view, the recycling of historic buildings, at which Henriquez is adept, is not only an opportunity to reveal and augment the past: it's a pragmatic imperative.

The themes of Henriquez's architecture, which implies powerful narrative capability, all come together in his design for the Environmental Sciences Building. 'I wanted to get the idea of the future across, and of respect for nature,' he said. He also had memory to deal with in the person of the late Ron Thom, who designed the university's master plan and most of the buildings on the Trent campus.

Not all of the master plan was realized, however. So Henriquez decided to build some of the pieces that hadn't been built—'fragments of Ron Thom's intentions', he calls them. He's kept the footprint that Thom intended, but overlaid it with new meaning. One fragment, for instance, reappears at one end of the building as a barn suggestive of the campus's agricultural past. It will be used as an animal-care facility.

Henriquez has interpreted another of Thom's fragments, a sloped wall, as a ramp rising to meet the centre's roof. He calls it the Ground Hog Ramp, and it's not for human use. Rather, it will be covered with earth and serve as a hotel for 'small creatures' displaced by construction. The roof, meanwhile, will be planted with grass and clover so as to embody the lesson that man is one of 'a community of living things'. Although not designed by Thom, a soon-to-be-abandoned railway line on the site has also been incorporated into the scheme, appearing to split the buildings where it crosses. More prosaically, the building attaches on all three floors to an existing physics and chemistry facility.

The past comes in many shapes and guises. Taken one by one, Henriquez's moves may seem overly personal, sometimes even corny. But the scheme as a whole is just the opposite. It's an elegant composition that easily contains the symbols and minutiae of meaning with which it has been invested. There are grand gestures too. The heart of the centre is a sphere-shaped forum for assembly and ceremony, surrounded by display cabinets for 'nature's representatives', in Henriquez's words, and topped by an ocular skylight. Henriquez considers the space a metaphor for both eye and cosmic sphere. It also promises to be a wonderful, light-filled room. The scheme acknowledges that narrative must serve architecture, and not the other way around. You don't have to be a displaced groundhog to appreciate the Environmental Sciences Building. It's much more than the sum of its symbols.

Henriquez has gone much further in interpreting his mandate than his client could possibly have expected. He's even designed a graduation ceremony that would focus on a proposed grove of oak trees to be planted, incrementally, over hundreds of years. The ceremony is complicated. It involves seedlings, a railway car, a sacred wall, water from the nearby Otonabee River, and a tower made of stone blocks housing time capsules. But as with the building proper, Henriquez' intention is simple. He's a humanist, and he's determined to drive us to an awareness of what it means to be human.   *— November 1989*

Canadian Embassy, Washington, DC

Washington might be the Prince of Wales's dream come true, but neoclassicism in such dense concentration can be oppressive. A visitor to the broad avenues of the power precinct may be forgiven for wishing the temples of the ancients had been held up by suspenders instead of columns. In Washington, columns come in rows, clumps, and plethoras. Walking Pennsylvania Avenue, it's hard to know what century this is, which is not to deny the graceful splendour of early nineteenth-century Greek Revival architecture. It's the absence of the twentieth century that confuses and disorients. Postmodern classicism is acceptable, but most everything else is not. New buildings look exactly like old buildings. Someone has forgotten to wind the clock.

Modernism is in such short supply that Gordon Bunshaft's Hirshhorn Museum, a monumental concrete doughnut raised on four massive piers, the whole protected by rectangular walls, actually appears friendly. The museum was designed in the late 1960s, and looks it. That is one of its principal charms. I.M. Pei's East Wing of the National Gallery of Art, completed in 1978, is another aggressive sculptural piece. In a different city, it might not seem so daring. In Washington, both it and Bunshaft's bagel are exceptional by their refusal to compromise with historicism.

Catty-corner to the East Wing stands the new Canadian embassy, designed by Arthur Erickson. (Technically, it's a chancery in that it's basically an office building rather than an ambassadorial residence, but they're calling it an embassy anyway.) Although awarded through a tarnished selection process, the project shone with promise. Here was a civic building slated for a prime site on the ceremonial route stretching between the White House and the Capitol Building. Here was a chance for Erickson, master of the bold stroke and the defiant gesture, so long the symbol of modern Canadian architecture at home and abroad, to deliver the stuff of which his reputation was made.

For one reason or another, Erickson didn't go the route of Bunshaft or Pei, or even of Arthur Erickson, at least not the Erickson of the Museum of Anthropology, the Bank of Canada, and Roy Thomson Hall. For true analogues, consult his unbuilt projects in the Middle East, such as the Kuwait Insurance Company building, designed in the same year the embassy was awarded. In any event, Erickson took on classicism in Washington, and lost. His $90-million monument seems stuck in mid-identity crisis. It has a bold, angular shape made by the horizontal planes of the upper stories that frame the site. From a distance, it has presence. At night, all lit up, it is thought to look wonderful.

But step onto the plaza around which the bulk of the building wraps like a U, and the heart sinks. It's as if Erickson had gone shopping for columns at a Pennsylvania Avenue garage sale and, ending up with more than he could use, couldn't resist strewing them around anyway. There's an entrance pavilion, or peaked glass roof, resting on four stubby concrete columns. Call it a Greek shack. A hideous colonnade of six 50-foot-high fluted aluminum columns stretches along the driveway. It supports, up top, the world's longest planter and a skinny glass canopy that looks misplaced. Finally, over toward Pennsylvania Avenue, there's a nothing-special rotunda with twelve medium-sized concrete columns, one per province and territory, set above a cascading fountain. Nothing is in balance. Nothing flows. The space is called a forecourt, but what it's meant to communicate, other than discomfort, is anyone's guess.

Maybe the Pennsylvania Avenue site wasn't such a blessing after all. It's been fumbled. The colonnaded driveway wants to make a big deal out of the minor public park on which it fronts. Nothing doing. The entrance off Pennsylvania wants to be grand, but the narrower frontage along this side of the site didn't co-operate. And because of the clutter on the plaza, the finer points of the building, such as the tiered façade of the office floors, get lost. All too frequently, Erickson's big moves terminate in miscalculations. There are two handsome sliding doors of bullet-resistant glass and chromed stainless steel that open onto the forecourt from a large reception room. Through these, people are encouraged to spill outside. But if they spill too enthusiastically, they may end up in a wave pool. Only a couple of feet separates building from water.

Inside the building, more of the same dynamic. Condominiums have nicer lobbies. Centre stage is occupied by a round, lumpy piece of concrete upholstered in red leather. It was designed by Erickson's firm. The colour

Canadian Embassy, Washington, DC

recalls those waxy lips once found at the corner drugstore. Through the chrome-framed doors ahead curves a mighty cantilevered staircase made of the Adair marble with which the embassy is clad. The climax of this major piece is a drab library and reading room. With the exception of the cheerful cafeteria, where hangs a sensational photo-work by Michael Snow, the public areas are singularly lacking in energy.

Where is the Erickson we all thought we knew? You'll find him on the top floor. Ambassador Derek Burney's office and private terrace are the best things going in the embassy, not least because the forecourt is invisible from the sixth storey. The office has the shape of a half-moon, and the view from the windows to Capitol Hill is spectacular—so much so that the ambassador switched his salon and dining-room in order to give the dining-room the better vista. (Unfortunately, he neglected to rearrange the furniture in the salon: it looks like a rec-room in the sky.)

Outside, on the terrace, you're reminded of the post-and-beam architecture that inspired some of Erickson's best work. The power of the horizontal is unimpeded. All is simplicity. Light makes music with stone. Memories of the embarrassing mess below almost vanish. For a while you can forget that, like too many architects in mid-career, Erickson has lost his compass. He's on the verge of disappearing into a historicist maze.   —*November 1989*

Rousseau House, Montreal

Jacques Rousseau, preparing to make the tour of La Maison Coloniale, his new house and more, begins by pointing out a pair of workboots in the hall. He bought them back in April 1988, when construction began. 'These boots were made for walking,' he thought. 'These boots will walk me to the work site.' They took a break for a year, while Rousseau, the second recipient of the Canada Council Prix de Rome, was living in Italy, working on a project relating to Montreal and 'what architecture can bring to society today'. They saw action again last May, when he returned to Montreal and the construction site. Now they are mementoes.

Rousseau has moved in with his wife and son. The building is finished except for a few details that will wait until spring. It's a daring piece of work, as houses designed by architects for themselves tend to be. Only a few practitioners design their own houses from scratch. Those who do, by definition, are making a statement. La Maison Coloniale is no exception. It's an experiment for living—a theoretical proposition embodying themes that are personal to Rousseau, a man of poetry and intellect. The house occupies a small corner lot, only 9.4 metres wide and 15.5 metres long, in Mile End, an old immigrant neighbourhood in central Montreal. Tight site notwithstanding, it looks big and strong, almost fortress-like. The principal material is concrete. There are four stories, including one that's half-buried in the ground. Each floor consists of a long, wide corridor bounded on one side by a blank wall and leading, on the other side, to a pair of rooms. There are eight rooms, then, each 4.2 metres square, but varying in height and the width of their openings. The rooms have no doors. On the outside, they are expressed as two towers protected by low stone fences, the entry announced by a deep overhang and fin. Front and back elevations are identical.

Rousseau has taken full advantage of the corner and, indeed, of every available inch of site. The low fences, for example, built along the lot line, allow for the creation of a deep channel between fence and house that will eventually take lilac trees. An enclosed courtyard was made by the space between the two towers. 'We took all the zoning we could,' says Rousseau. 'The house expresses the permissiveness of zoning.'

But it expresses much more than that. Rousseau had three separate programs in mind when he designed the place. One element is a family house, another is a small office or atelier, and the third is a gallery for exhibiting the atelier's work and the work of others. So the rooms are flexible. Those downstairs and on the main level suggest office or atelier, Rousseau hasn't decided which. Office implies a conventional set-up. Atelier would indicate a preference for designing furniture and objects as well as buildings, and for involving artists in different media in projects.

One of the things preoccupying Rousseau, 42, is the direction he should be taking. 'How can someone practise somewhere near the fringes, and build something with a conventional reference as well as a marginal reference? One idea I took to Rome was what kind of practice to come back to. The idea of the atelier is growing. I want to build up the conventional but keep the margin.' Having a gallery would allow him to keep that margin, or 'invest [in] the fringe'. He explains: 'Canadian architecture is unpublicated. There are ideas, materials, an intellectual challenge you have to take on.'

He took all of them on in the house. With the exception of one contractor, his construction crew consisted of film and comparative literature students. 'For them, building in concrete was not knowledge,' says Rousseau. 'We were sensitive that we'd be learning. We began with brutal formwork and learned sophistication. From the bottom of the house to the top, you sense the mastering of the trade.' Correct. In the entry hall, and on the lower parts of the façade, the formwork is crude, but rich/crude. The forms were lined with chipboard, which left fascinating marks, like fossils. Indentations made by hardware appear as rows of intaglio squares. Near the top of the house, the severity of concrete is softened by an all-over pattern reminiscent of waves.

To every material, a meaning. 'Chipboard is related to the compression of matter, to compost,' says Rousseau. 'Outside, the concrete reveals a different kind of sedimentation. Remember the fine concrete finish of the sixties? In the sixties, they achieved a non-talking relationship with a brute material;

Rousseau house

they achieved a friendly user image by slick concrete work. Now that's all faded away. We have privileged brick and stone, but brick and stone are materials of application, not shapers. So taking up concrete again was nice. It was acknowledging that there was another way of entertaining the material. The idea of texture came. We had to domesticate the paste, to engage a soft relationship with the viewer.'

Many, many other things engage the viewer. Take the third level, for instance, which is practically all sunshine and window. The room at the front is a 'dining/talk room', the one at the back is the kitchen. This is part of the family element of the house, but there is no living-room as such. 'The conventional living-room is not basic for us,' says Rousseau. 'It will take different lives.' The dining-room will function as a living-room. So will the kitchen, which contains a huge circular counter/table fitted with a sink and appliances. In other words, walls have been liberated from appliances and vice versa. Moreover, both kitchen and dining/talk room were conceived as sunrooms: since Rousseau was dealing with such a small site, he decided to bring the balconies inside.

But the corridor will take on the role of living room, too. It's been fitted with steel frames that will take seating. Most astonishing of all, it has a garage door at either end. 'Imagine,' says Rousseau, 'in the summer, we close the doors downstairs and open the garage doors to the sounds. The garage doors are the true openings in the house. The house is not noisy. It is vibrant. Architecture has frequency. In this house, the frequency was planned. My idea was to vibrate the air around this small lot. I'm flirting with the idea that air, on an architectural level, could be thought of as a historical material. In North America, openness is as important as brick and stucco.'

On the top floor are two bedrooms. Here, the corridor has been treated as a service area. Down the middle are laundry room, bathtub, toilet. At one end is a seating area with armchairs. But to say that Rousseau and his family are living over the shop is imprecise. 'Living percolates through the other program,' says Rousseau. 'There's penetration of everyday life. An atelier shouldn't be dependent on a residence, but a residence can be dependent on an atelier.' Percolator? Tuning fork? Laboratory? Crafted object? La Maison Coloniale partakes of each. It's a reimagining of the conventional, four-storey Montreal greystone house that tests contemporary architectural thought and practice. Rousseau's workboots should be bronzed.   — *December 1989*

The Seagram Building, New York

The recent designation of the Seagram Building as a New York City landmark might have been foreseen. The 39-storey skyscraper designed by Mies van der Rohe for Joseph E. Seagram and Sons was *de facto* a landmark in 1958, the year of completion. It was Mies's first—and only—building in New York, and it is one of the paramount works of the International Style anywhere. The tower stands parallel to Park Avenue, on a large, slightly elevated plaza of pink granite and marble. Back in 1958, 'plaza' was not a noun invariably preceded by 'wind-swept'. It was accurately defined as a precious amenity beset on all sides by expensive real estate. The Seagram plaza, bare but for two symmetrical pools and a flagpole, signalled generosity. It astonished. At the time of its design, there was no comparable open space in mid-town Manhattan except for the mall at Rockefeller Centre.

Besides allowing restful space and a buffer from traffic, the plaza heightened the processional drama programmed into the Seagram building. Walking toward it, you barely sense its presence. As Phyllis Lambert, founder of the Canadian Centre for Architecture, once put it: 'You don't know what is there and you come upon *it*—with a magnificent plaza and the building not zooming up in front of your nose so that you can't see it.' Lambert was responsible for Mies's commission. She talked her father, Samuel Bronfman, out of a wedding-cake building for his New York headquarters and into a modern masterpiece. She personally selected Mies for the job over such as Frank Lloyd Wright and Le Corbusier, arguing: 'Mies forces you in. You have to go deeper. You might think this austere strength, this ugly beauty, is terribly severe. It is, and yet all the more beauty in it.'

The Seagram Building is still forbiddingly beautiful, as New York's landmarks commission has acknowledged. There is still a shock as you come upon *it*—a skyscraper clad in bronze and tinted glass, severely disposed and profoundly classical. It's more than a tall shaft on a big sidewalk. Mies extended the tower to the back with a 10-storey bustle, which is flanked on either side by a 4-storey wing. In the space between wing and tower he put a side entrance. In this way, he both compensated for the leasable space eaten up by the plaza and crossed an axial plan with a bold volumetric composition. For such strength and clarity of vision to have remained in focus for thirty years can hardly be surprising: Mies's bottom line was eternity.

The big surprise, and an unpleasant one for the Teachers' Insurance and Annuity Association, present owners of the Seagram Building, was the designation of the Four Seasons Restaurant inside—'the setting of settings in the building of buildings', as the *Wall Street Journal* once called it. The Four Seasons is only the second restaurant in New York ever to be declared an official landmark, the first being Gage and Tollner in Brooklyn, which has ornate Victorian interiors. The interiors of the Four Seasons are ornate, too—but in the manner befitting the strong minimalist statement made by the Seagram Building, where ornateness is a function of a restrained palette of rich materials, boldly and imaginatively used. Every detail counts, from the flatware designed by Ada Louise and Garth Huxtable, to the leaves on the trees that change with the seasons.

The Four Seasons occupies a monumental room at the base of each of the wings of the Seagram Building. Their dimensions were created by thickening the transfer girders that spanned the wings and by eliminating a column in each room. The thought, originally, was to lease them as car show-rooms, but Samuel Bronfman decided to go with a restaurant. Mies handed the design to Philip Johnson, with Phyllis Lambert as project architect. Turning two huge spaces with 20-foot ceilings and windows into dining rooms proved some trick, not least on account of having to dig the plaza to insert cloakrooms and washrooms where needed. Handsome as these are, it is the restaurant that leaves the impression.

If you're cool, you will lunch in the Bar Room rather than the Pool Room. If you're lucky, you will be seated at a corner table on the balcony where you can see everything and everybody—and beyond. For the full flow, you will come in through the main door of the Seagram Building, between the splashing pools, under the huge canopy. The plaza is behind, with only glass to separate it from you. You're inside, but you're still outside, too. Through the lobby and up a staircase at the rear—and you realize that another kind of space is in store. Directly ahead is a canvas backdrop painted by Picasso for Diaghilev's production of *Le Tricorne*. Johnson and Lambert acquired it from the Museum of Modern Art as a centrepiece for the hall connecting Bar Room and Pool Room. Through the glass doors, and you're in Picasso Alley, as it's been dubbed. To the right, and you're in the Bar Room. The immensity of the place is shocking.

The view from the table is magic. Walls are panelled in sleek French walnut inlaid at regular intervals with thick vertical stripes of bronze. The grain of the wood is Art Nouveau. Windows are covered with see-through metallic drapery—strand upon curving strand of fine aluminum, brass, and copper chain. Air rising from the heating and cooling vents causes them to shimmer. The streets shimmer, too. Above the bar hangs a sculpture of slender anodized metal rods by Richard Lippold—another scrim. Through the veils of mesh, the powerful grid of the curtain wall comes into view, then the grid of the plaza, then the city grid. What emerges from these disciplined superimpositions of geometry is a sense of being in New York and apart from it in a grand oasis, protected and secure. The sound is just right—waves of tinkle and conversation that never cohere into clatter or words.

The achievement was to make of abstraction a somewhere—a clubbable place that wears its age gracefully. Tom Margittai and Paul Kovi, who bought the Four Seasons in 1973, favoured designation. So, obviously, did the landmarks commission. The owners of the Seagram Building argued for the freedom to lease the space for other uses in the future. How nice that they were overruled. There are lessons to be learned from all of this, especially by those who've been misled into believing that modernism, urbanism, and comfort are incompatible. They should be dispatched to the Four Seasons immediately and strapped into one of the Brno chairs. We should all be so lucky. — *March 1990*

Kawamata Project, Toronto

The photograph is dated 1972. It shows three musicians standing on Yonge Street having themselves a good old time. The one wearing glasses is holding a trumpet. The one with the hat is strumming a guitar. They're both looking at the balding one: he's squeezing an accordion. People are hanging around, listening to the sounds, or walking on by. There are umbrella-shaded café tables on the sidewalk, a fluttering of pennants above, a sign advertising vermouth, and a muddle of wooden tubs planted with flowers and spindly trees. Whatever may be going on, it's taking place against the backdrop of a tavern sandwiched between two big stone banks. The caption reads: 'Street entertainers at [the] Colonial Tavern's sidewalk café . . . during the 1972 mall.'

The postcard is dated 1989. It was printed in Tokyo, and it says on the back: 'Kawamata Project at Colonial Tavern Park. 201 Yonge Street, Toronto. July-October 1989. 45 feet wide, 105 feet depth, 60 feet high. Organized by Mercer Union, A Centre for Contemporary Visual Art.' On the front is an image by architectural photographer Peter McCallum. Framing the picture are two stately neoclassical banks. Between them, where once stood buskers and street furniture, where once stood the Colonial Tavern, is what looks to be a construction site on the rampage—a whirlwind of lumber whipping around the space between the banks, twisting along the length of one, wrapping around the columns of the other, gusting over the sidewalk. Pile of sticks, house of cards, here today, gone tomorrow: a project, to be sure, and a lot of other things besides. Public art, architecture, mirage. Energy, poetry. Jazz.

Who, looking at the photograph of 1972, could have predicted the postcard of 1989? The images are related, but how? The answer is not so simple. The Kawamata Project is gone, just as the Colonial Tavern is gone. Images are all that remain of either one. That's life in the big city. Buildings come, buildings go. Artists blow into town and blow out again. But one thing is clear. If it weren't for Kawamata's structure, which went up last summer and came down last fall, there would be little likelihood of giving thought, now, to the history of the Colonial Tavern.

In brief, referring to Paul Dilse's recent architectural history *Toronto's Theatre Block*, there was once a jazz and blues bar called the Colonial Tavern. It was built in 1961 on the site of a three-storey Victorian building originally known as the Athlete Hotel. The architect was Bruce Etherington. The

Colonial's immediate neighbour to the north was the Bank of Toronto, designed by E.J. Lennox, architect of Old City Hall, and completed in 1906. Directly to the south was Darling and Pearson's Canadian Bank of Commerce, built in 1905. Just two storeys high, the Colonial stood out nonetheless. It was one of only two modern kids on the block, the other being the head office of Peoples Credit Jewellers, a sleek, sculptural affair of 1950s vintage.

The Colonial was understated by comparison. It was a neat, flat rectangular building whose façade was divided into four concave bays of ceramic tile, each with a display window, separated by marble piers. The entrance was to the south, marked by a wide bay of curved glass and steel. The place had two signs, one running up and down, the other straight across. There was nothing noisy about the Colonial except the acts that made it a musical landmark. Billie Holiday, Carmen McRae, Thelonious Monk, John Lee Hooker, and many others came to play.

Ironically, the Victorian and neoclassical architecture on Yonge Street survived while the new and modern languished. Peoples Credit Jewellers was renovated and reskinned beyond recognition; it became Canada's Gold Supermarket. The Colonial, meanwhile, was demolished to pave the way for a redevelopment scheme known as the Theatre Block concept, which has not yet been realized. It proved fatal for the Colonial that it neighboured not only on banks but also on Massey Hall, which is just around the corner, and the Elgin and Winter Garden theatres down the street. In the mid-1970s, an addition to Massey Hall was proposed. Soon afterward, the province announced its intention to acquire and restore the Elgin and Winter Garden. Politicians and planners saw an opportunity to consolidate the block and 'revitalize' the area.

Plans were commissioned, drawings issued forth. In each case, the Colonial had been made to disappear. One drawing showed the site reworked as a glass-roofed pedestrian arcade leading to an enlarged Massey Hall; a later one had it as a landscaped passageway connecting to an elaborate series of mid-block courtyards; yet another presented it as the forecourt of a covered plaza linking a group of massive highrises.

In 1983 the city secured ownership of the Colonial from the developers of the Eaton Centre across the street. Plans went ahead for its demolition despite an offer by a non-profit group, Jazz Watch, to restore and operate the building as a jazz museum. By this point the club had been remodelled several times over, and had lost its identity as a jazz mecca. Alderman Michael Gee argued demolition was 'essential to the revitalization concept' and, moreover, declared the building had 'no historic or architectural merit'. He was wrong on both counts, but Toronto had spoken.

The Teperman hoardings went up in 1987. Down came the Colonial. The property was landscaped, to put it politely, as a temporary park pending the realization of some grand scheme—another BCE Place, maybe, or another

Kawamata project

Bay-Adelaide Centre—beloved by planning authorities. 'It will be transformed into something, but into what is still not clear,' says Marc Baraness, director of architecture and urban design with the City of Toronto, further noting that the two banks, which are also owned by the City, will be renovated to public use. But from late last July through early October, Colonial Tavern Park was something else. It was the Kawamata Toronto Project.

Tadashi Kawamata is a Japanese artist in his mid-thirties who has gained international recognition through the many installation works he has built around the world. Moving from one big city to another, on sites of his own selection, using scavenged lumber and working with local assistants, he creates temporary structures—parasites and cancers, to use his own terminology—of haunting beauty and ambiguity; engaged, confrontational, inquiring. One of his best-known works was constructed in Kassel, Germany, in 1987. There, in the middle of the city, with ten assistants, he flung a wooden membrane over the bombed-out remains of a historic church. It was after experiencing this ghostly web of debris that Steven Pozel, then director of Mercer Union, started working to bring Kawamata to Toronto.

The artist was immediately attracted to Colonial Tavern Park as a site of operation because the tavern had only recently been wrecked and people still remembered it. 'That's why I chose the place,' he said. 'It still has time, memory. For me it's like a floating place. People still recognize the name. The first time I saw it, it seemed like a gap in the teeth, completely empty. My primitive idea is to continue the buildings'—rejoin the banks, restore the streetscape—'and people will be able to go through the inside of the structure.' He used original wood from the Colonial, donated by Teperman, to build. 'It's like a snake that eats its own tail,' he commented.

Kawamata's way with words made headlines well in advance of his way with wood. Especially controversial was his description of his work as 'visual terrorism'. The phrase was accurate, if impolitic. What he was saying, at heart, as that he wanted to shake Toronto out of its dogmatic slumber. 'Normally, in a city we are always trying to reduce intrusive noise,' he explained. 'My construction is like that noise. . . . I make a noise but its meaning is just like a big happening. . . . Because the city is based on a very tight structure, the artist must always make something to resist it.'

Resisting the grid, whether that grid be physical, social, or psychological, wasn't just a theme of the Colonial Tavern Park project. It was built right into the structure. The space created behind the whirling wall of sticks on Yonge Street, an urban room filled with vibrations, inspiring of calm, was made by a grid that was subverted, over and over again, by swirls of sticks that seemed passionately bent on escape. Things were no different when the piece was observed from Yonge Street. Tall vertical poles—stick columns that mimicked the hefty columns of the banks—marched regularly along the sidewalk, but the rush of lumber surging through them paid no heed.

The project resisted the will to classify, but it did provoke, especially when it became known it had been budgeted at $80,000. A message scribbled on the hoardings one night said: '$80,000 for shit.' (Kawamata's assistant, Mika Kioke, photographed it: it was part of the piece.) A letter to the art critic of the *Toronto Star* ended with: 'But Mr Kawamata's art I will never understand—do you? if so, above your name at the head of your column it says ART and it should really say GARBAGE.' (That too went into the file.) Others were inspired to sketch the structure at sunset, take pictures, study the shadows, wander through, bring their friends.

Kawamata made noise; he also built bridges. He brought architects and visual artists together. Structural engineer Morden Yolles contributed his services free of charge. More surprisingly, the architectural firm of Kuwabara Payne McKenna Blumberg sponsored an exhibition of drawings and maquettes at Mercer Union. 'That very rarely happens,' said Pozel. 'One of the unforeseen long-term benefits may be collaboration with architectural firms—co-sponsorships. I think the Kawamata project will affect a generation of architects and artists in this city. It's of that significance.'

It even affected people who didn't see the structure but only its after-images—photographs and maquettes—and not just in Toronto but even in Montreal, where they were shown at La Galerie Brenda Wallace in December. 'I had a memory of the last time I heard music at the Colonial Tavern,' said Montreal painter, sculptor, and musician John Heward, who visited the show. 'I'm not sure of the date, or even the decade, but it was Jimmy Rushing, the man who was called Mr Five-by-Five. He descended a circular stairway from the second floor, and made a majestic progress to the stage. That reminded me of Kawamata's circular movement.'

The finale came on 10 October, when the piece was dismantled. Over a week, Colonial Tavern Park became a shocking emptiness. All the energy that Kawamata had stirred up was driven underground, and so suddenly! People must have had similar feelings when the Colonial went down, and that's how Pozel sees it, too: 'I came back to Toronto after a trip to Japan and it wasn't there. I was devastated. I had a really empty feeling within myself. All that layering and building—it filled space in such a dramatic way. Kawamata's ideas really came home when the piece was taken down. It was an urban warning. Buildings twenty years old are coming down. The intensity of change in Tokyo became a real warning here. We're knocking down things . . .' Kawamata's noise keeps echoing. There's a musician—and what a performance!   — *March 1990*

Photograph Credits

Page 1 Herb Nott; 9 Steven Evans Photography Inc.; 11, 12, 21 Panda Associates; 23 Frederic Urban; 25 Panda Associates; 34 Canadian National, Public Affairs; 44, 45 Courtesy The Colborne Architectural Group; 67 Frank O. Gehry & Associates, Inc. 91 James Dow; 94 Steven Evans Photography Inc.; 98 Burton Kramer; 106 Courtesy The Power Plant, Harbourfront; 114, 115 Gabor Szilasi, courtesy Collection Centre Canadien d'Architecture/Canadian Centre for Architecture, Montréal; 121, 122 Courtesy Betty Goodwin; 125 Samuel Jack Hayward Studio, Montreal, courtesy Collection Centre Canadien d'Architecture/Canadian Centre for Architecture, Montreal; 140 Steven Evans Photography Inc., courtesy A.J. Diamond, Donald Schmitt and Co.; 147 Steven Evans Photography Inc.; 152 Courtesy Francesco & Aldo Piccaluga Inc.; 156 Courtesy City of Mississauga, Public Affairs; 166 Robert Fillion, courtesy National Gallery of Canada; 176 Courtesy Cleeve Horne; 191 Courtesy A.J. Diamond, Donald Schmitt and Co.; 194 Alain Laforest, courtesy Collection Centre Canadien d'Architecture/Canadian Centre for Architecture, Montréal; 198, 199 Courtesy Canadian Museum of Civilization; 204 (c) copyright Fiona Spalding-Smith Photographer; 207 Piotr Andrews; 213 Peter MacCallum, courtesy Mercer Union, Toronto.

Buildings and Projects Designed by Peter Dickinson

This list is intended for people who would like to view Peter Dickinson's architecture. Also recorded are demolished works. Precise dates for all projects, other than those noted in the text, are difficult to pin down. Papers are scattered, records incomplete or unavailable. In order to protect the privacy of residential clients, homes are not listed.

As chief designer at Page and Steele (May 1950 to January 1958):
Apartment building at 561 Avenue Road, Toronto.
Benvenuto Place Apartments, 1 Benvenuto Place, Toronto.
Beth Tzedec Congregation, 1700 Bathurst Street, Toronto.
Canadian Red Cross Society Headquarters, Toronto (demolished).
Church Street Public School, 83 Alexander Street, Toronto.
City of Ottawa Police Building, Ottawa, Ontario.
High-rise apartment towers, Regent Park South, s.s. of Dundas Street East, w. of River Street, Toronto.
Humber Valley Village Junior Middle School, 65 Hartfield Road, Etobicoke, Ontario.
Juvenile and Family Courts, 311 Jarvis Street, Toronto.
London Teachers' College, London, Ontario.
Lyndwood Public School, 498 Hartsdale Drive, Mississauga, Ontario.
Midland-Penetang High School, Midland, Ontario.
Mutual Benefit Insurance (preliminary design), 500 University Avenue, Toronto.
Office building for Babcock-Wilcox Co. and Goldie-McCulloch, Galt, Ontario.
Office building at 111 Richmond Street West, Toronto.
Office building at 2 St. Clair West (preliminary design), Toronto.
Office building at 55 Yonge Street, Toronto.
O'Keefe Centre (attributed to Earle C. Morgan and Page and Steele), Front and Yonge Streets, Toronto.
Oxton/Oriole Apartments, 240 Oriole Parkway, Toronto.
Park Plaza addition, Avenue Road at Bloor Street, Toronto.
Queen Elizabeth Building, Exhibition Place, Canadian National Exhibition, Toronto.
Range Road Apartments, Ottawa, Ontario.
Toronto Teachers' College (now part of Centennial College of Applied Arts and Technology, East York Campus), 951 Carlaw Avenue, East York, Ontario.
Wawanesa Mutual Insurance Company, 1819 Yonge Street, Toronto.
Westbury Hotel, 475 Yonge Street, Toronto.

West Glen Junior Public School, 57 Cowley Avenue, Etobicoke, Ontario.
Workmen's Compensation and Rehabilitation Centre (now called Worker's Compensation), 115 Torbarrie Road, Downsview, Ontario.

Peter Dickinson Associates (January 1958 to October 1961):
Additions to Loyola College, Montreal, Quebec.
Apartment building at 500 Avenue Road, Toronto.
Canadian Imperial Bank of Commerce, Windsor Plaza, Montreal, Quebec.
Champlain Secondary School, Pembroke, Ontario.
Continental Can Building, 790 Bay Street, Toronto.
Elm Ridge Golf and Country Club, Ile Bizard, Quebec.
Four Seasons Motor Hotel, 415 Jarvis Street, Toronto (demolished).
K.L.M. Royal Dutch Airlines Ticket Office, Toronto (demolished).
Office building at 1420 Sherbrooke Street West, Montreal, Quebec.
Office building at 801 Bay Street, Toronto.
Ontario Hospital Association Building, 24 Ferrand Drive, Don Mills, Ontario (demolished).
Prudential Insurance Company of America Building, 4 King Street West, Toronto.
Regis College, a seminary for the Jesuit Fathers of Upper Canada (now the Ontario Theological Seminary and Ontario Bible College), 25 Bally Connor Court, North York, Ontario.
Trans-Canada Pipelines Building, 150 Eglinton Avenue East, Toronto.
Tweedsmuir Apartments, Tweedsmuir Avenue, Toronto.
William G. Miller Public School, Scarborough, Ontario.

PDA projects completed by others after Peter Dickinson's death:
Inn on the Park Four Seasons Hotel, Leslie and Eglinton Streets, North York, Ontario.
Lothian Mews, Bloor Street, Toronto (demolished).
Telegram Building (now The Globe and Mail), 444 Front Street West, Toronto.

Competition entries:
Ontario Association of Architects Headquarters, 1950.
Coventry Cathedral, 1951.
City of Ottawa Police Building, 1954 (built 1957).
Toronto City Hall, 1957.
Liverpool Cathedral, 1959.
Ottawa Builders' Exchange, 1960 (first place; not built).

Index